Taylor's Guides to Gardening

Roger Holmes, Editor

Frances Tenenbaum, Series Editor

HOUGHTON MIFFLIN COMPANY
Boston · New York · London   1993

Taylor's Guide to Natural Gardening

Copyright © 1993 by Houghton Mifflin Company

Taylor's Guide is a registered trademark
of Houghton Mifflin Company.

Library of Congress Cataloging-in-Publication Data
Taylor's guide to natural gardening / Roger Holmes, editor.
       p.   cm. — (Taylor's guides to gardening)
    Includes bibliographical references and index.
    ISBN 0-395-60729-9
    1. Natural landscaping.   2. Natural landscaping — United States.
3. Organic gardening.   4. Organic gardening — United States.
I. Holmes, Roger.   II. Series.
SB439.T33   1993   92-16334
635.9'5173 — dc20   CIP

Printed in Japan

DNP   10   9   8   7   6   5   4   3   2   1

Drawings by Steve Buchanan

Cover photograph by David E. Benner

Contents

Contributors

Roger Holmes, the general editor of this book, was a general editor of *Taylor's Guide to Gardening in the Southwest* and the editorial consultant for *Taylor's Guide to Gardening Techniques.* He was the founding editor of *Fine Gardening* magazine. Trained as a cabinetmaker in England, Holmes builds furniture in addition to working as a freelance writer and editor. He gardens for pleasure at his home in Woodbury, Connecticut.

Melody Mackey Allen, author of the butterfly section of the wildlife essay, is the executive director of the Xerxes Society (10 Southwest Ash St., Portland, Oreg. 97204), the only international organization dedicated to invertebrate conservation. Among its publications is the book *Butterfly Gardening,* which includes contributions from Allen. She has also been a field representative of the Nature Conservancy and has served as the director of the Monarch Project.

Nancy Beaubaire, author of the essay on organic pest and disease control, is managing editor of *Fine Gardening.* As a home gardener and owner of a landscape business, she has used organic methods for more than twenty years. She lectures on various gardening topics and is an active member of the Natural Organic Farmers Association in Connecticut.

Meredith Bradford Clebsch wrote the essay on the Eastern Woodlands and consulted on that region's encyclopedia entries. A former Peace Corps volunteer, she and her husband established Native Gardens in Greenback, Tennessee, where they propagate and sell more than 200 species native to the southeastern United States.

Rita Buchanan, an editorial consultant for this book, was trained in botany and horticulture. She has worked and gardened in Texas, Colorado, Virginia, Connecticut, England, and Costa Rica. A general editor for *Taylor's Guide to Gardening in the South,* she was a founding editor of *Fine Gardening* and now writes and edits for *The Herb Companion* and other publications.

Steve Buchanan illustrated this book. He specializes in natural history subjects. His work has appeared in *Horticulture, Garden Design, Fine Gardening, Scientific American, Organic Gardening, The Herb Companion,* the *New York Times,* and several books.

Kevin Connelly, author of the essay on the California Floristic Province and consultant on that region's encyclopedia entries, is a professional landscape gardener specializing in California native plants and drought-tolerant gardens. He has established wildflower plantings for private and public gardens, including the Theodore Payne Foundation in Sun Valley, Earthside Nature in Pasadena, and the El Alisal Garden at the Lummis Home State Historical Monument in Los Angeles. Kevin is a regular contributor to the *Los Angeles Times* and *Pacific Horticulture* and is the author of the book *Gardener's Guide to California Wildflowers.*

John Diekelmann, author of the essay on the Great Plains and consultant on that region's encyclopedia entries, is an architect and landscape architect specializing in ecologically based landscaping. He is co-author of *Natural Landscaping: Designing with Native Plant Communities.* He lectures and writes and has contributed to the *New York Times* and *Garden* magazine, among other publications.

Kim Hawks, author of the essay on growing wildflowers and native plants and that on creating meadows and woodland gardens, owns Niche Gardens in Chapel Hill, North Carolina, where she sells nursery-propagated plants and publishes an award-winning newsletter, *Niche Notes.* After receiving a degree in horticultural science, she worked as a horticulturist, plant propagator, and nursery manager before establishing her own business in 1985. She has written for *Fine Gardening, Grower Talks,* and *The Herb Companion.*

Carleen and **Sam Jones,** authors of the essay on the Coastal Plain and consultants on that region's encyclopedia entries, are co-owners of Piccadilly Farm, a nursery in Bishop, Georgia, that grows hostas, hellebores, and other perennials for the Georgia Piedmont. Carleen has developed a large trial and display garden at the nursery. Sam, now retired, was a botany professor and plant taxonomist at the University of Georgia. He is co-author of *Native Shrubs and Woody Vines of the Southeast* and *Gardening with Native Wild Flowers.*

Mark Kane, co-author (with Roger Holmes) of the introductory essay, is executive editor of *Fine Gardening*. He has been gardening since 1972, first on an 80-acre Missouri farm and now on a city lot in Waterbury, Connecticut. He wrote extensively about natural gardening as a contributing editor of *Organic Gardening*.

Judith Phillips, author of the essay on the Western Deserts and consultant on that region's encyclopedia entries, is a landscape designer and co-owner of a nursery specializing in drought-tolerant native and locally adapted plants in the Albuquerque area. The author of *Southwestern Landscaping with Native Plants,* she is active in a variety of environmental, natural landscaping, and native plant organizations. She is developing her own garden, 20 acres near Socorro, New Mexico, as a wildlife habitat.

Craig Tufts, author of the bird section of the wildlife essay, is director of urban wildlife programs for the National Wildlife Federation (1400 16th St. NW, Washington, D.C. 20036). He is the federation's senior naturalist and oversees its Backyard Wildlife Habitat Program. He is also the wildlife gardening specialist for "The Victory Garden" on television.

Gayle Weinstein, author of the essay on the Western Mountains and the Pacific Northwest and consultant on that region's encyclopedia entries, is president of Eletes, a design and consulting firm in Denver, Colorado, specializing in native plants and regional designs. A former director of plant collections at the Denver Botanic Gardens, she is the author of *Rocky Mountain Landscaping Alternatives* and co-author of *Woody Ornamentals for the Midwest.*

Preface

If the term is new to you, "natural gardening" may be a bit puzzling. What, you may ask, could be *un*natural about gardening? Tilling the soil, tending plants — many of us feel closest to nature when we're gardening.

Yet you have only to compare a garden to an untended stretch of countryside to realize that nature's way with plants and the gardener's way can be very different. So different, in fact, that we sometimes seem to expend most of our gardening efforts trying to prevent nature from having her way.

Natural gardening is about lessening this struggle, about learning to work with, rather than against, nature. It's about growing plants adapted to the conditions nature sets. It's about reducing or eliminating the use of chemicals to feed our plants and to fend off the pests and diseases that afflict them. It's about designing our gardens and landscapes to complement the natural surroundings.

Not everyone is drawn to natural gardening for the same reasons. Some find the beauty of native plants and wildflowers irresistible but are quite happy to grow them in traditional beds and borders. Others enjoy the challenges of maintaining their soil with compost and manure and of outwitting rather than overpowering pests. Still others are moved by the look of wild places — a mountain meadow, woodland hillside, desert arroyo, coastal dune, or prairie streamside — to create something having the same spirit on their property.

If you share some of these interests or if you're just curious, we hope this book will answer most of your questions about natural gardening and will encourage you to give it a try. Whether you experiment with a few native plants or transform your entire gardening philosophy, you'll find natural gardening rewarding.

How to Use This Guide

Natural gardening is more an idea than a method. It asks you to think about gardening in a particular way and allows you to choose among many methods for putting your insights into practice. You can also be involved at various levels. You might begin by growing a few wildflowers or native plants in existing beds and borders. If you're bitten by the natural gardening bug, you might eventually transform your entire landscape. Whether you remain a dabbler or become an enthusiast, we feel this book will help you along your way.

How This Guide Is Organized

Like most of the books in the Taylor's Guide series, this one contains essays and a large selection of plants, shown in color plates and described in an encyclopedia. The essays present the ideas underlying natural gardening and offer guidance about methods. As one of the most important ideas is to grow plants that are well adapted to local conditions, the plants we've selected are all native to North America and cover a wide range of garden and landscape uses.

The Essays

The first essay presents the basic concepts of natural gardening, including ideas about designing natural plantings and landscapes. Six regional essays follow, introducing proven garden performers among North America's indigenous plants. Nature doesn't heed state boundaries, so our regions comprise areas in which plants have adapted to climatic and other conditions in similar, distinctive ways. (The map on p. xiv is based on the floristic provinces identified by Henry Gleason and Arthur Cronquist in their book *The Natural Geography of Plants*.)

The essay on attracting wildlife gives you practical suggestions for enticing birds and butterflies into the garden. Many wildflowers and native plants are no more trouble to grow than other garden plants. But some require special attention to propagate and maintain. The essay on growing native plants will help you over the occasional cultivation hurdle. The next essay tells how to establish two of the most popular natural landscapes, meadows and woodland gardens. The final essay introduces methods of controlling pests and diseases without the aid of synthetic substances; as with other aspects of natural gardening, pest control involves every phase of gardening, from selecting new plants to keeping a regular watch on old ones.

The Plants

Natural gardeners look for plants that are well adapted to the conditions in their gardens. These plants can be from any-where; China and Australia, for example, have provided nu-merous plants ideally suited to conditions in various parts of the United States. Increasingly, however, gardeners are dis-covering a wealth of attractive, highly adapted plants practi-cally in their own backyards. No matter where you garden on our vast continent — an arid, alkaline desert, a cool, moist woodland, or a windswept coastal bluff — you can find North American native plants that will thrive there. We present a selection of these plants in this book.

Choosing from the thousands of excellent candidates was not easy. We selected more than 300, emphasizing those that are likely to be readily available from major local nurseries or established mail-order suppliers. We looked for plants with more than one noteworthy characteristic (attractive foliage as well as flowers, for example) and with garden interest in more than one season (flowers in summer, colorful bark in winter).

We also tried to balance our choices among plants for dif-ferent landscaping purposes — providing shade or screening views, covering ground, serving as a background or a focal point in a planting. We sought plants that could work as well in traditional beds, borders, and foundation plantings as in informal or naturalized settings.

The term "native plant" may be new to some readers. Plants imported to North America from elsewhere are often called "exotics," whereas those indigenous to our continent are called natives. When grown in the Midwest, however, a plant native to the Atlantic seacoast is as much an exotic as a plant from China. In the regional essays, native plants are those indigenous to the region. Elsewhere, native refers to plants indigenous to North America.

The same sort of confusion can occur with the term "wild-flower." Strictly speaking, wildflowers can be native plants, indigenous to a locale, or exotics, introduced plants that have adapted so well to their new surroundings that they now grow wild. All the wildflowers discussed in this book are native North American plants, so we use the terms "wildflowers" and "native plants" interchangeably.

Native plants have some special characteristics. Grown in conditions similar to those of their native habitats — dry or wet, acid or alkaline soil, sun or shade, sheltered or exposed — they usually require little maintenance and irrigation. They resist fungus diseases and are relatively free of insect problems. As you use this book, it is helpful to remember that the path to understanding native plants leads through their natural habitats; once you're familiar with the conditions in which a plant has evolved, you'll be better able to decide whether you should grow it.

Color plates

To give you a sense of the many possibilities for natural landscaping, we begin this section with views of gardens from around the country. Then, to help you choose individual plants, we provide a collection of plant portraits. These will give you a good idea of a plant's foliage, flowers, and, in some cases, growth habit. The portraits are arranged by plant type: trees, shrubs, wildflowers (herbaceous annuals and perennials), and grasses and vines. A short comment on the plant's use or character accompanies each plate, along with its botanical and common names, height, and hardiness zone rating, and the page on which you'll find its encyclopedia entry.

Plant encyclopedia

If you're intrigued by a plant mentioned in an essay or one you see on a garden visit, consult this section. The encyclopedia contains descriptions of each plant shown in the color plates as well as additional cultivars and related species. The listings are arranged alphabetically by genus. (If you don't know the botanical name, consult the index, where botanical and common names are cross-referenced.)

The encyclopedia entries. Each genus is briefly described, followed by detailed descriptions of selected species and cultivars. These entries present the plant's desirable characteristics — foliage, flowers, growth habit — provide suggestions for using it in the landscape, and comment on how to grow it. (Many entries are accompanied by a sketch of a particular species, often highlighting a noteworthy characteristic.)

Hardiness zones. Plants vary considerably in their ability to withstand cold temperatures. Those native to high-elevation northern regions, for instance, can survive bitter cold, many degrees below zero, while some tropical plants may die when touched by the slightest frost.

In the early years of this century, horticulturists began to correlate the cold-hardiness of plants with gradients of temperature as plotted on a map. The zone map on p. xvi, which represents ten temperature zones for North America, is based on one recently revised by the U.S. Department of Agriculture. The zone rating for each plant indicates the lowest temperatures at which the plant can usually be expected to survive. A plant rated for zone 5, for instance, should survive minimum temperatures between −10 to −20 degrees F. If you live in zone 5 or a higher-numbered zone, cold shouldn't kill the plant in your garden.

When selecting plants, remember that zone ratings indicate cold-hardiness *only*. Many other factors — heat, wind, rainfall, alkaline or acid soils, to name a few — are at least as important. These factors are mentioned in the plant descriptions; if you're in doubt about a plant's suitability for your location, ask a knowledgeable person at a local nursery.

Appendices

The appendices introduce some of the many excellent resources for natural gardeners. For a library of helpful reference books, see "Further Reading." "Sources of Supply" lists a variety of suppliers of plants, seeds, and natural controls for pests and diseases. There's no better way to learn about plants and how to use them than to visit superb gardens. "Public Gardens" provides a selection of noteworthy examples in each region.

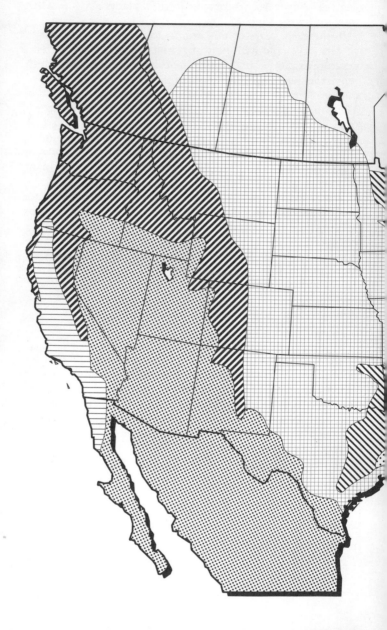

Western Mountains and Pacific Northwest

California Floristic Province

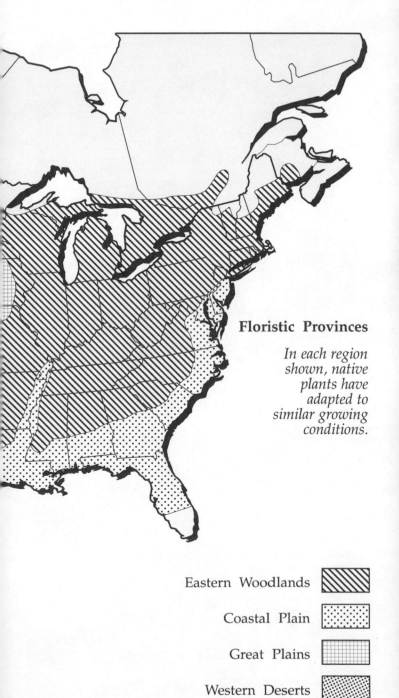

Floristic Provinces

In each region shown, native plants have adapted to similar growing conditions.

Eastern Woodlands

Coastal Plain

Great Plains

Western Deserts

ZONE 1	BELOW		−50°F	
ZONE 2	−50°	TO	−40°	
ZONE 3	−40°	TO	−30°	
ZONE 4	−30°	TO	−20°	
ZONE 5	−20°	TO	−10°	
ZONE 6	−10°	TO	0°	
ZONE 7	0°	TO	10°	
ZONE 8	10°	TO	20°	
ZONE 9	20°	TO	30°	
ZONE 10	30°	TO	40°	
ZONE 11	ABOVE		40°	

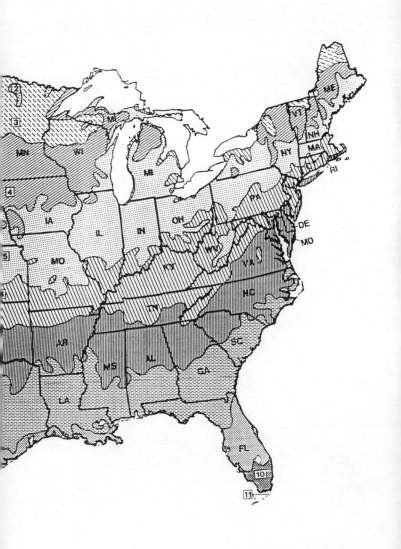

Gardening Inspired by Nature

Gardeners have long regarded natural landscapes with a combination of delight and envy. We revel in the beauty of a wild place — unplanted, untended, and enduring — but not without reflecting on the effort it takes to make our little patch at home bloom and prosper even half as well. In a sense, natural gardening can be said to spring from this commonplace observation. By paying more attention to how nature does things, we can enrich our gardens with some of the grace and endurance of wild places while being kinder to the environment and less wasteful of nature's resources and our own efforts.

Working in partnership with nature isn't a new idea, but it has had a spotty history in North America. For new immigrants to the continent's vast wilderness, nature seemed more obstacle than inspiration. Forests quickly reclaimed hard-won clearings, prairie fires swept away crops sowed in newly broken sod, drought turned plants to dust. Wherever the rigors of life permitted gardening for pleasure, people did their best to re-create the gardens they remembered from a "home" that was often across the continent or the ocean.

Many of our ideas about gardens and many of the plants we grow are legacies of these remembered gardens: the English cottage garden, with its careless profusion of blossom; the formal French garden, with its bedding plants precisely deployed beneath manicured shrubs; the Spanish courtyard garden, with its roses and spreading shade tree. Even that staple of the suburban landscape, the close-cropped lawn, is an English import. Our gardens, like our country, are filled with immigrants from the Far East, Europe, the Americas, Africa, Australia — lilies, roses, camellias, flowering crab apples. The list goes on and on.

While imported garden styles and plants have undoubtedly enriched our domestic landscapes, they have also exacted a price. Many of the plants require heroic measures to survive in their new homes. The arid Southwest is not kind to most lawn grasses, for example, and great quantities of water and fertilizers are necessary to carpet a desert yard with turf. And, in a country of spectacularly diverse natural beauty, reliance on a few popular gardening styles and a standard palette of plants has homogenized our domestic landscape. With their conventional swath of lawn, clipped hedges, shade trees, and tidy flower beds, suburban developments have become almost identical from coast to coast.

Natural gardening offers alternatives. By looking to nearby wild places for inspiration, we open possibilities for countless new landscape styles. By heeding local conditions of climate and topography, we can reduce the amount of labor and resources necessary to maintain a garden. Finally, by working in partnership with nature, we grow closer to it and become more aware of its workings and its wonders.

If natural gardening sounds good to you but you don't want to remake your entire landscape, don't worry. You can choose the level of involvement that suits you. You may want to start by introducing a few native plants into your existing beds and borders. You may continue by "naturalizing" part of your lawn — in the Midwest, make a small "prairie" with native grasses and wildflowers; in New England, establish a small woodland garden. These relatively small changes may be enough for you. Or you may get hooked by this approach and create a landscape so natural looking that visitors will wonder when you plan to start gardening.

Basic Principles

The principles of natural gardening are simple. First, become familiar with the climate and conditions in your region and on your property. Then seek out plants that are adapted to those conditions — plants that grow well without irrigation, fertilizer, or pesticides. (We'll discuss naturalistic design later.)

Growing the Right Plants

Choosing plants adapted to the conditions in your garden is perhaps the most important principle of natural gardening. These plants give their best without special care. They survive the stress of winter cold in northern states or of summer heat in the South. In arid regions they tolerate drought, and in the humidity of the South and Pacific Northwest they resist the fungal diseases that affect leaves and roots. Everywhere they are resistant to pests and require pesticides only in rare instances.

Plants adapted to your area may be native to the field next door or to another continent. Throughout the world there are regions with climates and conditions that resemble those in one part or another of the United States. Plants imported from these regions can be as tough and carefree as the best of our native plants. In fact, many introduced plants — daylilies and hostas, forsythia and lilacs, Norway spruce and Japanese maple — are far better known than the equally handsome and resilient plants native to North America.

North American Native Plants

Spurred by the growing interest in natural gardening, neglect of our native plants is beginning to end. With its wide range of climates, North America has one of the richest plant populations of any continent. Every region has a distinctive flora, providing garden-worthy plants for every landscaping need. The prairies, for example, offer bright, long-blooming perennials, such as black-eyed Susans and purple coneflowers, tall prairie grasses, and tough, drought-resistant shrubs and trees.

Adaptation to local conditions is only one of the attractions of native plants. As more gardeners come to value natural diversity for its own sake, the variety and relatively restrained beauty of natives offer a welcome alternative to the relentless tendency of highly bred garden staples to become larger, brighter, and showier. These gardeners have seen enough of dahlias with flowers the size of pompoms. They prefer the cheerful, carefree New England aster, whose flowers are showy but not overbearing.

The excitement of discovery also fuels the interest in native plants. Wildflower societies, specialty nurseries, and botanical gardens are continually bringing new native plants into cultivation. Once in the garden, their performance can be surprising. Some have proven to be unexpectedly adaptable. The Louisiana iris, for instance, is native to wet regions along the Gulf Coast from Texas to Mississippi, but adventurous gardeners in zone 5 are growing the plant with success, and it even appears capable of enduring some drought. Many plants are surprisingly vigorous. Freed from competing with its wild neighbors for resources, a native penstemon may double in size and make a dramatic show of vivid flower spikes. The mountain laurel that grows with lanky, reaching branches in a woodland thicket will grow full and dense in a sunny garden and bloom more profusely.

Sparing the Environment

Natural gardening aims for self-sufficiency. Though you'll never fully achieve this goal — there are always weeds to pull, young plants that need watering through a drought, outbreaks of pests to control — you can minimize maintenance and the need for pesticides, fertilizer, and water.

Reducing pesticides

Natural gardening practices reduce the need for pesticides in several ways. Many native plants have developed defenses against pests and diseases common in their habitats. Also, when grown in conditions to which they are well adapted, plants suffer fewer of the weakening stresses that make them more vulnerable to pests and disease. Growing a varied selection of plants encourages a diversity of insects and birds. Along with harmful insects, the natural garden harbors their predators. (For more on this topic, see the essay "Organic Control of Pests and Diseases.")

Water conservation

Natural gardens often require very little watering. Almost by definition, adapted plants are able to make do with the water nature provides. In arid regions of the country, natural landscaping has acquired a new name, xeriscaping (coined from *xeric,* the adjective for plants that tolerate dry climates). Xeriscape gardeners follow one main precept: grow plants that need little or no watering. The most noticeable effect of a switch to xeriscaping is the shrinking of water-hungry lawns, replaced by ground covers, perennials, shrubs, and trees native to dry climates. Even a modest xeriscaping makeover cuts watering in half. Growing only adapted plants can eliminate watering altogether except to establish young plants.

Fertilizing

Natural gardeners rely largely on organic matter to provide nutrients for their plants, supplemented by occasional light applications of nitrogen, phosphorus, and potassium fertilizers. Mulch is the main source of organic matter, supplying nutrients steadily in small quantities as it breaks down. Renewed each year, it builds soil fertility and improves soil structure. Much of the mulch in a natural landscape comes from the plants themselves — leaves and composted fall cleanup — but you will probably have to import organic matter, too, especially if your garden has few shrubs and trees or is new and needs several years of heavy mulching to improve the soil and discourage weeds. Small amounts of fertilizers are enough to help maintain the lawn, help transplants get established, and correct temporary soil deficiencies.

Maintenance

In a natural landscape, maintenance of established plantings is largely a response to growth or decline. The lawn needs mowing, but it's smaller and takes less time. You prune shrubs and trees that develop awkward branches, crowd their neighbors, or choke the gutters. You divide daylilies that have grown too dense and deadhead the coreopsis to keep it blooming and attractive. When the occasional plant dies, you replace it. Once a year, you renew the mulch throughout the garden. In fall, you clean up dead stems and litter and add them to the compost pile.

Naturalistic Design

You can garden naturally in traditional gardens and landscapes. But if you're adventurous, you'll want to take the next step and plant some or all of your landscape naturalistically. Inspired by the diversity and drama of wild places, you can design your property to reflect the distinctive character of your region and to offer food and shelter for wildlife.

Diversity

Wild places include a diversity of plants. Competing for light, nutrients, and water, different plants adopt different strategies. At almost any moment in a woodland, prairie, mountain meadow, or desert arroyo, some plant is flowering, setting seeds, emerging from the soil, declining, or going dormant. Nature's diversity offers a principle for naturalistic design: grow a wide range of plants, of different types, heights, shapes, and flowering times. If you choose plants that are also attractive in periods of dormancy, your garden will be interesting and vivid during all seasons of the year.

Drama

The drama of wild places arises from nature's habit of painting with broad and thin brushes. In the wild, an extensive colony of one plant grows alongside, above, or under a rich collection of different plants. The aspens of Colorado cover entire hillsides, their fluttering leaves and pale, bare trunks dramatically shaping the view, while at their feet grows a sea of varied understory plants.

In naturalistic design, you mix broad stands of the same or similar plants with smatterings of different plants. You set out azaleas in threes and fives, if you have the room, and surround them with a variety of spring bulbs and perennials. You place a single blue dogbane at the front of the garden, where its low-spreading fountain of arching, bottlebrush stems will contrast vividly with drifts of black-eyed Susans and purple coneflowers. You back a sweep of daylilies with tall, clumping grasses whose stiff rustling leaves and dry seed heads persist through the winter.

As you're planning and planting, keep in mind that plants in the wild arrange themselves according to growing conditions. In the arid Southwest, sagebrush and cactus stand apart with bare soil between; in New Orleans, abundant rain and mild winters produce a lush growth of brambles, ferns, and magnolias beneath 70-foot-tall sweet gums. Remember that you don't need to copy these associations and spacings exactly to elicit the same effect in your garden.

Wildlife

A natural landscape invites wildlife. Choose plants that offer food and shelter to a range of creatures, especially bees, butterflies, and birds. Instead of a tidy, clipped yew hedge, which offers at best a few fall berries and nesting sites for small birds, plant a mixed hedge of unsheared, fruit-producing shrubs — viburnums, blueberries, hollies, serviceberries. No garden is too small for a pond, even if it's just a barrel sunk in the ground. Ponds encourage frogs, toads, and lizards, which play a role in controlling unwanted insects, and they allow you to grow water plants. To invite birds, set out a birdbath and a bird feeder. Install arbors and trellises and train vines over them to provide nesting sites and food. (See the essay "Gardening for Wildlife" for more on this subject.)

Regional character
Every region of the country contains a wealth of varied habitats that can provide inspiration for natural landscapes. In Kansas City, for example, you might take the prairie, remnants of which remain in the nearby Flint Hills, as your starting point. A sweep of lawn and foundation plantings around the house will preserve the neighborhood conventions. Then devote wide, unmowed borders around three sides of the property to grasses, deep-rooted perennials such as the purple coneflower, and drought-resistant shrubs and trees. In spring, sand cherries and native plums will bloom as profusely as the celebrated flowering cherries of Japan.

Getting Started

Before you take the first steps toward natural landscaping, consider your energy, time, and dreams. Beware of rushing toward a complete transformation of your landscape. The pleasure of gardening lies as much in the voyage as in the destination, so set out at a pace you can enjoy and savor your progress.

First, ask yourself what you want most from your garden — outdoor rooms for leisure, cut flowers, wildlife habitat. Think of small desires as well as large. If you're interested in naturalizing part or all of your property, consider how your neighbors will react to a nontraditional appearance. Maybe you'll decide to maintain the lawn and foundation plantings in the front yard and install a meadow in the back.

Make yourself familiar with the climate and characteristics of your region and of the particular conditions on your property — where the snow lingers latest in the spring, where the water collects after a rain. (See "Growing Wildflowers and Native Plants" for more on these topics.)

Next, learn which plants suit these conditions. Start a list of trees, shrubs, vines, and perennials. Cast your net wide. Seek out nurseries that specialize in native or adapted plants for your region. Visit those nearby, and send for mail-order catalogs of others (see "Further Reading" in the appendix). Visit botanical gardens and arboretums and ask the staff for advice. Call the nearest branch of the Cooperative Extension Service. Attend meetings of the native plant or wildflower society in your state. Visit local gardeners who practice natural landscaping; their advice and camaraderie can be invaluable.

If possible, explore nearby wilderness areas. Very few people will want (or be able) to reproduce a natural habitat faithfully. But even if you landscape only a small portion of your property naturally, the time spent studying a wilderness habitat can be enormously rewarding.

After all this preparation (much of which continues long after you've begun to make your garden) comes the design. The simplest way to think about naturalistic design is to imagine your lawn shrinking. Where can you convert lawn to plantings? Almost certainly you can use the borders of your property and the foundation of your house. Look also along paths and sidewalks and beside the garage. Can you make island beds here and there? It is possible to make an effective natural planting — a meadow, woodland, or bog garden — in a relatively small spot. If you like the way this limited effort turns out, you can expand, converting more lawn or traditional beds and borders as you go.

As your natural landscape grows richer, so will the rewards of caring for it. Birds will take refuge on your property. The inchworms that once plagued your oak trees will vanish to feed your new visitors. Once the plantings are established, you can spend the time you save on maintenance combing nurseries for new plants to try or traipsing around your favorite wild places in search of new inspiration.

Eastern Woodlands

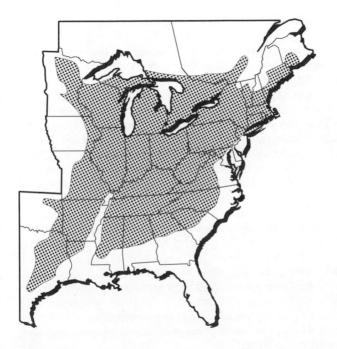

It may not be obvious from the streets of New York or Cleveland or the rolling farmlands of Pennsylvania or Kentucky, but most of the eastern half of the United States was once covered by forest. For millennia, Native Americans lived in dynamic equilibrium with the seemingly endless woodland. Then, in just three centuries, European immigrants completely transformed the landscape. Today there are still large wooded tracts, but Longfellow's "forest primeval" is gone. Luckily for gardeners, many superb native plants survived to add grace and beauty to our lives.

Despite the profound changes, conditions in this region still promote lush growth. Cleared land reverts readily to forest; New England is more heavily forested today than when it was intensely farmed. The reversion process takes time; if you sold the lawn mower today, you would probably not live to see the return of more than a very few of the original forest inhabitants. But natural gardeners try to speed up nature's pace to increase the diversity of wildflowers and native plants in their landscape or to "freeze" it at a certain stage. Natural meadows, for instance, are rare and usually short-lived in the East. Unless maintained by grazing, periodic fire, disease, or mowing, meadows are soon invaded by shrubs and small trees on their way to reestablishing the forest.

A Thumbnail Portrait of the Region

The Eastern Woodlands is a large region characterized by deciduous trees, which drop their leaves in winter. Oaks, hickories, and maples are the most common today. Early settlers would also have included chestnut, which has been devastated by blight in this century. To the west is prairie, where there is too little precipitation to support a woodland. To the north, where temperatures are lower and growing seasons shorter, evergreens dominate. To the southeast is the Coastal Plain, where warmer temperatures do not provide a sufficient dormant period for deciduous species; there, pines take over.

Climate
Climate varies widely across the region, brief droughts are not uncommon, and the growing season is fairly long. Plants with established root systems, particularly trees and shrubs, rarely need much irrigation. Average rainfall is quite high, resulting in lush growth and high humidity. Though we find humid conditions uncomfortable to work in, plants thrive in them; with less evaporation and transpiration, a given amount of rain will support more plant growth in the humid East than it might in the Southwest.

But ample water isn't an unmitigated blessing. High humidity and frequent rains increase disease problems, which can be worsened by poor air circulation in overcrowded plantings. Bacteria and fungus thrive in moist conditions, increasing the potential of rot. Regular rains may leach nutrients from the soil, and low-lying areas may flood in season or drain too slowly, depriving roots of oxygen.

The lie of the land
Topography has a tremendous influence on what grows in a region. Compared to the steep, sharp features of the geologically younger West, the East is a quilt of weathered, worn hills and valleys, gullies and hollows. Hillsides shed water and

cold air faster than valleys. South-facing slopes warm up faster in spring and retain heat longer in autumn. Each type of site will support a very different range of plants.

Soils

The region's soils are as varied as its other features. On top of a ridge, the soil may be shallow and dry; at the bottom, it may be deep and crumbly, rich enough to make meadow plants grow tall and leggy. It may be porous gravel, perfect for a rock garden, or clay that is always too wet or too dry to work. In wooded areas, the leaves of summer become winter's forest floor, a layer of organic matter deposited over time. Sometimes this layer is fairly thick and fertile; all too often it is thin and lacking in nutrients. It's almost always a good idea to add organic matter to your soil to increase its capacity to hold water and to encourage microorganisms that build fertility. In the South, high temperatures increase the speed at which humus breaks down, so adding mulch is a good idea at any time.

Wildflowers of the Eastern Woodland

It should come as no surprise, given the region's size and diversity, to find a vast selection of native plants for the garden. Some of the best are discussed below, grouped according to their tolerance for shade, sun, and wet spots.

Spring in the shade

In a region covered with forest, you'd expect to find a great many shade-tolerant plants. Of these, many prefer good, well-drained soil with plenty of organic matter. Drainage is particularly important for early spring flowers, many of which arise from fleshy roots and corms that may rot if waterlogged.

Jack-in-the-pulpit (*Arisaema triphyllum*) is a mainstay of the woodland scene, effective as a single specimen or in small groups. The tubers are well suited for planting among low ground covers, like green-and-gold (*Chrysogonum virginianum*) or partridgeberry (*Mitchella repens*). Jacks are fascinating for more than their unusual appearance. A given plant may produce male flowers one year on the clublike spadix (the "Jack") and female flowers the next. In some years the seed head will ripen into a large cluster of bright red, berrylike fruits in late summer, while in other years there will be only flowers.

The humus built up on the forest floor by decades of rotting

---

*Plant names preceded by an asterisk (*) are cited in the encyclopedia.

leaves and wood is most often acid (pH below 7). But some woodland natives, including the early bloomers sharp-lobed hepatica (*Hepatica acutiloba*) and bloodroot (*Sanguinaria canadensis*), require more alkaline (pH above 7) conditions to stay healthy. It is not uncommon to find celandine poppy (*Stylophorum diphyllum*) in more basic soils in the wild, yet it seems equally at home in moderately acid soils in the garden. Celandine poppy — not to be confused with the invasive celandine (*Chelidonium majus*) — is one of the easiest and most rewarding plants for a shady spot. Its large, bright yellow flowers light up dim corners for much of the spring and even sporadically through the summer if it's not too dry. Good bedfellows include Virginia bluebells (*Mertensia virginica*), columbine (*Aquilegia* spp.), foamflower (*Tiarella cordifolia*), and creeping phlox (*Phlox stolonifera*).

Continuously blooming perennials are few and far between and are especially appreciated for brightening shady spots after the spring extravaganza has subsided. Bleeding heart (*Dicentra eximia*) blooms most heavily in midspring, but its arched stems continue to dangle rosy pink hearts above intricate pale green foliage right up to frost. You'll be rewarded if you take a minute to pot a few for a shady porch or window box. (Be sure to replant them in the ground in the fall.)

One of the most versatile native perennials is columbine (*Aquilegia canadensis*). The flowers, reddish orange with tubular yellow centers, seem to hang upside down, but this doesn't deter hummingbirds from visiting. The deeply dissected lobed leaves will last well into a mild winter. Columbine is widely tolerant of all types of conditions and seems to thrive on neglect. Planted at the top of a stone wall or rock garden, it will easily naturalize wherever the seeds tumble. This casual mingling can create some very pleasant associations throughout the garden. Celandine poppy, foamflower, and bluebells in particular seem to appreciate its company. Color and leaf shape are extremely variable in the wild and usually repeat in seedlings; if you see a columbine you like, collect some seed and see what happens.

In the "can be tricky but worth it" group is fire pink (*Silene virginica*). In the wild it is a poor competitor, relegated to impoverished, gravelly soils, where it is often stingy with blooms. In the garden, however, given a very well drained, dryish spot in sun or shade, its timorous, unassuming rosette will ignite a hundred or more flashy, red, starlike flowers that last for two months or more. If it gets an early start, you may enjoy combinations with foamflower, alumroot (*Heuchera americana*), dwarf iris (*Iris cristata*), *Phlox divaricata,* or celandine poppy. Later you can usually count on it to be blooming along with eared coreopsis (*Coreopsis auriculata*),

green-and-gold, sundrops (*Oenothera fruticosa*), and butterfly weed (*Asclepias tuberosa*).

One of the best ground covers for all but the driest or wettest
areas in part sun or shade is green-and-gold (*Chrysogonum
virginianum*). Blooming heavily most of the spring, *C. v.* var.
virginianum then continues to produce its sunny yellow, star-
shaped flowers until frost. The most common green-and-gold,
C. v. var. *australe,* ceases blooming with the arrival of summer.
It is quite easy to maintain in average garden conditions, filling
the spaces between tree roots (if it's not too dry) and easily
substituting for small patches of lawn in the shade.

Natives for summer shade

Although grasses are more likely to be adapted to open,
sunny situations, several of our handsome natives choose
shade. Commonly used en masse as ground cover on shady
slopes and in open woodland is river oats (*Chasmanthium
latifolium*). It is excellent for naturalizing and relaxing the
garden. Like the surface of a pond, the drowsy blades seize
the slightest summer breeze in ripples and waves, tempting
your thoughts away with them. In a scaled-down planting, the
seed heads swing freely and are easily seen against a dark
stump or wall. For a grasslike texture in moist shade, consider
members of the sedge family. Plantain-leaved sedge (*Carex
plantaginea*) is one of the best native sedges to use as a low
edging along a shady path or arranged in groups, possibly over
bulbs.

To enliven the quiet green of the summer shade garden, try
black cohosh (*Cimicifuga racemosa*), astilbe (*Astilbe biter-
nata*), and goatsbeard (*Aruncus dioicus*). In early to mid summer, all feature white flowers, some rising up to 6 feet, above
bold, 2- to 3-foot-high foliage. Black cohosh, or bugbane, is
one of the more refined wildflowers, with strong, branched
wands of flowers and interesting seed heads that often last
through winter in the garden. The full foliage skirts of astilbe
and goatsbeard are perfect for filling gaps and as a foil at the
rear of spring beds. Their bright flowering plumes last several
weeks.

Sheltered in summer beneath dense canopies of leaves, most
understory plants stop blooming. As you survey the greenery,
you may ask yourself why you didn't plant more impatiens.
Fortunately, there are some very good native summer-flowering
alternatives.

Among the latest plants to bloom under considerable shade
are white wood aster (*Aster divaricatus*), buff goldenrod (*Solidago sphacelata*), and white snakeroot (*Eupatorium rugo-
sum*). Their light-colored blooms are easily spotted in the
obscure reaches of the withering autumn garden. Since spring

the lush, mounded foliage of the white wood aster and false goldenrod have so perfectly framed all of the earlier performances that it is almost a surprise when they appear as the last act. Nearly pure stands are often found in the wild, their arching flower stalks reaching out from a trail bank or road edge, and they work best when similarly placed in the garden.

As a matter of fact, our native impatiens, called jewelweed (*Impatiens capensis* and *I. pallida*), are also at home in moist shade. Tall, loose annuals reaching 4–6 feet, their fascinating orange or yellow flowers last from early summer through fall and are irresistible to hummingbirds and bumblebees. Also called touch-me-nots because the ripe seedpods explode when touched, tossing their young far and wide, jewelweeds are extremely prolific and may be best enjoyed if allowed to ramble along a creek bank or fill a damp ditch. The juice from crushed leaves and stems has long been used for the relief of rashes such as poison ivy.

Spring in the sun

All too often, would-be wildflower gardeners in the region consider only the spring-blooming flowers of the woodland. But as the forest canopy closes in, plants looking for the energy to flower must follow the sun out into the fields and roadsides. These plants are candidates for a whole new garden.

Commonly there is a "great green lull" in the garden between the glitter of spring and the flash of summer. The wild indigos are some of the most interesting and sturdy perennials for this potentially slow period. Wild blue indigo (*Baptisia australis*) is in the same family as the true indigo and has also been used in dying and in medicines. Three-part leaves, held along many stiff, branched stems, are attractive throughout the season. Foot-long racemes of indigo-blue, lupinelike flowers rise above the shrubby mound of foliage. The tiny seedpods that replace the faded flowers inflate quickly to dry into bulging "rattles." White wild indigo (*Baptisia pendula*) is very similar but has contrasting catbird-gray stems and creamy white flowers. Baptisias flower best in full sun but also do well at the edge of a wood or in light shade. The slow-growing plants will eventually spread 6–10 feet or more, making a perfect specimen plant or a neat and respectable background plant. Once established, you couldn't ask for more carefree, disease-resistant plants.

Penstemons (*Penstemon* spp.) are favorite plants for naturalizing in dry areas, especially when combined with sundrops (*Oenothera* spp.). Penstemon's lavender to blue snapdragon-like flowers mix perfectly with the large, bright yellow sundrops. Both plants are fond of harsh conditions, full to part sun, dryish and well-drained soils. Though some-

what short-lived as individuals, penstemons are prolific seed-
ers; plant them near the top of a slope and allow gravity to
complete the design. If not crowded, they will renew themselves indefinitely for years. Purple coneflower (*Echinacea
purpurea*) and butterfly weed (*Asclepias tuberosa*) are noteworthy among other showy wildflowers of the roadside and
fields.

Eastern wildflowers for wet spots

If you are lucky enough to have a pond, creek, pool, or
natural wetland, you can enjoy another fascinating world of
gardening with its own native plants. An enormous number
of plants can be grown in the water, but many are native to
more southern or even tropical regions. If your plant palette
is limited by winter hardiness, keep in mind that plants growing at the edge of the water rather than in it increase your
choices dramatically.

Stream or pond banks and low spots that retain moisture
year-round can usually be counted on to support a wealth of
interesting plants if relatively undisturbed. If you don't have
a naturally wet area, you can create one simply by digging a
hole about 2 feet deep and lining it with heavy plastic. (Poke
several holes about halfway down and cover the holes with
screens to allow some drainage.) Then replace the soil,
amended with compost or peat if needed to help retain moisture. If you have only a few plants or a few minutes, simply
bury a tub to its rim and plant in that. To keep it moist, place
your "bog" in a spot to which water drains naturally or at the
end of a downspout.

Some of the best hummingbird attractors are found in open
wet areas. Cardinal flower (*Lobelia cardinalis*) is at home in
moist or wet fertile soil in full or part sun, whether at the edge
of a creek or pond or in a garden bed. In midsummer the
flower stalks begin to extend, reaching 3–5 feet by late July,
when they burst into flaming red torches that last for six to
eight weeks.

If you can grow cardinal flower, try turtleheads (*Chelone*
spp.), which can handle light shade and damp soil admirably
and will draw attention back into the cooler reaches of the
garden from late August until frost. *Chelone lyonii* offers clusters of deep pink flowers, *C. glabra* has creamy white flowers,
and the flowers of *C. obliqua* are pinkish white. Naturally
occurring plant associations that perform flawlessly in wet
conditions in the garden include cardinal flower, turtlehead,
and bee balm (*Monarda didyma*) with hibiscus (*H. coccineus, H. militaris,* or *H. moscheutos*) or with cinnamon fern
(*Osmunda cinnamomea*), marginal shield fern (*Dryopteris
marginalis*), or royal fern (*Osmunda regalis*).

Woody Natives

In the Eastern Woodlands, trees and shrubs often come with a house. Oaks, maples, hickories, and ashes may provide a ready-made structure for the landscape. Even if you find the choices unsuitable, existing trees and shrubs are excellent indicators of what the site can support. Choosing larger woody plants to replace or add to existing ones is often only a matter of preference, as most are widely adaptable and easily obtained. A few well-placed evergreens, such as hemlock, American holly, or southern magnolia, will be attractive year-round and will serve as winter windbreaks and wildlife shelters.

In addition to the well-known canopy-forming trees, the region offers a diverse selection of desirable understory trees and shrubs. Freed from intense competition for space, light, and nutrients, what may look like straggly sticks in the wild often become classic specimens in the garden.

In the wild, sourwood (*Oxydendrum arboreum*) appears to offer little aside from its striking, deeply fissured gray bark. But in the garden, given a little room in full sun or part shade, it develops into an extraordinary specimen with something to contribute all year. In early summer, panicles of white, beadlike flowers drape gracefully over the foliage, like hundreds of maidens' hands waiting to be kissed. (Honeybees are more than happy to oblige.) Through the summer the clusters of fruits ripen into dry, tawny lace. As early as midsummer the leaves begin mottling with burgundy, turning later to glorious yellows, oranges, reds, and purples. In winter, sourwood's bark and distinctive branching pattern gives it a wizened, Oriental appearance.

Sassafras (*Sassafras albidum*), like sourwood, does well in acid, loamy soils and is quite drought tolerant. As an individual, sassafras is always impressive, but if allowed to spread and form a colony, it provides a real treat in the winter landscape. Plant sassafras where you can enjoy the buttery yellows and electric oranges of the leaves in the fall and the distinctive candelabra patterns of the branches in the winter.

Informal shrub borders or groups of shrubs gently contain or direct your field of view toward points of interest or away from imperfections. One of the best medium-to-tall shrubs for this and other uses is sweetshrub (*Calycanthus floridus*). With its slowly running habit, it forms dense clumps of deep green, glossy foliage about 4–10 feet high. All parts of sweetshrub have a delicious, spicy scent when crushed. (In the past, when women had to use lye soap — not known for its sex appeal — they crushed and tucked the maroon flowers in their cleavage, hence the name "sweetbubby bush," still common in some parts.) If the fragrance is important to you, choose your plant carefully, since the potency varies considerably.

A superb shrub or small tree for the shade or sun garden is bottlebrush buckeye (*Aesculus parviflora*). It is among the first to leaf out in spring, from huge buds that are not infrequently mistaken for flowers. Its coarse branching perfectly spaces the large, palmate leaves, giving the plant a tidy but relaxed look. For about three weeks in midsummer the wide white "bottlebrush" flowers extend above the leaves. In humusy, mulched soil, bottlebrush buckeye spreads to form a loose colony, which can serve as an anchor for the rest of the garden. Place a comfortable log or bench nearby to enjoy the hosts of butterflies and other pollinators attracted to the buckeye in spring.

Sweet bay (*Magnolia virginiana*) is a medium-size tree or multitrunked shrub whose lush foliage and clean form enhance just about any situation. The leaves resemble those of rhododendrons and are evergreen to semi-evergreen in the southern parts of its range. The leaves rustle in the wind, and a glance at a sweet bay will tell you whether it's balmy or breezy. Groups of sweet bay are especially pleasing in sun or shade, though if allowed ample space, a single plant will enrich even the most ho-hum surroundings.

Coastal Plain

On winter days when sub-zero temperatures and deep snows blanket the northern states, warm breezes fresh from the Gulf Stream whisper among the grasses of the Atlantic seaboard, and the graceful live oaks along the Gulf Coast are lush and green. While their northern friends are only dreaming of spring, gardeners along much of the Coastal Plain can be working among their plants and enjoying their gardens.

Enhancing the pleasures of year-round gardening are the region's wonderful native plants. European gardeners have long admired and sought many of these natives, but only recently have they become widely available here. Where once only a few nurseries offered native plants, today you can readily find all sorts of common and unusual species. Grown in containers, they can be transplanted at any time of year and are far more likely to survive than plants dug from the wild. With so many native species to choose from, the region's gardeners can develop landscapes reflecting the character of their natural surroundings, whether next to the sea, inland among the pines, or along the numerous wetlands that transect this low-lying region.

A Regional Overview

The Coastal Plain extends some 3,000 miles along the Atlantic seaboard and Gulf Coast, from Cape Cod to Texas. For most of its length, it is a relatively narrow band; then it plunges north into the heart of the continent, following the floodplain of the Mississippi River into southern Illinois.

Sloping toward the sea, the Coastal Plain is a diverse area of low relief, typically 200 feet or less above sea level. At the shore, numerous salt marshes, sounds, bays, inlets, and marshy river deltas punctuate miles of sandy beaches. Wetlands are common, and in many areas the water table is at or near the surface. The large rivers that cut across the region have extensive floodplains.

The soils of the region are varied. In the Sand Hills of South Carolina and Georgia, the soil is almost pure sand. Sticky clays characterize the alkaline prairies of the Blackbelt in Alabama and Mississippi. Near the coast of the Carolinas is acidic peat soil, while extensive regions of sandy loam from southeastern Virginia to eastern Texas were once covered by towering longleaf pines. Throughout the region, rivers have deposited fine silt along their waterways.

The Coastal Plain favors its native plants, and its gardeners, with a climate that provides both adequate rainfall during the long growing season and relatively few extremes of temperature in both winter and summer: it is cooler in summer and warmer in winter than much of the continental interior. Thus gardeners on Long Island can grow plants normally used much farther south, and Gulf Coast gardeners can grow many subtropical species. The high humidity in summer and the warm, wet winters probably limit plant selection more than winter cold.

Because of the strikingly different conditions in the region, it is more useful to discuss the plants by natural habitat rather than the more common categories of annuals, perennials, and so on. If your home, for example, is on a dry, sandy beach exposed to the harsh effects of sun, wind, and salt spray, it makes sense to choose your plants from those that have evolved under such conditions. Adapted to the prevailing environmental stresses, these plants are more likely to thrive and to require less maintenance than others, giving you more time to enjoy the delights of living on the coast. The motto of the natural gardener might well be, "If life gives you lemons, make lemonade."

Coastal natives and other regions

Many Coastal Plain species have widespread garden appeal and are hardy in many sections of eastern North America. For example, Ashe magnolia (*Magnolia ashei*) from the panhandle of Florida is hardy as far north as Chicago. Bottlebrush buckeye (*Aesculus parviflora*) from the Coastal Plain of Alabama and Georgia is widely grown in southern New England and in much of the Midwest. A recent record freeze in the middle and upper South proved a number of Coastal Plain natives to be much hardier than some widely grown exotics. Some people have suggested that many southeastern natives pushed south by glaciers during the Ice Age have an inherent adaptation to colder climates.

Seaside Gardening

Coastal Plain gardeners who live near the sea are likely to encounter one or more of the following habitats.

Dunes
In strong contrast to the rocky shores of northern New England, the shoreline from Cape Cod to Texas is a practically unbroken expanse of sand. This greatly admired strip of beaches is continually being shifted by water currents and wind, and its native plants have adapted to the dry, sterile sands, strong winds, and salt spray.

To hold the sand in place around beach homes, gardeners use several native grasses. From Virginia northward, they plant American beach grass (*Ammophila brevillariata*); from North Carolina southward, they use sea oats (*Uniola paniculata*). Sea oats is the handsomer of the two; its golden seed clusters are unforgettable in summer and autumn, waving against the azure sky. Cape beach grass (*Ammophila* cv. Cape) is especially salt tolerant, robust, easy to plant, and quick spreading. For color in the beach landscape, use blanket flower (*Gaillardia pulchella*). Its showy pinwheel flowers of bright yellow, red, and orange make a striking accent among the beige grasses and the white to golden sands.

Foremost among the shrubs that withstand salt spray and constant wind are wax myrtle (*Myrica cerifera*) in the South and bayberry (*Myrica pensylvanica*) from North Carolina to Cape Cod. These dense, aromatic, evergreen shrubs bear attractive gray fruit, require little maintenance, and do not attract deer. *Yucca filamentosa,* another hardy, picturesque native shrub, also grows well on sand dunes.

Maritime forests
Moving inland, you encounter the taller trees and shrubs of the maritime forests, which develop on the well-drained soils

*Plant names preceded by an asterisk (*) are cited in the encyclopedia.

of barrier islands, narrow peninsulas, and other bodies of land near the sea. A bit more protected from the elements than the dunes, these are prime areas for gracious living along the coast.

Live oak (*Quercus virginiana*) dominates the maritime forests from North Carolina southward. A picturesque tree, live oak commonly has a short, massive trunk, large, spreading branches, and a low, rounded crown. Its small gray-green leaves are evergreen, and its curved and bent branches are often festooned with Spanish moss and clumps of ferns. On Long Island and the coast to the north, the maritime forests are dominated by American holly, red oak, white oak, and beech.

Common along the entire coastline, red cedar (*Juniperus virginiana*) is used as an evergreen windbreak or screen. The berrylike cones are consumed by cedar waxwings and many other birds and mammals, and the thick foliage provides nesting sites and excellent cover for cardinals, robins, brown thrashers, and other birds. In southern maritime forests, the evergreen southern magnolia (*Magnolia grandiflora*) grows fast and is happy near the coast. Cabbage palm (*Sabal palmetto*), a striking tree with a bushy head of large, fanlike leaves, and saw palmetto (*Serenoa repens*), an equally effective shrub, add a tropical effect to southern coastal gardens. Other useful trees for these sites include American holly (*Ilex opaca*) and flowering dogwood (*Cornus florida*).

Devilwood (*Osmanthus americanus*), an excellent evergreen shrub, makes a good screen for coastal areas. With long, light green leaves and fragrant flowers, it will grow to 20 feet or can be liberally pruned. Another good screening plant for the coast is *Ilex vomitoria*, or yaupon holly, with small, evergreen, boxwoodlike leaves and clusters of red berries in fall and winter.

Salt marsh edges

Marshes flooded twice daily by the tides can be places of unusual beauty. Masses of yellow-green salt marsh grass (*Spartina* spp.) and the narrow black stems of needle rush (*Juncus roemerianus*) contrast handsomely with the blue waters.

A number of desirable native plants are suited to a garden next to a salt marsh. One of the best is the perennial seashore mallow with the complicated name of *Kosteletzkya virginica*. Large clumps of it will reward you in August and September with hundreds of lovely pink flowers about 3 inches across. Several fine selections of switch grass (*Panicum virgatum*), a low-maintenance, fine-textured grass for marsh edges, are available. For a shrub, select groundsel tree (*Baccharis halimifolia*), which grows about 6–10 feet tall, with gray-green leaves. The female plants have striking, silvery seed heads in fall and early winter.

Gardening near Fresh Water

The freshwater habitats in the region include ponds, marshes, and wooded streams.

Ponds

Freshwater ponds, natural and manmade, are common in many parts of the Coastal Plain. There are numerous native plants for gardeners blessed with a pond, but before you dive into water gardening, consult a good book on the subject and remember that many attractive aquatic and wetland species grow rapidly and can become weedy.

Among the better native species for open, sunny water, 2–3 feet deep, are *Nymphaea odorata,* the familiar white-flowered water lily, and the less common yellow American lotus (*Nelumbo lutea*), whose unusual flat-topped seed heads can be used in dried arrangements. Other desirable natives for open water include the yellow pond lily (*Nuphar advena*), with waxy yellow flowers, the early-spring-blooming golden club (*Orontium aquaticum*), and floating heart (*Nymphoides aquatica*), an interesting floating plant with tiny water lily–like flowers.

Freshwater marshes

Marshes — open, sunny areas covered by herbaceous vegetation and water to a depth of 6 inches or less — are also common in the Coastal Plain, occupying areas as vast as a lake or as small as a drainage ditch. With the cultivation of just a few of the region's many attractive, well-adapted natives, these boggy sites can become interesting and unusual wetland gardens. (The plants discussed below grow in marshes or wet places in the wild, but many can also tolerate occasional drying out in the garden.)

Wetland irises come immediately to mind. One of the most widespread species is blue flag (*Iris versicolor*). Its blue flowers appear for several weeks in the spring, and the foliage remains attractive throughout most of the growing season. Not surprisingly, the southern version (*Iris virginica*) is called southern blue flag. One of the Louisiana irises, *Iris fulva,* or red iris, has bronze-red flowers and is also easily grown in wetland situations.

Wild red mallow (*Hibiscus coccineus*) is a striking, red-flowering species from southern marshes. Unlike its relative the rose mallow (*Hibiscus moscheutos*), whose flowers are rose-colored to white, the wild red mallow is not prone to insect damage. The easily cultivated swamp rose (*Rosa palustris*), with pink flowers 2 inches in diameter, is always found in marshy situations.

Wooded streamsides

Low-lying areas in the Coastal Plain that are subject to flooding (or were in the past) are often covered by trees. The streams and rivers typically found in these areas carry heavy loads of silt and are muddy much of the year.

Gardeners living in this habitat can choose from a number of interesting trees. Bald cypress (*Taxodium distichum*), a long-lived tree reaching heights of 70–100 feet, with soft, featherlike green branches and bronze-red autumn colors, makes a handsome ornamental tree for residential lawns and public landscapes. Hardy well to the north of its native range, it grows rapidly on moist, well-drained soil, much faster than in its swamp habitat. Its relative the pond cypress (*Taxodium ascendens*) is often planted for its interesting form and twisted trunk.

Water tupelo (*Nyssa aquatica*) is a large, picturesque tree with swollen buttresses at the base of its trunk. A common wetland species of the Coastal Plain, it is often planted along the edges of ponds and oxbow lakes. Two additional species of *Nyssa* are useful in low-lying sites. Ogeechee-lime (*Nyssa ogeche*) is a small tree, 20–30 feet tall, with multiple crooked stems. *Nyssa sylvatica* var. *biflora,* commonly called swamp gum or swamp tupelo, reaches 50–80 feet. Its dense foliage, which turns brilliant red in autumn, makes it an excellent shade tree. Other good trees for lowland sites are red maple (*Acer rubrum*), water ash (*Fraxinus caroliniana*), and pecan (*Carya illinoensis*). Shrubs for these sites include swamp dogwood (*Cornus foemina*) and possum haw (*Viburnum nudum*). Cross vine (*Bignonia capreolata*) is a choice flowering vine for lowland gardens.

The Coastal Flatwoods

Gardeners within 25 to 50 miles of the coast are likely to reside in a habitat loosely called the coastal flatwoods. Low-lying and poorly drained, with very acid soil, these areas are dominated by one or more species of pine with an abundant understory of shrubs, a number of which have found a place in horticulture. Of these shrubs, some are evergreen and many exhibit winter hardiness much to the north of their natural ranges.

Attractive flowers and fine-textured foliage recommend

sweet bay (*Magnolia virginiana*) for many landscape situations. The silvery lower surfaces of the leaves are especially attractive, and some selections retain their leaves in winter. Sweet bay can form a small tree but is often pruned as a shrub. Loblolly bay (*Gordonia lasianthus*) is a magnificent native shrub with a treelike habit, showy white flowers, and evergreen leaves. It grows well in the Piedmont and mid-Atlantic states. Sweet pepper bush (*Clethra alnifolia*) is excellent for a damp spot, although it will grow in almost any soil. Grown well in full sun, it is a remarkably beautiful shrub with alluring clusters of perfumed flowers.

One of the easiest of the native azaleas to grow is *Rhododendron austrinum*, the yellow wild azalea or Florida azalea. Its abundant yellow to orange flowers are among the first of the wild azaleas to bloom in the spring. Leucothoe or fetterbush (*Agarista populifolia*) is a superior evergreen plant for the South. Its arching branches and bright green leaves provide a wonderful texture in the landscape. With heavy pruning, it can be maintained as a large foundation plant. For tasty berries in summer and scarlet and crimson color in autumn, plant highbush blueberry (*Vaccinium corymbosum*).

The Longleaf Pine Belt

Much of the region from southeastern Virginia into eastern Texas was once covered with longleaf pine (*Pinus palustris*), the most distinctive of southern conifers. It reaches 80–100 feet tall and 30 inches in diameter, with needles 10–18 inches long. Natural fires were common in its habitat, and the original forest stands were open and parklike, with a prairielike ground cover of grasses and herbaceous plants called forbs. Longleaf pines are still common in the region today, and a few natural gardeners manage their pine forests with fire to recreate the natural landscape, producing places of uncommon natural beauty.

In the South, the end of summer brings a new beginning with the flowering and fruiting of native grasses and forbs. Many of these are also common to the Great Plains, including big bluestem (*Andropogon gerardii*), little bluestem (*Schizachyrium scoparium*), Indian grass (*Sorghastrum nutans*), blazing star (*Liatris spicata*), and sweet goldenrod (*Solidago odora*).

Among the shrubs that naturally occur under the pines are the previously mentioned wax myrtle and an evergreen holly called inkberry (*Ilex glabra*). Both are adapted to fire; the dwarf selection *I. glabra* 'Shamrock' is suitable for foundation plantings.

Gardening in Dry, Sandy Areas

Areas of water-deposited sand occur throughout much of the Coastal Plain. Supporting a sparse, dry vegetation of scrub oaks and pines, these habitats are called sand hills or sand ridges. The most extensive are the Fall Line Sand Hills, extending from Fort Bragg, North Carolina, to Columbus, Georgia. Several very nice perennials are adapted to these dry, sterile, sandy sites. Golden aster (*Pityopsis graminifolia*) has silvery foliage and numerous golden flowers in the fall. For color earlier in the season, try sand milkweed (*Asclepias humistrata*) and sandhill lupine (*Lupinus villosus*).

An excellent, long-flowering shrub for sandy sites is red basil (*Satureja coccinea*), which bears scarlet flowers on 3-foot stems. Other shrubs to consider are deerberry (*Vaccinium stamineum*), sparkleberry (*Vaccinium arboreum*), and prickly pear (*Opuntia humifusa*). For shade you can turn to longleaf pine or other pines native to your area.

The Southern Hardwood Forest

Although casual visitors may feel they are traveling through a sea of pine trees, many areas of hardwood forest exist in the region. While the northern hardwood forests are known for their perennial spring flowers, their southern counterparts boast numerous handsome shrubs and trees that are excellent for landscaping.

Foremost among the trees are the magnolias. The evergreen southern magnolia (*Magnolia grandiflora*) is widely planted as a specimen tree for its showy, fragrant flowers and large, shiny evergreen leaves. Fast growing, it is hardy throughout much of the region. Bigleaf magnolia (*Magnolia macrophylla*), with 24- to 30-inch leaves and large, creamy white flowers, is also notable.

American beech (*Fagus grandifolia*) is one of the dominant species in the hardwood forest and warrants a place in the landscape if space allows.

Among the many outstanding shrubs native to the hardwood forest is the oakleaf hydrangea (*Hydrangea quercifolia*). A large shrub with attractive peeling bark, interesting foliage, and large clusters of flowers, it is at its best massed in a border. The bottlebrush buckeye (*Aesculus parviflora*), a graceful, dense shrub nearly 6 feet tall with white flowers in a long "bottlebrush" cluster, is excellent for massing or on its own as a specimen. Masses of red buckeye (*Aesculus pavia*), a large, open shrub often reaching 12 feet, are attractive along woodland edges or in shrub borders. Valued for its mid to late

summer flowers, plumleaf azalea (*Rhododendron prunifolium*) is a large, graceful shrub. Its vibrant orange to scarlet to
deep red flowers make it an excellent choice for the shady
southern garden. For honeysuckle-scented flowers in early
spring, try *Rhododendron canescens*. Finally, Ashe magnolia
(*Magnolia ashei*) is an excellent shrublike magnolia that, as
mentioned earlier, is hardy as far north as Chicago.

The Southeast's Prairie Soils

There are several prairies in the Coastal Plain, and their neutral
to slightly alkaline soils originally supported deep-rooted perennial herbs. The largest of these natural prairies is the Blackbelt of Alabama and Mississippi, a band about 50 miles wide
from, roughly, Montgomery, Alabama, to Columbus, Mississippi. Smaller prairies exist in Mississippi, Arkansas, Louisiana, and Texas.

Gardening conditions here have much in common with
those of the Great Plains, including many native plants. Among
the recommended grasses are big bluestem (*Andropogon gerardii*), broom sedge (*Andropogon virginicus*), and little bluestem (*Schizachyrium scoparium*). Herbaceous perennial
flowers include compass plant (*Silphium laciniatum*), purple
coneflower (*Echinacea purpurea*), prairie coneflower (*Ratibida pinnata*), blazing star (*Liatris spicata*), black-eyed
Susan (*Rudbeckia fulgida*), prairie mint (*Pycnanthemum flexuosum*), and sunflower (*Helianthus flexuosum*).

Great Plains

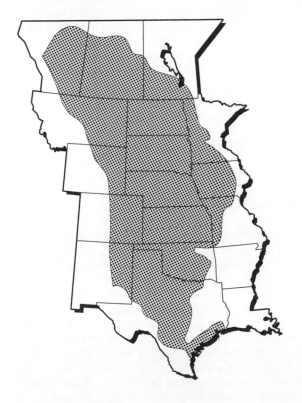

The Great Plains, like the earth's great oceans, are at the mercy of unpredictable and extreme forces. For thousands of years the region's flora and fauna and its scattered communities of indigenous peoples engaged in a windblown dance of survival. Then, in the space of a century, the continent's vast expanse of indigenous grasslands disappeared beneath the plow. Today only a tiny fraction of untouched prairie remains.

The accomplishments of modern agriculture are undeniable. Never in history have so few managed to feed so many. But the agricultural revolution was not achieved without cost. Erosion, pollution, and the destruction of habitats and their indigenous plants and animals have all taken their toll. Many people in the region are seeking ways of living in greater harmony with their surroundings, ways that restore some of the balance that has been lost.

Whether moved by concerns about the wider environment or captivated by the beauty of the prairie, home gardeners and landscape professionals are increasingly looking to the continent's disappearing grasslands. The view can be inspiring. The prairie's subtle colors, shades of gray, and fine textures resonate with the qualities of the finest paintings of the French impressionists. In the midst of this subtlety, coarser foliage or brightly colored flowers bring to mind the forceful gestures of the great paintings of our own school of abstract expressionism. Set against a seemingly endless horizon, the prairie landscape reveals nature's wealth, and its finitude.

Some gardeners are moved enough to create a slice of prairie in their own backyard. If that is not for you, prairie grasses and wildflowers make wonderful additions to more traditional landscapes. One of the most popular perennials today, the purple coneflower (*Echinacea angustifolia*), is a prairie native.

A Grassland Portrait

The North American grasslands are landscapes of great complexity, the product of glaciers, climate, fire, the grazing of animals, and the practices of indigenous peoples.

The Great Plains comprise about a fifth of the land area of the coterminous United States. To the west are the evergreen forests of the Rocky Mountains, whose trees, shrubs, and low-growing plants penetrate halfway across the plains on hills and escarpments. On the east, plants of the deciduous hardwood forests can be found along rivers well out into the grasslands. To the north, the prairies extend into Canada; to the south, through Texas to the Gulf of Mexico. The land is flat or gently rolling; only the Black Hills of South Dakota rise to what can be called mountains. Wetlands are rare, occurring along rivers, in depressions known as prairie potholes, and occasionally as springs. The high evaporation rate can produce waters of high alkalinity or salinity.

The Great Plains appear to the uninitiated, as they did to early explorers, as a landscape of interminable monotony. Closer inspection, however, reveals subtle differences, reflected in the three distinct subregions: shortgrass, mixed-grass, and tallgrass prairies.

The shortgrass prairie
Dominated by grasses adapted to dry conditions (10–20 inches of precipitation per year), the shortgrass prairie once

*Plant names preceded by an asterisk (*) are cited in the encyclopedia.

covered an area of about 237,000 square miles from the Rocky Mountains on the west to the northeast corner of Colorado and the northwest portions of Texas. The most common grass is blue grama (*Bouteloua gracilis*), followed by buffalo grass (*Buchloe dactyloides*) and needle-and-thread grass (*Stipa comata*).

The mixed-grass prairies

East of the shortgrass prairie, two mixed-grass prairies once occupied some 217,000 square miles. The northern mixed-grass prairie extended from the Canadian prairie provinces through Montana, the Dakotas, eastern Wyoming, and into parts of Nebraska. It is characterized by little bluestem (*Schizachyrium scoparium*), needle-and-thread, Junegrass (*Koeleria pyramidata*), and blue grama, among others.

The southern mixed-grass prairie lies between the 98th and 100th meridians, passing through the center of Kansas, Oklahoma, and Texas and into northeastern Mexico. Here, moisture during the growing season is somewhat more dependable than in the prairies to the west and north. The main grasses include little bluestem, sideoats grama (*Bouteloua curtipendula*), and blue grama. In their moister areas, both mixed-grass prairies may include elements of the tallgrass prairie to the east.

The tallgrass prairies

Three tallgrass prairies, north, midcontinent, and south, once covered some 220,000 square miles, but less than 1 percent remains today. The northern prairie extended from Canada through western Minnesota, eastern North and South Dakota, and northwest and north-central Iowa. The dominant grasses were big bluestem (*Andropogon gerardii*), prairie dropseed (*Sporobolus heterolepis*), and Indian grass (*Sorghastrum nutans*), among others. The midcontinent prairie, which extended from Iowa through eastern Nebraska, Kansas, and Oklahoma, was dominated by little bluestem, big bluestem, Indian grass, and sideoats grama. The southern prairie, in Texas, was dominated by little bluestem, big bluestem, and Indian grass, among others. Growth in this southern area was (and is) more robust, because of moisture from the Gulf of Mexico.

Climate

The differences in the grasslands described above are inextricably wedded to climate. As you move from west to east the rainfall increases, and with it the height of the dominant grasses. Similar species will be taller in the east than in the west, independent of genetic differences, because they get more moisture. Plants in the western portions of the Great Plains are also subject to greater stress from other factors. In addition to low soil water, the growing season is subject to high soil and air temperatures, drying winds, and abrasion from wind-blown detritus. Winter brings temperatures well below freezing and irregular snow cover, exposing dormant plant parts to desiccating and destructive winds.

Soil

The soils of the region are diverse. Glacial deposits of sand and gravel are common in the north. To the south, sandstone and shale are the foundation for soils. The central part of the region has windblown loamy soil and sand, while the soils of the southern plains vary from fine sands to heavy clay loams.

While some of the region's soils are among the most fertile in the world (those of the Platte Valley, for example), others are more problematic. Heavy clay, which is found throughout the region, is especially difficult. Claude Barr, perhaps the foremost horticulturalist of the Great Plains, has described his experience in growing dry-country plants in almost pure clay as "years of battling the clinging wet gumbo." Plowing, grazing, and construction have all taken their toll; compacted clay is particularly nasty stuff. Soil amendments — sand, limestone, peat moss — offer one solution; deep-rooted prairie plantings another. Direct-seeded and mulched, they can preclude the need for soil amendments in all but the most extreme conditions.

Gardening with Great Plains Natives

The flora of the Great Plains, like its peoples, is thought to be a group of relatively recent arrivals. Species from the West and the Southwest extend to about the middle of the region; species from the East and the Southeast extend to that same midpoint. Along the river valleys, eastern and western species range even farther.

The grasses that once blanketed the Great Plains inspire the naturalized landscapes of the region, providing both backbone and backdrop for sunlit plantings. Completing the dynamic picture are a group of plants that have traditionally been known as wildflowers but, in prairie parlance, are more accurately called forbs. Forbs add color and texture to the landscape as well as providing, along with the grasses, food and shelter for wildlife.

Most of the Great Plains natives discussed here and listed in the encyclopedia will grow throughout the region, although many are not indigenous to the entire area. But if you want a landscape that is as free of maintenance as possible, select plants adapted to the conditions of your site. One of the major reasons that indigenous plants do not thrive is our failure to provide them with an appropriate habitat. To learn about the best plants for your area, visit native plantings and prairie restorations nearby. (Ask local or regional native plant societies or botanical gardens for information.)

Grasses

Native grasses range in size from diminutive species no more than 6 inches tall to giants reaching 8 feet or more. Some form a continuous sod; others rise like fountains from discrete clumps. Their flowers, though usually minuscule in comparison to those of other garden plants, are no less beautiful. While many grasses go dormant in a dry season, others remain green through all but the driest summers and produce fall colors that rival those of many trees and shrubs in their brilliance. For many people, the red-bronze autumn color of Kansas's Flint Hills is a sight never to be forgotten.

Shorter grasses, such as blue grama (*Bouteloua gracilis*) and buffalo grass (*Buchloe dactyloides*) make handsome, drought-tolerant lawns, allowing you to blend a traffic or play area into a prairie planting of taller grasses, forbs, and shrubs.

Midheight grasses, such as little bluestem (*Schizachyrium scoparium*) and prairie dropseed (*Sporobolus heterolepis*), are backbone plants. Little bluestem is especially attractive in the fall; illuminated from behind by low-angle sunlight, its fluffy seed heads look like a field of sparklers. The fine textures of prairie dropseed are beautiful on their own or as a backdrop for other plants.

The tall grasses, while no less attractive, may not be appropriate for small sites. In addition to their stature, they have a propensity to spread. Nevertheless, if you have the space, a path through stands of big bluestem (*Andropogon gerardii*) and Indian grass (*Sorghastrum nutans*), stems and seed heads waving in the wind, provides an unforgettable experience.

Grasses have several other useful qualities. They help control weeds in a formal planting or naturalized landscape simply by taking up the space that weeds would otherwise occupy. Many native plants, having evolved in tightly knit community groupings, grow long and leggy when planted alone. Clumps of native grasses can support floppier neighbors.

Forbs

The Great Plains offers a selection of handsome forbs. These herbaceous plants provide color from earliest spring through latest fall.

Spring

The drier prairies are the home of a wide variety of low-growing forbs. One of the earliest is the pasque flower (*Anemone patens*). This furry plant's ground-hugging flowers open almost as soon as the ground has thawed, and their yellow centers are soon teeming with numerous tiny insect pollinators. Quickly following the arrival of the pasque flower is prairie smoke (*Geum triflorum*). Named for the wispy appearance of its seed heads, its pendulous red flowers also provide pollen for prairie insects and an early splash of bright color.

Spring in the Great Plains is often dry and windy. Most shade-tolerant plants do not thrive when exposed to drying winds even in amended, regularly watered soils. Nevertheless, spring finds flowers in the region's shaded landscapes. The blue woods violet (*Viola sororia*) is among the most tolerant plants for a ground cover in a shaded location. Red baneberry (*Actaea rubra*), spring beauty (*Claytonia virginiana*), and downy yellow violet (*Viola pubescens*) can be grown in locations protected from the drying and battering effects of the prairie winds. Red baneberry, with white flowers in spring and glossy bright red fruit in July and August, can give a small shaded area its own special character.

As the days lengthen, the plants do, too. Among the many prairie plants that bloom at taller heights as the season progresses is the prairie lily (*Lilium philadelphicum* var. *andinum*). This species, with red to orange chalicelike flowers on stems 15–18 inches high, becomes rarer as the prairies diminish. Difficult to start from seed (and you'll probably have to collect your own; get permission from the landowner first), this beautiful plant presents a challenge to dedicated native plant enthusiasts. During the first growing season each seedling, which must be protected from all manner of herbivores and disturbances, produces a tiny bulb; four years later, if all goes well, you'll be rewarded with the first flowers.

Summer

On the drier prairies, summer sees fewer blossoming species. On the moister prairies, however, the greatest number and variety of forbs bloom in late July and early August along with many of the prairie grasses. (It is pollen from introduced grasses, such as timothy and the ubiquitous Kentucky bluegrass, rather than from natives, that elicits allergic reactions.)

The compass plant (*Silphium laciniatum*), made famous by the naturalist Aldo Leopold, is a large, stout plant often mistaken for a thistle. The common name reflects the tendency of its leaves to orient themselves along a north-south axis. Landscape and garden design tradition tells us that this plant is too large and coarse for the refined wildflower garden. Children, who enjoy touching the large, scabrous leaves and wandering through a forest of the 6-foot stems, remind us that such edicts are not always correct. Despite the children's presence, butterflies, attracted by the sunflower-like blossoms, go about their business.

Other flowers of the summer prairie include yucca (*Yucca glauca*), gayfeather (*Liatris pycnostachya*), blazing star (*Liatris spicata*), prairie coneflower (*Ratibida pinnata*), the wild onions (*Allium cernuum* and others), the sunflowers (*Helianthus* spp.), perennial blanket flower (*Gaillardia aristata*), the biennial black-eyed Susan (*Rudbeckia hirta*), and the annuals showy partridge pea (*Cassia chamaecrista*) and plains coreopsis (*Coreopsis tinctoria*).

The region's wetlands also bloom in summer. Two of the most striking wetland plants, cardinal flower (*Lobelia cardinalis*) and marsh milkweed (*Asclepias incarnata*), are effective hummingbird and butterfly attractors, ideal for a small pond or birdbath.

Fall

Fall brings the asters (*Aster* spp.) and the goldenrods (*Solidago* spp.). Goldenrods, like native grasses, have been wrongly associated with allergy-producing pollen; the real culprit here is the giant ragweed, denizen of the disturbed ground of cultivated fields and river floodplains.

The colors of the fall flowers are at home in the russets and golds of the prairie grasses. An especially complex and subtle combination of flower and foliage, color and texture, is silky aster (*Aster sericeus*), aromatic or savory-leaved aster (*Aster oblongifolius*), and little bluestem (*Schizachyrium scoparium*). Both asters are low-growing and fine-textured. Both are in bloom (silky aster begins first) when little bluestem is turning its fall color. Fall forbs of the region's driest areas include pitcher sage (*Salvia azurea*), with exquisite blue flowers, and Rocky Mountain zinnia (*Zinnia grandiflora*), whose prolific yellow flowers carry over from the heat of summer.

Prairie Fire

Fire is an integral part of the prairie life cycle. It burns away old thatch and debris and releases nutrients, helping to create conditions that stimulate the substantial root systems of prairie plants to send up new growth. It also minimizes the effects of woody plants, which, if allowed to grow unchecked, would overshadow the prairie plants. Before the influx of immigrants to the prairies, lightning set off prairie burns and Native Americans intentionally set fires to aid their hunters.

This does not mean that today's prairie gardener should casually throw matches at the landscape. Small prairie gardens can easily be cared for without fire. Pulling tree and shrub seedlings by hand and mowing in spring are substitutes. Grasses and forbs left standing provide food for birds through the winter.

If you're interested in burning, you'll probably need a permit; you should certainly discuss your plans with neighbors and your fire department. Some officials wholeheartedly support the practice, and volunteer fire departments have used these burns as practice exercises. Other officials reject the practice out of hand. The pamphlet *How to Manage Small Prairie Fires* (see "Further Reading") describes fire as a beneficial but dangerous tool. The main danger is being lulled into a false sense of security.

The prairie, with its sudden fires and windblown, sunlit dance of plants, is a region of risk, but one of rewards, too. When we see prairie birds sprinkling the seeds of a native plant on the snow-covered landscape, we connect with America's past and the possibilities for its future.

Western Deserts

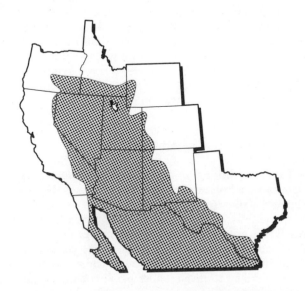

Deserts, filled with extremes, are challenging places to garden. Summer days regularly top 100 degrees F while the nights, lacking insulating cloud cover or stabilizing humidity, are in the comfortable 70s. Winters are generally mild, but storms often bring drastic drops in temperature; swings of up to 60 degrees F are common.

Water is scarce. Rainfall is infrequent, and intense sunlight and drying winds evaporate the precious stuff with startling speed. There are defined rainy seasons when moisture is expected, but there are no guarantees that it will come. An area averaging 8 inches of yearly precipitation may receive 12 inches one year and only 4 the next. A single storm may drop a third of the year's rain in an hour or two, a deluge the parched soil cannot absorb.

Soils are another harsh reality. Alkaline and virtually devoid of organic material, most desert soils are certainly not suitable for gardening. Within each desert, dramatic changes in topography create strong variations in soil and microclimate. Cold air and moisture sink to lower ground, leaving steep, boulder-strewn slopes and gravel-plated hilltops warmer and drier. Arroyos, dry riverbeds in the desert, channel the cold air and water runoff toward basins, where the tallest trees grow in sand, silt, or heavy clay soils, providing shade and buffering the winds. Rocky or sandy soils are usually well drained unless underlaid with caliche, a cementlike hardpan. Where soils drain poorly, salts build up, limiting plant communities to salt-tolerant species such as saltbush and alkali sacaton.

Urbanization has also created microclimates. Buildings and pavement store and reflect heat, tempering winter lows and raising summer highs, as well as creating new drainage patterns for runoff. Although the removal of topsoil during development is not as devastating as it is where soils are loamy, site disturbance often results in soil compaction or surface instability, leading to erosion and invasion by weeds.

Desert Plants: Adaptation to Adversity

Given the harsh conditions, you might think that the southwestern deserts are a botanical vacuum for gardeners. Not so. Deserts support a surprising diversity of small trees, shrubs, wildflowers, and grasses as well as the stereotypical cactuses and yuccas. These are opportunists, plants that evolution has equipped to cope with and even exploit desert conditions. Their unique flowers, forms, and fragrances command attention, and their ability to thrive under harsh conditions and offer the amenities of shade, stability, and habitat have earned them a lasting place in the cultivated landscape.

Adaptation to drought provides a good example of how desert plants cope with difficult conditions. Many plants are described as drought tolerant, capable of surviving short periods with little water. Desert plants must either avoid drought, coordinating their life processes with the short periods when water is available, or endure drought, surviving long periods with limited moisture.

Drought evasion

For many desert plants, drought evasion is built into the seed. Equipped with impermeable coats and growth regulators keyed to temperature, light, and available moisture, these seeds won't germinate unless conditions are suitable for the survival of the seedlings. Dryland annuals such as owl's clover (*Orthocarpus purpurascens*) and gold poppy (*Eschscholzia mexicana*) germinate, bloom, and reseed in rapid response to seasonal rains.

Drought evasion involves other strategies as well. Long-lived

*Plant names preceded by an asterisk (*) are cited in the encyclopedia.

trees and shrubs such as desert olive (*Forestiera neomexicana*) and ocotillo (*Fouquieria splendens*) are drought deciduous, dropping their leaves when water is scarce. Going a step further, palo verdes (*Cercidium floridum* and other species) and joint fir (*Ephedra* spp.), leafless much of the time, have chlorophyll in their stems, enabling them to photosynthesize without leaves.

Drought endurance

Drought endurance also takes many forms. Plants such as chamisa (*Chrysothamnus nauseosus*), prostrate indigobush (*Dalea greggii*), and Texas sage (*Leucophyllum frutescens*) have silver leaves that reflect light and heat. Self-shading, they require less water. Creosotebush (*Larrea tridentata*) and Arizona rosewood (*Vauquelinia californica*) have waxy or resinous leaves that reduce moisture loss by evaporation and transpiration. Many of these plants have relatively small leaves, giving a light, airy feel to the landscape while making them more water efficient. The ultimate in efficiency are those plants with succulent leaves, stems, or roots, such as cactuses, yuccas, bush morning glory (*Ipomoea leptophylla*), and giant four o'clock (*Mirabilis multiflora*), which absorb moisture copiously when it is available and store it as insurance against the dry times sure to follow.

Desert Environments

Adaptation to adverse desert conditions has produced a palette of plants that range from subtle to bold in form, texture, and color and that have a tough constitution. Desert plants can also be quite particular about where they will grow. Gardeners who want to develop a self-sustaining landscape need to understand the peculiarities of their site so that they can choose a companionable community of plants. The region contains too many microclimates to discuss here, but a look at the larger picture should be helpful.

There are four distinct deserts in the southwestern United States: the Great Basin, Mohave, Sonoran, and Chihuahuan. While they share the characteristics of summer heat, intense sunlight, pervasive drought, and soils more suitable to adobe bricks than to a garden, there are many differences between them that are reflected in local plant communities.

The Great Basin

The region's northernmost desert, the Great Basin is the highest in elevation at 4,000–6,000 feet and the coldest, with winter lows of 0 to −20 degrees F. Much of the 6–8 inches of annual precipitation is winter snow, with occasional localized summer rain. Shrubs dominate the vegetation and include sagebrush (*Artemisia tridentata* and others), saltbush (*Atriplex canescens*), chamisa, desert olive, joint fir, yucca, Apache plume (*Fallugia paradoxa*), and relatively few species of cactus. Where summer rains occur, grasses provide ground cover. The cities of Reno, Nevada, Salt Lake City, Utah, Cortez, Colorado, Farmington, New Mexico, and Winslow, Arizona, are part of the Great Basin desert.

The Mohave

The smallest desert, the Mohave provides the transition between the Great Basin and the Sonoran Desert, ranging in elevation from below sea level at Death Valley to 4,000 feet. Relatively cold winters, with nights 0–10 degrees F, contrast with extremely hot summers. Most of its 2–10 inches of annual precipitation falls as rain or snow in winter. In years of ample moisture and favorable temperatures, annual wildflowers provide the dazzling displays that are the Mohave's hallmark. The Joshua tree (*Yucca brevifolia*) is closely identified with the Mohave, as are mesquite (*Prosopis glandulosa* and *P. pubescens*), creosotebush, saltbush, brittlebush (*Encelia farinosa*), joint fir, and teddy bear cholla (*Opuntia bigelovii*). Barstow, California, and Las Vegas, Nevada, are Mohave cities.

The Sonoran Desert

The Sonoran is the warmest desert, with winter lows ranging from 30 to 0 degrees F. It is also the lowest, spanning elevations from near sea level to 3,000 feet. Annual rainfall varies from 2 inches in the lower Sonoran, where some areas are covered with a rocky pavement devoid of plants, to 12 inches at the upper limits, where cactus is a dominant feature. Because rains tend to be less seasonal here, there is a greater diversity of trees, shrubs, and wildflowers. Trees include desert willow (*Chilopsis linearis*), honey mesquite (*Prosopis glandulosa*), ironwood (*Olneya tesota*), and palo verde. Shrubs include creosotebush, ocotillo, brittlebush, and fairy duster (*Calliandra eriophylla*). Among the wildflowers are desert zinnia (*Zinnia grandiflora*), mallows (*Sphaeralcea ambigua* and *S. coccinea*), evening primroses (*Oenothera berlandiera* and others), and penstemons (*Penstemon ambiguus* and others). The saguaro (*Carnegiea gigantea*), giant of the cactus family, is also native to the Sonoran Desert. Palm Springs, California, and Phoenix and Tucson, Arizona, lie within this desert's borders.

The Chihuahuan Desert

At its northern limits, the Chihuahuan Desert is nearly as cold as the Great Basin, with winter nights reaching 10 degrees F, occasionally dropping to −15 degrees, and nearly as high, with elevations ranging from 2,500 to 5,000 feet. Annual precipitation varies from 5 to 14 inches. Winter snows are common, but most moisture comes as summer monsoons, which also cool things off for a while. Chihuahuan cactuses tend to be smaller in stature and therefore less conspicuous than the Sonoran species. Trees, shrubs, and wildflowers are well represented, including desert willow, mesquite, creosotebush, ocotillo, chamisa, Apache plume, littleleaf and threeleaf sumac (*Rhus microphylla* and *R. trilobata*), Texas sage, desert zinnia, blackfoot daisy (*Melampodium leucanthum*), bush morning glory, giant four o'clock, and bush penstemon (*Penstemon ambiguus*). Still expanding into semiarid grassland, this desert also supports a bounty of warm-season grasses, including Indian ricegrass (*Oryzopsis hymenoides*), sand lovegrass (*Eragrostis trichoides*), sacatons (*Sporobolus wrightii* and others) and gramas (*Bouteloua curtipendula, gracilis,* and others). Tombstone, Arizona, and El Paso, Texas, lie along the desert's southern U.S. border; the northern limit extends almost to Albuquerque.

Gardening with Desert Plants

The earliest settlers in the desert Southwest sought relief from the heat and dust of an uncompromising wilderness in courtyard gardens enclosed by walls. By the middle of the twentieth century, a booming population of newcomers was using powerful water-pumping technology to transplant the gardens of their past to an environment otherwise poorly suited to such efforts.

In those days of inexpensive water and labor, large shade trees, formal bluegrass lawns, and foundation plantings of ornamental shrubs and exotic flowers became the symbols of civilization on the western frontier. Homeowners without the time or inclination to maintain this ecological overhaul created "rock lawns," a uniform expanse of gravel mulch broken infrequently with a few scattered yuccas, cactuses, pinyon pines, or junipers. Mislabeled "southwestern landscaping," such displays paid stylized tribute to perhaps the single most uninviting type of desert ecology.

As recently as ten years ago, the options for desert gardeners seemed split between the extremes of grass or gravel. However, recent interest in natural landscaping points toward another course, an approach that allows gardeners to work with, rather than against, the desert's often harsh conditions. Water, no longer viewed as an unlimited resource, is closely managed in such gardens. Using well-adapted native plants, natural gardens have greater diversity and subtlety, more movement and softer edges, than either the "exotic" or the "southwestern" styles of the past.

Desert plant communities as garden models

Natural landscaping is open to a variety of interpretations. A few gardeners attempt a virtual recreation of natural habitat. Others are less stringent, choosing to reflect regional character by imitating the form rather than by reproducing the content of the landscape.

Gardeners seeking a self-sustaining landscape emphasize native integrity by using local plant communities as exclusive models. Locally native plants will establish on site more quickly and suffer the vagaries of weather with less stress. Such gardens form links with larger natural areas in a system of greenways needed to keep wildlife populations genetically viable.

In desert plant communities a handful of species, usually shrubs, dominate, merging with one another and feathering out at the perimeters of the stand. In the Great Basin, for example, bigleaf sage and chamisa cloak hundreds of miles at a stretch with an aromatic blanket of silver. Creosotebush dominates much of the other deserts on rolling, gravelly hills and sandy, alluvial fans. Saltbush dominates areas with strongly alkaline or saline soils in all the deserts. Groves of small trees occupy low spots, where they benefit from additional runoff during rains. Wildflowers are incidental grace notes in the landscape, usually very local in distribution compared with the shrubs.

Many of these natural land forms and plant associations translate effectively to the garden. Groves of small desert trees placed in broad basins near buildings and patios offer dappled shade and use runoff from rooftops and paved surfaces to great advantage. Shrub masses serve as tall ground cover, borders, and screens, where their personalities lend resonance to the landscape. Many desert plants seem to explode into color as spring temperatures rise or after seasonal rains, transforming otherwise nondescript shrubs into blazing bouquets. Perennial wildflowers and grasses are the carpet, their colors and textures adding depth to the landscape.

Shade for desert gardens

Large, thirsty ashes, mulberries, and especially ill-adapted maples are being replaced by smaller trees, such as Chinese pistache (*Pistacia chinensis*) and claret ash (*Fraxinus oxy-*

carpa), both exotic species. Groves of smaller native trees, such as desert willow (*Chilopsis linearis*), mesquite (*Prosopis* spp.), palo verde (*Cercidium* spp.), ironwood (*Olneya tesota*), and desert olive (*Forestiera neomexicana*), provide light shade for patios, and sunscreens for windows. Such deeply rooted and water-efficient trees can be used near foundations and paving without fear of structural damage. Because they love heat, they thrive on the reflected warmth from walls and paving that would undermine less tolerant plants.

When selecting trees or any other plants, remember that where you are ultimately determines the choice of plants. The site may suggest a grove of trees for shade or as a focal point. In Reno, desert olive or mountain mahogany (*Cercocarpus ledifolius*) may be the best choice. In Albuquerque, desert willow is a third option. Near El Paso, desert willow or goldenball leadtree (*Leucaena retusa*) will work well, and in Phoenix, mesquite, palo verde, and ironwood add to the possibilities. Each place, then, is its own, with the stubborn integrity that is the desert.

Where space or time is limited, you may want to build shade rather than grow it. Ramadas (simple post-and-beam shade structures) make south- or west-facing patios comfortable immediately. A layer of cooling foliage can be provided with the addition of a few well-placed vines, including climbing roses, honeysuckle, woodbine (*Parthenocissus inserta*, a desert native and close relative of *P. quinquefolia*), western virgin's bower (*Clematis ligusticifolia*), or yellow jasmine (*Gelsemium sempervirens*).

Plants for outdoor living spaces

Shaded patios and decks, partially enclosed by walls or shrub borders, buffer the vastness of the open desert. Walls that create enclosures for people also provide protected microclimates for plants that might otherwise not adapt to the site. Cherry sage (*Salvia greggii*) is pushed to its limit of hardiness in the far northern reaches of the Chihuahuan Desert. Planting it near a wall that will insulate it from unusually cold weather may make a life-or-death difference. Even when the situation is not potentially fatal, the protection of a wall or fence may keep broadleaf evergreens such as yellow jasmine from wind-burning in winter.

The fine textures of threadleaf sage (*Artemisia filifolia*) and fernbush (*Chamaebatieria millefolium*) are an effective foil for a rough mass of stuccoed adobe. Threadleaf sage grows against rock outcrops at Arches National Monument in Utah, fernbush along rock ledges at the Grand Canyon, where its soft grace contrasts with the bold features of the natural landscape. Using plants in garden situations similar to their native habitat not only satisfies their site preferences but also evokes in the viewer an emotional response like that experienced upon encountering the plant in the wild.

Plants themselves may become walls for outdoor living spaces. Leafy natural barriers are cooler than manmade ones. When it contains plants of mixed height and density, a shrub border works as a visual barrier yet allows air to circulate, capturing the breeze of a summer evening. Sited so that they're backlit by the slanting light of early morning or late afternoon, the silver seed heads of mountain mahogany (*Cercocarpus ledifolius* and *C. montanus*), the feathery pink seed heads of Apache plume (*Fallugia paradoxa*), and the flowers of pink fairy duster (*Calliandra eriophylla*) are striking.

More interesting than formal hedges, shrub borders are also an effective means of contrasting plants for color or texture. In Great Basin or upper Chihuahuan Desert gardens, a mixed border of threeleaf sumac (*Rhus trilobata*) and winterfat (*Ceratoides lanata*) is especially effective in autumn, when the sumac leaves turn shades of scarlet and the woolly white seed heads of winterfat reach their prime. In spring and summer, the silver foliage of winterfat is a foil for the dark green sumac. Add a foreground planting of pineleaf penstemon (*Penstemon pinifolius*), whose scarlet flowers will attract hummingbirds from May through September. Mix the penstemon with the soft silver foliage of fringed sage (*Artemisia frigida*) to echo the fall color display of the sumac and winterfat. In lower Chihuahuan, Sonoran, or Mohave desert gardens, creosotebush (*Larrea tridentata*) with a foreground of prostrate indigobush (*Dalea greggii*) or mixed with Texas sage (*Leucophyllum frutescens*) offers a similar play of colors. After a rain, Texas sage provides a burst of lavender flowers, and creosotebush is especially fragrant.

The proximity of deserts to semiarid grasslands encourages the use of native grasses as ornamental plants. Where a less substantial border is desired, plant a sweep of strongly vertical tall grasses, such as giant sacaton (*Sporobolus wrightii*), little bluestem (*Schizachyrium scoparium*), or sideoats grama (*Bouteloua curtipendula*). Or plant a mass of softly pliant sand lovegrass (*Eragrostis trichoides*), Indian ricegrass (*Oryzopsis hymenoides*), or bamboo muhly (*Muhlenbergia dumosa*). No plants express grace in movement or distill in a small space the grandeur of the high plains like the grasses.

Along with grasses, wildflowers form the carpet in the outdoor living area. They tend to be specific in the conditions they prefer. Chocolateflower (*Berlandiera lyrata*), prickly poppy (*Argemone squarrosa*), blanket flower (*Gaillardia aristata*), and pitcher sage (*Salvia azurea*) colonize swales, where they soak up extra runoff during storms. Bush morning glory (*Ipomoea leptophylla*), blackfoot daisy (**Melampodium leucanthum*), white tufted evening primrose (**Oenothera caespitosa*), and many penstemons drift up slopes, where the soil drains quickly. Giant four o'clock (**Mirabilis multiflora*) rests at the base of pinyon and juniper, where birds deposit seeds and the evergreens provide shelter for the young seedlings. Globe mallows (*Sphaeralcea coccinea*) and desert zinnia (**Zinnia grandiflora*) persist even when soils are disturbed repeatedly.

Desert annuals require soil disturbance as well as the perfect match of moisture and temperatures to prosper. Since weeds invade disturbed areas readily and are far less demanding about other conditions than most showy annual wildflowers, staging a display with annuals requires more effort than one with perennial wildflowers. Some gardeners rise to the challenge; others prefer to leave annuals to nature, reveling in the magic when conditions are right, relying on perennials when times are tough.

Lawns

Traditional bluegrass lawns are shrinking. Better adapted fescues or native buffalo grass (**Buchloe dactyloides*) and blue grama (**Bouteloua gracilis*) are being substituted where turf is needed for play areas. Drip-irrigated shrubby ground covers are alternatives where grass is unnecessary but a green space is desired.

While "rock lawns" are hardly a thing of the past, the natural landscaping alternative takes its cue from more inviting desert plant communities. Abandoning the level, sodded lawn frees you to work with the natural contours of the site, perhaps exaggerating some to form a meandering dry streambed, a desert arroyo. The streambed can be functional, carrying runoff to plants during rainstorms and, when dry, connecting spaces in the garden as a path. Here, the "rockscape" (gravel mulch lining the path and retaining the slopes) becomes a real desert pavement with a purpose. Dense, twiggy shrubs such as chamisa (**Chrysothamnus nauseosus*), Apache plume (**Fallugia paradoxa*), and sumac (**Rhus* spp.), massed at bends along the meander and where runoff channels into the streambed, slow the water down by filtering out sediment, stabilize the soil, and provide color and textural interest, just as they do along natural drainages. Chamisa also provides late summer nectar for butterflies. Wastewater is a resource, an arroyo is a garden, and we are more connected to our surroundings in the process.

Growing Desert Natives in Other Regions

Given the peculiarities of desert climates, the temperature extremes, and the scarcity of water, some dryland plants are
poor prospects for gardens elsewhere. There are few hard
boundaries in nature, however, and plants from the transitional zones — where the deserts blend with surrounding regions — are the best prospects for gardeners outside the
region.

Indeed, the normal range of some desert plants may span
several regions. Desert zinnia (*Zinnia grandiflora*), for example, is also commonly called prairie zinnia and Rocky
Mountain zinnia, and it is native to both those areas. Some
southwestern natives may have potential well beyond their
transitional ranges. Desert willow (*Chilopsis linearis*) and
cherry sage (*Salvia greggii*) may prove garden-worthy across
the Southeast, to the delight of hummingbirds and their ad-
mirers. Very few desert natives belong in the eastern woodlands, where light levels are comparatively low, the soil has
too much water and organic matter, and the winters are long
and cold. But southwestern wetlands, an atypical desert habitat, offer some possibilities.

Gardeners wishing to sample the plants of another region
should be aware that some plants, held in check by climate or
critters in their own habitat, may run rampant in new locations. The South already has kudzu; we need to exercise a bit
of caution when spicing up the ecological stockpot. There are
also limitations beyond the practical. Rough-hewn desert char-
acters may lose their punch amid lush fields and forests. Fine-
textured desert plants may come across as horticultural wimps
without a bold backdrop of vast blue skies and blazing sun
for contrast.

When we see our gardens as part of a larger system and
make that connection evident in the flow and character of its
plantings, introductions from too far afield become intrusive,
disturbing the natural harmony we're seeking. Every region
has many wonderful plants, providing limitless opportunity
to create gardens that are deeply satisfying, not only because
they are beautiful, diverse, and easy to care for, but also because they reflect the vitality we all hope to see restored to
our planet.

Western Mountains and Pacific Northwest

This region is dominated by some of the most dramatic mountains in the world, with steep cliffs, gorges, canyons, mesas, and swift rivers. From the Coast Ranges along the Pacific Ocean to the majestic Rockies, stretching from the Yukon south to the Mexican border, the mountains provide striking natural settings and a wide variety of native plants.

Inspired by the rugged outcrops and scree slopes of the mountains, rock gardeners grow native sedums, phlox, and penstemons. Woodland gardeners plant columbines, bleeding hearts, and lupines as well as a wide variety of evergreen and deciduous shrubs and trees from the region's forest communities. Mountain meadows, lovely in spring, summer, and fall, have provided numerous garden plants, and "meadows" large and small are increasingly seen in the domestic landscape.

Before examining the region's diverse habitats and plant life more closely, let's look at some of the factors that determine what plants grow where.

Climate

This region includes several major climate zones and, within them, a number of minor climates. In addition, countless microclimates affect plants in areas as large as a mountain meadow or as small as a streamside niche. We can give only a broad outline of the major climates here. (For a thorough examination of the region's climates, see *The Western Garden Book,* listed in "Further Reading.")

West of the Cascade–Sierra Nevada divide, the climate is maritime. Moderated by the nearby ocean, the temperatures are mild, with fewer daily and seasonal differences than beyond the mountains to the east. The mild winters bring rain to the coastal lowlands and snow to higher elevations. The summers are dry, and the frost-free growing season is long. Here on the coast, conifers reach their greatest size and longest life.

The climates of the Rocky Mountains, on the other hand, are most affected by the continental air mass. The winters are cold, the summers hot. Extremes in daily and seasonal temperatures are greater, the growing season shorter, and the relative humidity lower than on the coast. Drier and colder than the mountains to the west, the Rockies shelter fewer species of plants and smaller trees. Nevertheless, native plants demonstrate great variation. The Rockies extend 2,100 miles from north to south, and plants from the northern range require more moisture than those in the south. Plants at high elevations must be able to survive temperature swings of 30 degrees F or more from day to night. In the middle and southern Rockies, plants at high elevation must also cope with intense solar radiation, low relative humidity, and low precipitation.

Between the Cascades and the Rockies, the climate reflects both maritime and continental influences. Temperatures are still relatively mild, but colder in winter and warmer in summer than on the coast, and the area is far more arid.

Exposure and Elevation

Over the course of a year, the southern slopes of a mountain receive more light and heat than the northern, lengthening the growing season and reducing the accumulation of snow. Eastern and western exposures can also differ. Moist air blowing in from the Pacific is forced to rise as it encounters the western slopes of the Coastal Range and the Cascades. The air cools, moisture condenses, and rain falls before the air can cross the range. As a result, Seattle and other coastal areas receive between 60 and 120 inches of rain per year, while land on the other side of the mountains may receive only 10 to 20 inches. Although the air currents pick up some moisture again before they reach the Rocky Mountains, the Cascades and Sierra Nevadas get more rain than the Rockies.

Higher altitude generally means more precipitation, stronger winds, greater solar radiation, shallower soils, and cooler temperatures (about 5 degrees F cooler for every 1,000 feet you climb).

Gardening with Mountain Natives

Each of the many mountain environments, with its distinct climate and topography, provides a home for a community of plants and animals, and certain plants define the character of each habitat. For example, the shrublands of the Great Basin between the Cascades and Rockies are dominated by large sagebrush and a few other shrubs. Certain high-altitude forests are dominated by Engelmann spruce. Look more closely at a habitat and you'll discover other species — some less obvious, some less numerous — that are equally well adapted to the particular conditions found there. It seems appropriate to introduce the region's native plants by taking a tour of some of its significant habitats.

Rocky Habitats

Whether found on mountain ridges or alpine peaks, among rock outcrops, cliff faces, or rock debris (scree or talus), rocky habitats are difficult for plants. Exposed to strong winds, cold temperatures, and intense sunlight, plants must grow in shallow soil that holds minimal moisture and nutrients. Plants adapted to such conditions are usually perennials, slow growing and close to the ground with extensive root systems or deep tap roots.

Rocky sites on valley floors or at the base of steep slopes offer deeper soil and warmth from sunlight, which is absorbed and steadily radiated from nearby boulders. These are dry sites, and natives here are often succulents, which store water in fleshy leaves, or plants covered with white hairs, which reduce the rate of transpiration.

Two succulent groups widely used in rock gardens are stonecrops and bitterroots. Stonecrops (*Sedum lanceolatum* and others) are the more versatile of the two. Used in rock gardens, containers, or as ground covers, they are easy to grow, require minimal attention, and provide an interesting array of attractive, fleshy foliage and flowers. Bitterroot (*Lewisia rediviva*), Montana's state flower, is especially valued in rock gardens for its succulent foliage and large, striking, pink to white flowers, like water lilies.

Streamside Habitats

Along the region's waterways is a diverse collection of deciduous broadleaf trees and shrubs that provide the foundation and backbone for landscaping as well as a haven for wildlife. Streamsides are more protected than rocky habitats, and moisture is available throughout the year. Sufficiently watered, streamside plants adapt easily to a variety of garden settings. Many of these plants can be substituted for traditionally used, nonnative species; instead of forsythia, for example, try silver buffalo berry (*Shepherdia argentea*).

Streamside trees

Alders, fast-growing trees or shrubs generally found along mountain streams, gulches, and cold mountain lakes, are year-round ornamentals. Hawthorns, also planted alone or in groups, provide masses of white or pink flowers in spring, outstanding fall color, edible fruit, and interesting bark and form. They also attract birds to the garden. Rocky Mountain maple (*Acer glabrum*), a handsome shrub or small tree, has smooth gray bark when young, bright red winter buds, and delicate foliage that turns yellow in fall.

Streamside shrubs

A streamside species at home in wet and dry gardens is silver buffalo berry. A tall, rigid shrub to 15 feet tall, with striking, silvery, willowlike leaves, it is an excellent substitute for the Russian olive hedge. The small red fruit attracts birds. Western river birch (*Betula fontinalis*) has thin, smooth bark with a

*Plant names preceded by an asterisk (*) are cited in the encyclopedia.

bronze metallic sheen and colorful leaves in fall. As a large shrub, it is a good background plant or informal hedge or screen.

Unlike the pampered hybrid tea roses, wild roses require little care. Clustered wild rose (*Rosa pisocarpa*) and Wood's rose (*Rosa woodsii*) feature clusters of large, single pink flowers, bright red edible fruit, and slender, sparse prickles.

Streamside perennials

Because they grow in the shadow of larger plants, many streamside wildflowers are subtle. But a number of them attract immediate attention. Groups of arrowleaf groundsel (*Senecio triangularis*) are striking. From 3 to 6 feet tall, with clusters of small yellow flowers set off by long, triangular, dark green leaves, it is an excellent background plant for the perennial border. Goatsbeard (*Aruncus dioicus*) produces long spikes of tiny white flowers in early to mid summer. Its height (5–6 feet) and large, compound leaves, which give the plant a coarse texture, make it useful as a background plant for shady, moist spots.

Mountain Meadows

One of the most appreciated western landscapes is the mountain meadow. Found in valleys, on gentle slopes, at the tops of mountains or mesas, and in parklands and forests, these large, open spaces are dominated by grasses or sedges and splashed with a variety of colorful wildflowers. Staggered cycles of emergence, bloom, fruiting, and dormancy constantly change the face of a meadow and help plants to coexist.

Home landscapes inspired by mountain meadows can be very rewarding. They can substitute for formal lawns or provide a transition between lawns and informal plantings of trees and shrubs. Meadow wildflowers attract butterflies and birds. Even if you don't want to establish a meadow, many plants found in natural meadows are suitable for garden beds and borders.

Meadows vary considerably; a high-altitude meadow is very different from one at a lower altitude. Some meadow plants are more suitable for home gardening than others. The plants discussed below may not be the most numerous or obvious of those found in the wild, but they are good for creating the effect of a mountain meadow in the home landscape.

Meadows in spring

In early spring, grasses, sedges, and perennial wildflowers, still low to the ground, begin to green up. As the season warms, the first wildflowers appear: the fragrant golden yellow flowers of mountain wallflower (*Erysimum asperum*), the azure-blue flowers of Lewis flax (*Linum perenne lewisii*). Pungent wild onions add delicate clusters of starlike flowers. The pale pink flowers of Geyer onion (*Allium geyeri*) bloom from midspring to early summer; late spring sees the subtle white flowers of nodding onion (*Allium cernuum*). Many plants in the daisy family appear, including common yarrow (*Achillea millefolium*), whose flat-topped clusters of small white flowers continue long into summer.

Meadows in summer

Among summer meadow flowers are several familiar to many gardeners. Black-eyed Susan (*Rudbeckia hirta*) has a long history in flower beds and arrangements. Throughout the summer, blanket flower (*Gaillardia aristata*) bears numerous large gold and red pinwheels set off by orange-brown centers. In late summer, wild bergamot (*Monarda fistulosa* var. *menthifolia*) provides bright patches of very showy, rosy purple flowers on stalks 1–2 feet tall.

Meadows in fall

As the fall foliage turns, asters and goldenrods dominate the mountain meadow. Showy aster (*Aster conspicuus*), about 3 feet tall with bluish violet flowers, is a handsome meadow plant that is also useful toward the middle or back of a border. Goldenrods vary tremendously, but nearly all have clusters of tiny, bright golden yellow flowers. A tall native goldenrod, *Solidago canadensis*, grows 2 feet or more depending on conditions. Gayfeather (*Liatris punctata*) is a sleeper in the meadow. Its foot-tall, grasslike foliage is inconspicuous until the fall, when small powderpuffs of tiny pink to purple flowers rise along the stems.

Forest Communities

Forests in the region are found on steep slopes, hillsides, or level land. The stands of trees may be dense, shading out all but a few other plants, or open, sheltering a flourishing variety of understory plants.

As one moves east from the Pacific, forests cover the cool, humid lowlands and the mountains of the Coastal Ranges. Here the dominant trees are moisture-loving species such as Sitka spruce, western hemlock, coastal Douglas fir, and coast redwood. A little farther inland, the western slopes of the Cascades aren't quite as rainy and are still mild but with greater temperature extremes. They shelter Douglas fir, Engelmann spruce, alpine fir, giant arborvitae, and Pacific yew.

South of the Cascades, the Sierra Nevada forests are generally drier, with mixed stands of incense cedar, ponderosa pine, sugar pine, white fir, and Douglas fir. To the east, precipitation decreases and temperature extremes increase. The Rocky Mountain forests include drought- and cold-tolerant species such as ponderosa, limber, and lodgepole pine, and Douglas fir.

Forests change with elevation, too, which provides a useful way to examine the plants.

Plants of high-elevation forests

The cool temperatures and moist soils at higher elevations favor conifers such as Engelmann spruce, alpine fir, yew, mountain hemlock, lodgepole pine, giant arborvitae, and aspen. Generally speaking, pollution, higher temperatures, and the salting of snowy or icy roads make it difficult to grow high-elevation trees in cities. High-elevation conifers are usually too large for residential properties, though they make good screens where there is sufficient space. Many dwarf varieties are suitable for small sites.

At the feet of giant Engelmann spruce trees you will often find bunchberry (*Cornus canadensis*) growing on old stumps. Only 6–8 inches tall, it is a tiny copy of the great flowering dogwood of the northwestern and northeastern forests. Given the right conditions (cool, moist, slightly acid, organically rich soil), it makes an excellent ground cover.

In gardens, bristlecone pine (*Pinus aristata*) endures where lesser high-elevation trees fail. Although native to windswept peaks, this 30- to 40-foot tree adapts well to lower elevations and city life. Limber pine (*Pinus flexilis*), another tough, rugged, timberline tree, grows in semiarid areas of the Rockies and Sierras. A large tree, it has a slender, symmetrical form when young, but broadens with age.

Among the pines, you may find red-berried elderberry (*Sambucus pubens*), an impressive tall shrub with creamy white spring flowers and red fall fruit and, scattered in the sunny areas, patches of pearly everlasting (*Anaphalis margaritacea*), an attractive herbaceous perennial whose papery crisp white flowers are dried for winter ornament.

A striking scene in the higher mountains is an aspen forest surrounded by dark evergreen forests. Quaking aspen (*Populus tremuloides*), with its nearly white bark and flat, triangular leaves that flutter with the slightest breeze, grows throughout North America. In the mountains, it displays brilliant, golden yellow fall color; in warmer climates at lower elevations, however, the fall color is often disappointing.

The native Rocky Mountain columbine (*Aquilegia caeru-

lea), Colorado's state flower, is a stately perennial, 1–2 feet tall with blue and white flowers. It has a place in the lineage of many garden hybrids, especially those with long spurs. Western columbine (*Aquilegia formosa*) from the Pacific Northwest grows 1–3 feet tall and has graceful, nodding, coral-red and yellow flowers. An excellent plant for natural gardens, it attracts both butterflies and hummingbirds. Another exceptional garden plant native to damp, shaded spots in the Sierras, Pacific Northwest, and Coastal Ranges is western bleeding heart (*Dicentra formosa*). Its lacy, gray-green foliage and smoky pink flowers provide color in a shady garden from spring into early summer.

Plants of low-elevation forests and foothills

Low-elevation forests, dominated by pines, junipers, Douglas fir, and a variety of shrubs, have inspired many natural landscapers. Groups of ponderosa, Jeffrey, or lodgepole pines make handsome groves; singly, they make excellent specimen trees. A selection of garden worthy companion shrubs and a rustic mulch of fallen needles enhances the effect.

Douglas fir (*Pseudotsuga menziesii*), a large, pyramidal tree familiar to many as a Christmas tree, adapts well to the home landscape. Often planted with it are a variety of pines, including ponderosa pine (*Pinus ponderosa*), a large tree that grows in the transitional zones between the cool, high forests and low, warm areas of shrub and grasslands. Mature trees, with their colorful, deeply furrowed bark, are striking year-round.

Several shrubs from the low-elevation forests adapt well to garden settings and offer year-round greenery. Bearberry (*Arctostaphylos uva-ursi*), a low-growing broadleaf evergreen with glossy green foliage and red berries, makes an excellent ground cover. Creeping holly grape (*Mahonia repens*), another spreading broadleaf evergreen, is more upright, growing 1–3 feet tall depending on conditions, and versatile, able to withstand cold, dry weather in sun or shade.

Oregon grape (*Mahonia aquifolium*) is a fine broadleaf evergreen shrub, growing 6–8 feet tall with leathery, spine-tipped leaves. It has fragrant, bright honey-yellow flowers (Oregon's state flower) and dark blue berries. Snowbush (*Ceanothus velutinus*), an equally handsome broadleaf evergreen native, is covered from late spring to early summer with dense clusters of strongly scented white flowers.

For contrast with the broadleaf evergreens, you might plant junipers, with their needlelike or scaly foliage. Common juniper (*Juniperus communis*) is a useful foundation or specimen plant. Its height is variable, usually 2–3 feet, with a spread of between 5 and 10 feet.

The deciduous shrubs of low-elevation forests are numerous and varied. Flowering currant (*Ribes sanguineum*) is one of the most striking, with drooping clusters of pink to intensely red flowers. Several species of nine-bark (*Physocarpus*), a genus closely related to spireas and named for its layered, peeling bark, are useful spring-blooming shrubs. The region's native mock orange (*Philadelphus lewisii*, Idaho's state flower) is perfumed with snowy white blossoms in spring.

One of the brightest blue flowers of the Rocky Mountain foothills is the blue-mist penstemon (*Penstemon virens*). Growing in loose clumps a foot wide and 8 inches tall, this easy-to-grow plant is especially attractive in a grove of ponderosa pines. Harebell (*Campanula rotundifolia*) is a very reliable wildflower. Its slightly pendulous, delicate blue flowers are remarkably sturdy, able to withstand strong winds without breaking apart. Washington lupine (*Lupinus polyphyllus*), a parent of the commonly grown Russell hybrid lupines, has stately spires of blue, purple, or reddish flowers.

Woodland Communities

Between the moist conifer forests and drier grasslands or deserts are the region's woodlands. Sometimes called pygmy forests, they are more open than forests and feature smaller, more drought-tolerant trees (predominantly oaks, pines, and junipers) and many shrubs and wildflowers. The woodlands receive 10–20 inches of rainfall per year, little of it in the summer. Most native plants of these regions are relatively unknown in gardening, but those discussed here are excellent garden plants. In general, they prefer quick-draining rocky or gravelly soils; in highly fertile garden soils, they may become ungainly.

Curl-leaf mountain mahogany (*Cercocarpus ledifolius*) is a small broadleaf evergreen tree with light gray, stiff branches and short, spurlike twigs. The flowers are inconspicuous, but the fruits, each tipped with a feathery tail, are interesting. Everything appears twisted: the fruit, the leaves, and the overall habit of growth. It is a good choice for espalier, hedges, and mass planting as well as a picturesque specimen. In a natural garden, it combines well with ponderosa pine, manzanitas, Douglas fir, mock orange, rock spirea, fringed sage, June grass, and buckwheat.

Greenleaf manzanita (*Arctostaphylos patula*), a slow-growing shrub to 6 feet tall, can be found from the Sierras east to the high forests of the Rockies' western slopes. Practically maintenance free, it is a good specimen, foundation plant, or ground cover. Pinemat manzanita (*Arctostaphylos nevadensis*), a shorter, faster-growing relative, makes an excellent ground cover. One of the finest native shrubs of the western ranges is serviceberry (*Amelanchier alnifolia*). Its white flowers open in spring just before the leaves emerge; the edible, applelike fruits develop quickly and ripen by early summer. Ranging from 6 to 15 feet tall, it is an excellent shrub border or patio plant.

Of the woodland perennials, many of the buckwheats are desirable for their form, flowers, and low maintenance. Yellow buckwheat (*Eriogonum flavum*) has lemon-yellow flowers and gray, ground-hugging foliage. Sulfur flower (*Eriogonum umbellatum*) is highly variable, with creamy white to sulfur-yellow flowers rising above a rosette of dark green foliage.

Shrublands

Although shrubs appear in all the region's habitats, some areas are dominated by them. These communities, called brush, scrub, or shrubland, usually are found in dry, rocky foothills or transition zones too dry for forests or woodlands and too wet for grasses. (Many of the woodland shrubs, such as manzanita and mountain mahogany, could easily be included here.) The plants may be loosely spaced or in thickets. Chaparral communities, shrubs with thick, leathery, evergreen leaves, are found in areas with hot, dry summers and wet winters. Thickets of deciduous shrubs, such as scrub oak, are found in colder climates. Many shrubland plants are useful for foundation plantings, ground covers, hedges, screening, and wildlife.

Gambel oak (*Quercus gambelii*), which grows in dense shrub thickets in the wild but may become a tree of 20–30 feet in the landscape, offers fall color ranging from brown to red to burgundy. Sumacs, adaptable, easy-to-grow shrubs, provide some of the most outstanding fall color to be found. The lush green foliage of smooth sumac (*Rhus glabra*) turns brilliant red in autumn; that of threeleaf sumac (*Rhus trilobata*) changes to yellow, orange, and purple.

Shrub-Steppe Communities

From the rain shadow of the Cascades to the Rockies lies a large mosaic of grasses and shrubs. Here the maritime climate gives way to the continental, producing a semiarid region with warm to hot, dry summers and relatively cold winters.

The dominant plants are several species of sage and grasses such as fescue and wheatgrass. Sprinkled among them are valuable garden plants. Some, like yellow groundsel (*Senecio integerrimus*), have striking flowers; others, like prairie smoke

(*Geum triflorum*), with its nodding pink flowers that never fully open, are more modest. Plants that may go unnoticed in the wild make fine garden plants. Pussytoes (*Antennaria rosea*), a low, matted plant with gray foliage and clusters of furry, pink flowers, can be impressive in the garden, draping over rocks and creeping among stepping stones.

Bigleaf sage (**Artemisia tridentata*) is the tallest of the sages, growing to 6–8 feet. Its grayish silvery foliage and twisted form make it perfect for a "wild garden." Low sagebrush (*Artemisia arbuscula*), a similar but shorter (to 3 feet) plant, is easier to combine with other plants in a more formal setting.

California
Floristic
Province

Descriptions of California's native plants are typically loaded with superlatives — the height and girth of coast redwoods and giant sequoias, the age of bristlecone pines, and the rarity of Torrey pines. But many of the region's superlatively beautiful native plants have yet to receive all the recognition and popularity they deserve as garden plants. European gardeners enthuse over the dazzling blue flowers of our California lilacs, but why aren't they planted more often in this country?

Like many other questions about California, the answer has roots in the region's immigrant past. Drawn by the promise of work and wealth, a comfortable climate, and surpassing natural beauty, the population boomed and soon grew beyond what the arid land could support. To sustain domestic, agricultural, and industrial growth, huge dams and canals were built to funnel water from distant sources into the region.

The settlers, most from wetter climates, had their own ideas about how gardens should look. With seemingly endless supplies of water, they transplanted favorite plants from "home," and gardens grew lush. The native plants, however, lost out. Finely tuned to the local Mediterranean climate and its dry summer rest period, they suffered or died in heavily irrigated gardens.

Today water no longer seems limitless and conservation has become inescapable. Happily, the need to conserve water coincides with the public's growing interest in ecology, habitat preservation, and rare plant conservation. As gardens inevitably become drier, native plants are finally coming into their own. Gardens from which natives once were banished now have become their refuge.

Regional Characteristics

There really is something special about the West Coast, but it has little to do with the usual crowing of San Franciscans or Angelenos. It is a characteristic shared by any continental western coast at about 40 degrees north or south latitude: a gentle, ocean-dominated Mediterranean climate with cool, wet winters and hot, dry summers.

In California, the coastal influence is effectively limited by the high elevations of the Sierra Nevada and the Transverse and Peninsular ranges of southern California, beyond which lie the North American steppes and deserts. The Coast Ranges are not high enough to block all of the ocean's influence, but they do wring much moisture out of the air as it rises up their seaward slopes, leaving the leeward slopes and the Sacramento and San Joaquin valleys in a dry rain shadow.

For botanists, the part of North America where the Mediterranean climate prevails is known as the California Floristic Province. As the map opposite shows, the region does not coincide with the boundaries of the state of California. It excludes the redwood forest and the higher mountains and deserts, whose climates and plant communities are significantly different. (For convenience, however, we'll continue to refer to this botanical region as California.)

The region encompasses a wealth of diverse habitats and ecological niches where ancient, formerly widespread species, such as Monterey pine (*Pinus radiata*), make their last stand and where new species continue to evolve. For gardeners, this diversity of habitat translates into a great variety of gardening microclimates, each with special opportunities for growing native plants.

Climate

To generalize, the region divides into zones with cool summers, hot summers, and hottest summers. The immediate coastline is noted for its cool, often foggy, summer weather, which becomes warmer and drier as you proceed from north to south. Many of the showy native species from California's islands make top garden subjects here.

The intermediate valleys and adjacent hills are superb gardening country, with enough heat to satisfy even desert natives but still enough marine influence to grow coastal species. In the interior valleys and their surrounding hills, including the Sacramento and San Joaquin valleys, plant choices should be made with summer's fierce heat in mind. Here, most coastal natives would need afternoon shade and would serve best as minor elements, subordinate to species from heat-adapted chaparral, woodland, and grassland environments.

The Mediterranean climate is a stressful one for plants because high temperatures and consequent water loss are greatest precisely when water is least available. To make matters worse, strong, extremely dry winds called Santa Anas often plague southern California, and the whole region is subject to periods of prolonged drought, when the normal cool-season rains fail to arrive.

California plants have evolved several ways to cope with the climate. Some, like Cleveland sage and fuchsia-flowered gooseberry, lose all or part of their leaves in the dry season to minimize their water needs. Others, including several California lilac species, have small, tough evergreen leaves that give up little water. The leaves of many natives are covered with protective hairs or waxy substances to mitigate the desiccating effects of the sun. And a number of California annuals evade drought by passing the dry season in the form of seeds. These plants sprout with the fall rains and end the rainy season with a great crescendo of spring bloom. It is the Mediterranean climate that makes California a land of brilliant wildflowers.

Growing California Plants in Other Regions

California plants have always been a temptation for gardeners in colder climates. California annuals, which are cool-season growers in nature, can be used as summer annuals in cold-winter areas by sowing seeds when the danger of frost is past.

Native bulbs are easy to grow in containers, making them good candidates for cold-frame culture. The evergreen habit of most California shrubs is a mild-climate adaptation that renders them too tender for the coldest areas, but a few can be grown in zone 7.

Almost as important as hardiness is drainage. Many of the most desirable California species, from annuals to trees, are native to gravelly slopes, where water runs off quickly. When grown in summer-rain areas they should be provided with the sharpest drainage possible.

Cold-climate gardeners enticed by California natives should consult the beautifully written guide *Hardy Californians,* by Lester Rowntree, which helps sort out the intricacies of growing Mediterranean-climate plants (see "Further Reading"). Rowntree gardened in northern New Jersey between an idyllic childhood among California wildflowers and an adult career as a champion of the native flora.

A Seasonal Introduction to California Native Plants

Blessed with a mild climate, California gardeners enjoy a full year of activity. It therefore seems fitting to meet the region's native plants by following the seasons.

Most California plants bloom toward the end of the rainy season or shortly after the rains have finished, corresponding to late winter and spring. When cultivated in gardens, natives can be irrigated occasionally to give earlier flowering or a longer season of bloom. Though relatively few natives are summer or fall bloomers, by choosing plants carefully you can make a native garden with a satisfying succession of bloom in all seasons.

Autumn
In the natural scheme of things, early autumn is a time of waiting. The seeds of last spring's wildflowers are scattered in the dust while bulbs lie dormant in the cooler depths of the soil. Some shrubs are stubbornly evergreen, but others have shed their leaves in late summer to cope with the drought. All are waiting for the first rains, which may come in October or more likely November, although in some years there is simply no fall rain.

The imminence of the rainy season makes early autumn a time for action, not waiting, for gardeners. It is time to plant nursery stock so that plants can start to develop deep root systems to help them live through the following summer with little irrigation. It is also time to sow wildflower seed to have a brilliant display in the spring. Planted early in the fall, plants and seeds will get the benefit of the season's first cool, soaking rain.

The dry season extends into early fall, and in the equable climate of the immediate coast this period can be surprisingly colorful. A number of shrubs become virtually ever-bloomers, especially if given an occasional watering. The island tree mallow (*Lavatera assurgentiflora*), an evergreen shrub to 15 feet admired for its 2-inch pink flowers, silvery, maplelike leaves and rapid growth, has been cultivated since the days of the early missions. Smaller ever-blooming shrubs include woolly blue-curls (*Trichostema lanatum*) and the red-flowered bush snapdragon (*Galvezia speciosa*), all in the 3- to 6-foot range and all highly attractive to hummingbirds. Away from the coast, they require extra water to encourage long bloom and perhaps some afternoon shade in the hottest areas.

For many other natives, the late dry season is definitely a period of rest. Gardeners getting to know the native flora should realize that in California a deciduous shrub is not necessarily dormant in winter, as are those in colder climates. One of our finest flowering shrubs, fuchsia-flowered gooseberry (*Ribes speciosum*), is leafless in late summer and fall until rain or irrigation wakes it up. It flowers shortly after its shiny leaves appear, its bristly branches thickly covered with pendant, 1-inch red flowers with long, projecting stamens. Fuchsia-flowered gooseberry is an excellent plant for growing under native oaks, which should not be watered in summer in order to prevent oak-root fungus.

By November, the ripening berries of toyon or California holly (*Heteromeles arbutifolia*) are attracting migrating flocks of cedar waxwings to the garden. The huge trusses of scarlet berries, which stay on the 10- to 25-foot-tall evergreen shrubs for months, are traditional holiday decorations. As they begin to ripen, they accompany the russet tones of western sycamore (*Platanus racemosa*), and by New Year's the bright berries provide contrast for the blue flowers of the season's first California lilac (*Ceanothus* 'Ray Hartman').

Winter

Winter can be amazingly springlike in California, especially in the south. Wildflowers germinated by early fall rain or irrigation can start to bloom as early as Thanksgiving. It is not unusual to have a scattering of arroyo lupines (*Lupinus succulentus*) and California poppies (*Eschscholzia californica*) in the January garden, soon joined by baby blue eyes (*Nemophila menziesii*), a charming low-growing annual. Its

---

*Plant names preceded by an asterisk (*) are cited in the encyclopedia.

flowers, which resemble white-centered china-blue saucers, are a special treat of February and March.

In the Coast Ranges, a January and February spectacle is the bloom of the silk-tassel bush (*Garrya elliptica*). A selected male clone called 'James Roof' has become a popular garden plant for its dazzling display of foot-long pale green catkins.

March is memorable for the redbuds' peak bloom. Western redbud (*Cercis occidentalis*) is a winter-deciduous large shrub or small tree that bursts into a cloud of rose-purple pealike flowers beginning in February and lasting into April as the butterfly-shaped leaves appear. It makes an excellent multi-trunked patio tree; perhaps its only drawback is that it may bloom poorly for lack of winter chilling in the mildest parts of southern California.

Beneath a redbud you can add to the spectacle by sowing seeds of fivespot (*Nemophila maculata*), a March-blooming annual whose white petals are veined and spotted with deep violet. Other excellent early-spring-blooming underplantings are the purplish blue annuals arroyo lupine and yarrow-leaf gilia (*Gilia achilleaefolia*) or the perennials blue-eyed grass (*Sisyrinchium bellum*), a diminutive iris relative, and yellow-flowered sea dahlia (*Coreopsis maritima*), a rare species from the San Diego coast.

Spring: shrubs

In April, the native garden reaches its climax with the hybrid flannel bush or fremontia, *Fremontodendron* 'California Glory', a large evergreen shrub that may grow to 20 feet high and at least as wide, covering itself with 3-inch waxy, lemon-yellow blossoms. Any shrub of such proportions requires thoughtful placement, and fremontia even more so because it does not tolerate summer watering. It is, however, perfect for dry landscapes and especially for spacious slopes.

California is the home of a legion of *Ceanothus* species, many of them found wild only in extremely limited areas. These shrubs, usually called California or mountain lilacs (though they are unrelated to true lilacs), are famed for their fragrant clusters of tiny flowers ranging from palest powder blue to deep cobalt blue, violet, and white. At native plant nurseries you will find a broad range of ceanothus, wild species as well as new, and old, named cultivars and hybrids for landscape uses from low ground cover to small flowering tree.

The Carmel ceanothus (*Ceanothus griseus*) is best known for its low-growing forms, which are sometimes called Carmel creeper. The popular ground cover selection 'Yankee Point' bears clusters of medium-blue flowers and grows 2–3 feet tall with a spread of 6 feet or more. Taller selections useful as 6-foot specimen shrubs include 'Louis Edmunds' and 'Santa

Ana'. All are drought tolerant near the coast but appreciate some extra summer water elsewhere. In hot interior valleys they prefer some afternoon shade.

Ceanothus impressus, native to a small area of Santa Barbara and San Luis Obispo counties, combines excellent deep blue flowers and extreme drought tolerance. A 5- to 10-foot-tall shrub, it is perfect for dry gardens, but its hybrid offspring, 'Concha' and 'Dark Star' among them, have better tolerance of summer watering.

Spring: annual wildflowers

As if beautiful flowering shrubs weren't enough, April is also the peak month for wildflowers. Four species from the sunny, parklike oak woodlands that once dominated much of California combine to give a dependable blue, orange, and yellow color scheme to accompany fremontias and ceanothus. Deep orange California poppies and cheerful yellow and white tidy-tips daisies (*Layia platyglossa* subsp. *campestris*) contrast with the sky-blue spherical clusters of globe gilia (*Gilia capitata*) and the purplish blue spires of spider lupines (*Lupinus benthamii*). Plant these among drifts of the perennial purple needlegrass (*Stipa pulchra*) in a garden dominated by a majestic valley oak (*Quercus lobata*) and you will have recreated a piece of California that has nearly been lost.

Few native annuals prefer shade, but thanks to a couple of members of the mighty genus *Clarkia,* which has some 30 species in California, the shade garden isn't bereft of color. The dainty red ribbons (*Clarkia concinna*), whose flowers are elaborate rose-purple creations, is as comfortable in a traditional garden among camellias and azaleas as in its native redwood forest.

Mountain garland (*Clarkia unguiculata,* also called *C. elegans*) is a taller, coarser plant that will grow in sun or part shade and competes well with introduced annual weeds.

Spring: perennials

By late April, the perennial wildflowers and small flowering shrubs are hitting their stride. Scarlet bugler (*Penstemon centranthifolius*) and violet or blue foothill penstemon (*Penstemon heterophyllus*) make a vivid display on dry banks; the latter also adapts well to summer watering. Use foothill penstemon as a companion for its fellow members of the figwort family, the monkey flowers (*Mimulus* spp. and hybrids), a series of evergreen shrublets with flowers in many shades of red, orange, yellow, violet, and pink.

Douglas iris (*Iris douglasiana*) is a common plant of northern California's coastal prairies, so vigorous it is even considered a weed by some ranchers, albeit one with lovely blue-violet flowers. It has been crossed with other native species to create a class of hybrids called Pacific Coast irises. These have a wide range of colors, including yellow, gold, buff, bronze, blue, violet, and white, with many new varieties introduced each year. Mostly under a foot tall, these diminutive and adaptable plants produce their 4-inch flowers from March through May in sun or light shade with much or little water.

Island alumroot (*Heuchera maxima*), from the cliffs of Santa Cruz and Santa Rosa islands, bears stout, 2-foot stalks of whitish flowers and has proved to be another important species for plant breeders. This robust perennial has been crossed with other California species and with its cousin, the common garden coral bells (*Heuchera sanguinea,* a native of Arizona) to yield plants with the drought tolerance and impressive stature of the island species but in colors from light pink to ruby red.

Alumroots are pretty in light shade with canyon lupine (*Lupinus latifolius* var. *parishii*), an easy-to-grow perennial that attains 6 feet or more in height when bearing its robust flower stalks. The intensely fragrant, blue or lavender-pink blooms last well as cut flowers. In the landscape, canyon lupines need moisture through their blooming period but then go dormant in midsummer and can be dried off.

In scattered localities away from the immediate coast from Ventura County south to the Mexican border, May unquestionably belongs to Matilija poppies (*Romneya coulteri* and hybrids), whose 8-foot-tall stems are tipped with enormous white poppies with crinkled or pleated petals and a ball of golden stamens. More widespread than Matilija poppies and scarcely less spectacular is Whipple's yucca (*Yucca whipplei*), a characteristic plant of southern California chaparral. From its rosette of narrow, sharp-pointed leaves, gray-green to silvery blue, arises a 12-foot stalk bearing hundreds of waxy, cream-colored flowers.

In the chaparral of San Diego County, the finest of the native sages, Cleveland sage (*Salvia clevelandii*), makes a profuse display of lavender-blue blossoms from late spring to August. Anyone who has smelled the wonderful fragrance of its leaves on a warm breeze will know that it can be used in cooking in place of the European *Salvia officinalis*.

Combine all of these late bloomers in the garden with Matilija poppies in the background and the evergreen Cleveland sage in front to hide the poppies when you've cut them down after blooming. The superb architecture of the yucca provides an accent, and in the protective cover of its armed leaves plant the precious mariposa lily. This memorable planting would be at its best in May and June but could continue on into early August.

Summer

By June, most wildflowers have set seed and died down, but a famous flower from California's northern coastline is just getting started. Our grandmothers knew it by its former botanic name, *Godetia,* but it is now properly known as *Clarkia amoena.* Two common names, farewell-to-spring and herald of summer, properly describe its bloom period straddling the seasons. Its cup-shaped flowers are lavender-pink with a splash of bright red on each petal; seed of cultivated forms with flowers in various shades of salmon, rose, and pink are also available.

Summer is wild buckwheat season in California, which shelters some 75 species of the genus *Eriogonum,* from tiny annuals to 10-foot-tall shrubs. Some frequently cultivated perennials in this group include sulfur buckwheat (*Eriogonum umbellatum*) and Conejo buckwheat (*E. crocatum*), both low, mounded plants with gray leaves and brilliant yellow flowers. Of several ornamental shrubs included in the genus, the largest is giant buckwheat (*E. giganteum*), native to California's islands. It makes a fine garden subject with oval, fuzzy gray leaves and an immense bloom of graceful, intricately branched inflorescences of tiny, cream-colored flowers so elegant they are sometimes sold in florists' shops.

With summer at its height, perhaps four months after the last rainfall and with most of the native flora in a dormant state, hummingbird's trumpet (*Zauschneria californica*), also called California fuchsia, is just starting to bloom. This spreading, knee-high perennial produces a riot of narrow, tubular scarlet blossoms that last into the fall, bringing California's garden year full circle. As the clouds of the season's first storms pour in from the Pacific, hummingbird's trumpet is just shedding its plumed seeds to join those of all the other flowers that have been patiently waiting in the soil for the rains to begin.

Gardening for Wildlife: Birds and Butterflies

Gardens can be enjoyed for the creatures they attract as well as for the pleasures of growing plants. Indeed, some gardeners design their entire landscape with an eye to attracting wildlife. A backyard wildlife habitat may offer the scent of skunks in February, the tinkle of peepers in April, bluebirds at the nest box in May, ruby-throated hummingbirds vying for trumpet creeper nectar in July, katydids talking from oak branches on a warm September evening, and migrating monarch butterflies sipping nectar from the flowers of New England aster in an October meadow.

Of all the creatures enticed to the garden, none are more popular than birds and butterflies. They aren't difficult to attract; if you provide food, water, cover, and places where they can raise their young, they will respond. We'll discuss gardening for birds first, then butterflies.

Birds: Starting Out

First take stock of what you have. If you have been watching birds in your yard, you know which trees the orioles nest in or how the cactus wren cherishes your chollas for cover and nesting. Make a list of birds (and other wildlife), the landscape features they frequent, and when they do so. Add comments on how your family uses the yard. Then put your notes on a plan on graph paper, to scale. This plan will be the basis for decisions about additions and deletions to the landscape.

Never work in ink as you plot and plan. Next week that hickory could be hit by lightning. A goner? Perhaps, but consider having it topped, as a snag for a visiting American kestrel or a roosting bat or as a trellis for wild grape, trumpet honeysuckle, or Virginia creeper. A sudden freshet might convince you that the wet spot in the back corner has potential as a bog — or a frog garden. A plan is only as good as your willingness to change it.

Neighbors are important in your landscape scheme. A backyard wildlife habitat may not look like a traditional residential landscape. Take time to explain what you're doing and why. The time spent educating your neighbors is often as satisfying as that spent gardening and observing wildlife.

Providing Food

For most of the year, your landscaping is your most important bird feeder. Trees, shrubs, and other plants provide three key categories of food: berries and other soft fruits, seeds and nuts, and insects. Your goal should be to have food available from your plantings every month of the year.

Plant small trees and shrubs that offer a variety of fruit types. Large trees gulp immense quantities of water and monopolize sunlight; a yard dominated by a few large trees will offer a far less interesting variety of plants and foods for animals or people. Songbirds prefer berry-bearers to woody plants that bear acorns or other types of nuts. If you can choose between planting an elderberry or a hazelnut, go with the elderberry.

If possible, plant native species. You may need to do some research to find out which natives will both attract local birds and fill your landscaping needs. Viburnums, dogwoods, elderberries, sumacs, blueberries, hollies, cherries, and service-berries are among the best small trees and shrubs. Somewhat larger native trees that provide excellent bird foods include sassafras, tupelo, madrone, hackberry, and mountain ash.

Jays, other corvids, and a wide variety of quail, grouse, turkey, pigeons, doves, and waterfowl will eat soft fruits but also feed heavily on the hard-shelled fruits of many plants. Groups to consider for these larger and generally more rural birds include oaks, hazels, beech, hornbeam, and chinkapin.

Insects

Planting natives is also the best way to provide the third, and perhaps most important, category of food — insects and other small animals. All plants get buggy at certain times of the year. Native plants are more likely to sustain large, tasty populations of six-legged crawlers without suffering unacceptable damage from them. As nestlings, virtually all of our land birds rely heavily on invertebrates for food. (Chickadees, titmice, nuthatches, and woodpeckers eat chiefly insects but have rapacious appetites for seeds with a high fat content. Seeds with a high oil content serve as insect-food mimics.)

Among the better insect-laden woody plants that attract birds are alders and willows. Both grow as trees or shrubs of moderate size, and both may form dense stands in wet soils, solving the problem of what to do with that quagmire out back. Willows and alders offer great food value for butterflies, beaver, deer, and moose as well as dozens of bird species. Oaks and crab apples also support large numbers of the small insects that small birds eat.

In addition to buggy trees and shrubs, a good source of insects in winter is the withered and dead flowering stems of native meadow and prairie plants. If you can plant a meadow garden or prairie plot, choose a mixture of grasses and wildflowers. The grasses offer an abundance of seeds for sparrows and juncos, and they help hold up the larger wildflower seed heads through the winter. Many insect eggs and larvae overwinter among sunflower, goldenrod, and thistle seed heads — wonderful snacking sites for chickadees, wrens, kinglets, and downy woodpeckers.

Supplementary food

Most wildlife gardeners provide supplemental foods, placing purchased seed and suet, fruit, and sugar water in man-made feeders. These items are great fast food and can't be beaten in terms of concentrating birds, perhaps as many as 15 to 25 species, in a conveniently observable location. And there is no better way to attract sharp-shinned and Cooper's hawks and goshawks to your yard than to have 20 or 30 juncos or house finches huddled around a mound of seed. If you don't want to encourage predators, rearrange your feeders so that the potential prey can find dense cover nearby or leave your feeders empty until the predators move out of your area.

Cover

A well-planned and planted backyard wildlife habitat will, in time, be stocked with a great variety of food-bearing plants, providing the second most important element for birds (and all wildlife): cover. Virtually any structural feature that offers places to hide from predators or from cold or stormy weather will suffice.

Deciduous trees and shrubs, brush piles, stone walls, hollow trees, or water can all provide sanctuary, but the best cover, especially for birds, is in evergreen trees and shrubs. Of the shrubs, yews, hollies, and junipers offer excellent dense foliage throughout the year as well as food. Yew berries last for only a brief period, but those of junipers and hollies are generally present for 2 to 8 months. In some neighborhoods, the holly and juniper fruits may sustain bluebirds and other thrushes and waxwings late into a cold, insectless spring. Look for native species of trees and shrubs, but don't turn your nose up at varieties from Europe and Asia. Other plants that may also do double duty as food and cover include the mahonias, Carolina cherry laurel, and, in the Pacific Northwest, evergreen huckleberry and salal.

Among tree species, all evergreen conifers provide quality cover, but some, such as eastern red cedar and other upright junipers, are among the very best plants for the backyard habitat. Pines offer excellent cover and exceptional food for vireos, nuthatches, kinglets, and chickadees. Evergreen oaks in the West and Deep South provide cover and a diverse diet of insects. A single southern magnolia can hide a flock of robins in its cloak while offering important high-fat fruit for fall-migrating thrushes of every type.

Tree trunks and branches also provide cover. Certain tree species, such as tupelos, sycamores, and many oaks and maples seem to produce hollow specimens much more frequently than others. A good hollow tree is almost worth its weight in wildlife and is a resource well worth preserving.

Water

All wildlife species, from mountain lions to wasps, need water. Robins and starlings will be delighted if you simply provide a traditional birdbath and keep it clean and full. Many wildlife gardeners find that a small pool or pond attracts more wildlife to their yard than any other landscape feature.

Most wildlife species, and especially songbirds, prefer very shallow water for bathing and basking. For that reason, even an inch-deep terra cotta saucer filled to the brim may be shunned by a mourning warbler. Likewise, an otherwise attractive fiberglass ornamental pool, a natural pond, or a stream won't accommodate birds unless each contains a shallowly flooded island. You can also place small sections of a halved tree trunk in a pond or slow stream, anchoring them flat side up with nylon rope and cinder blocks. These "loafing logs" provide excellent resting, feeding, and basking areas for herons, sandpipers, waterfowl, and turtles.

If you can't find space for a pond, dripping water may still attract some birds. Warblers seem drawn to a very slow, splashy drip into a shallow container. There are drip-flow regulators on the market, and many of the excellent books on bird attraction provide diagrams for making your own regulator. Remember, however, that water is a vital commodity. Make sure that any drip device is properly controlled so that it does not waste more water than is required to attract the desired small songbirds.

Nesting Sites

If your property is small — less than half an acre or so — make a special effort to build or buy nesting boxes for birds and roosting or brooding boxes for bats and other wildlife. These structures take the place of dead or hollow trees, which may not be tolerated as readily in suburban and urban yards as in rural areas.

You can interest children in wildlife by helping them build or find and monitor a nest box. No matter what the species — pygmy nuthatch, prothonotary warbler, or house sparrow — the experience is unforgettable for kids. Two or three boxes placed in a suitable habitat on a small property should attract at least one type of nesting bird. A standard bluebird house design is suitable for a wide variety of other species, including violet-green swallows, house wrens, tufted titmice, and chickadees as well as white-footed mice and even an occasional flying squirrel. Whether you build or buy nest boxes, be sure that you can open the top, front, or side easily in order to check on the inhabitants every 2 weeks or so. Clean out the boxes between nestings or at the end of the summer.

Gardening for Butterflies

Butterflies, their jeweled wings flashing in a graceful, wind-borne dance, bring liveliness and color to gardens. By growing plants that attract butterflies, you can open a magic window on nature. As you become attuned to the movement and behavior of the butterflies, you will begin to observe life in your backyard at a finer scale. You'll become aware of the numerous creatures that seek food and shelter in your trees, shrubs, flowers, and soil and of the intricacies of their interactions.

Beginning a garden to attract butterflies seeking nectar is simple. A novice can create a basic butterfly garden rapidly and easily; experienced gardeners need only shift their focus slightly to attract butterflies. But you must guard against unrealistic expectations of quick success. The British naturalist Miriam Rothschild advises prospective butterfly gardeners to "abandon any romantic idea of creating a home for these angelic creatures — the best you can do is to provide them with a good pub." Although you've planted the right nectar flowers for butterflies, cold or windy weather may discourage their flight, and the number of butterflies that find their way to your plot may be disappointingly few. Bear in mind that only very big gardens containing natural habitats such as a woodland, thicket, or meadow will attract the broadest diversity of local butterflies. Butterfly life cycles depend on many factors beyond your control, and butterflies themselves cannot be confined or trained. Their visits remain unpredictable, always a small gift of nature.

Succeeding years of butterfly gardening, however, can be increasingly rewarding because the longer a nectar source is established, the more butterflies are likely to visit. If you become enchanted by the theater of biology in your backyard, you can expand and elaborate on the butterfly garden each year by adding shrubs, larval food sources, and native plants. The choices cover a range broad enough to keep the most sophisticated gardener engaged for years.

The essence of butterfly gardening is to plant perennial and annual flowers that are sources of nectar and the herbaceous plants, shrubs, and trees that provide food for the butterfly's larvae. But the pivotal step is deciding to stop waging chemical warfare in the garden. Butterfly gardeners learn to view partially eaten leaves differently when they discover that the feasting caterpillar soon becomes a beautiful butterfly. Spared a chemical demise, other insects and organisms will also populate the garden, many of them beneficial. Some help control pests; others pollinate plants or disperse seeds. (For more on gardening without chemicals, see "Organic Control of Pests and Diseases.")

The Butterfly's Life Cycle

A butterfly's or moth's life occurs in four stages, spanning an astonishing spectrum of change. The egg, which has a tough shell to protect the developing embryo within, comes in many sizes and shapes, depending on the moth or butterfly species. From the egg hatches the larva (a caterpillar), which can be dull or colorful, large or small, and bear horns or spines. Caterpillars have voracious appetites; Dave Winter, the secretary of the Lepidopterists' Society, calls them "eating machines."

After 3–6 weeks, during which the larva outgrows and sheds four skins, it begins the pupal stage, in most cases forming a chrysalis, which is frequently suspended from a leaf or twig. After 1 or 2 weeks of pupal development, the adult butterfly or moth breaks open the chrysalis and emerges. It pumps fluid into the veins of its wings, the wings harden and dry, and metamorphosis is complete.

You can observe these life changes at first hand in your garden and your neighborhood; visit undeveloped areas nearby as well. With the aid of good field guides, you can learn to recognize the eggs and larvae of specific butterflies and moths, the plants they visit for nectar, those the females choose for egg-laying, and those that provide food for the caterpillars. If you're just beginning a butterfly garden, this information will be invaluable for choosing the right plants to grow.

Getting Started

Butterfly gardening begins in spring with the choice of plants. For your first butterfly garden, you may want to concentrate on planting sources of nectar, leaving larval food plants for another year. If you've observed butterflies in your area, you'll have a good idea of which plants to grow. If not, consult a local nature center or your county extension agent. Butterfly gardening books also provide plant lists (see "Further Reading"). If you're not sure which butterflies inhabit your area, plant a selection of butterfly attractors and see what turns up. The list at the end of this essay will give you a good start.

If you are interested in plants and animals native to your region, seek out butterfly-attracting species. It is likely that over time a native garden will attract butterfly species you haven't previously observed. If you are in the suburbs, a native plant garden increases the chances of luring in stray butterfly visitors from the surrounding countryside.

Set the plants in sunny places well protected from the wind. Butterflies cannot fly if their body temperature falls below a certain level; you'll often observe them basking in the sun to warm their muscles for flight. Butterflies also gather around water, and a birdbath, pool, or large clay saucer will provide another opportunity for close observation.

Your garden's design — the plant arrangement and color grouping — is up to you. Butterflies are just as happy with a hodgepodge of plants as with an elegant composition. Some design principles, however, serve both aesthetic and butterfly-watching ends. Grouping several plants of the same species together concentrates sources of nectar as well as establishing major blocks of color. Arranging plants carefully by size can lend grace to the garden's structure, and it makes flowers and butterflies alike easier to see. Place large shrubs or trees in the background, with tall flowering plants immediately in front of them, intermediate-size plants next, low-growing plants at the front, and edging plants at the borders. You can also plant butterfly attractors among your vegetables or in ·borders around vegetables; you can create small hedgerows between your beds or around your back or front yard; and you can fill any unused flower bed space with attracting plants.

Keeping Going

When you're ready to plant your second butterfly garden, you will probably know the names and habits of most of the butterflies that came the previous year. With that in mind, you may want to research and plant larval food plants, which will attract some of the local egg-laying female butterflies. With diligent observation and good luck, you may be able to see caterpillars pupating and perhaps witness a butterfly emerging from its chrysalis in your own garden.

When you're planting, do as Laura Ingalls Wilder suggested in *Little House on the Prairie* and plant "one for the cutworm, one for the crow, one for the cabbage worm, and one to grow." Begin to think of your garden as a habitat, where certain plants are part of the food chain for the butterflies and other creatures you're trying to attract. Learn to accept chewed leaves.

Butterfly gardens also include trees and shrubs that provide larval food. As your interest increases, make room for them, then expand your selection of bigger butterfly-attracting shrubs, such as butterfly bush (*Buddleia davidii*). Enlist your neighbors; more butterfly gardens in a neighborhood mean more butterflies. When the Smithsonian Institution's National Zoological Park replanted all of its flower beds with butterfly nectar plants, they counted 13 different species of butterflies after three years.

For the small amount of time and effort required, butterfly gardening offers considerable rewards. It can brighten your surroundings and alert you to the biological intricacies of the world. Summer gardens are immeasurably enhanced by the colorful patterns and carefree, roller-coaster flights of these four-winged creatures.

Nectar Plants for Butterflies

Glossy abelia (*Abelia* × *grandiflora*)
Fernleaf yarrow (*Achillea filipendulina*)
Butterfly weed (*Asclepias tuberosa*)
New England aster (*Aster novae-angliae*)
Orange-eye butterfly bush, summer lilac (*Buddleia davidii*)
Jupiter's beard, red valerian (*Centranthus ruber*)
Daisies (*Chrysanthemum* spp.)
Cosmos (*Cosmos bipinnatus*)
Purple coneflower (*Echinacea purpurea*)
Joe-Pye weeds (*Eupatorium* spp.)
Sunflowers (*Helianthus* spp.)
Heliotrope, cherry pie (*Heliotropium arborescens*)
Daylilies (*Hemerocallis* spp.)
Lantana, yellow sage, hedgeflower (*Lantana camara*)
Lavender, English lavender (*Lavandula angustifolia*)
Blazing star (*Liatris spicata*)
Wax leaf privet, Japanese privet (*Ligustrum japonicum*)
Japanese honeysuckle (*Lonicera japonica*)
Mints (*Mentha* spp.)
Bee balm, Oswego tea (*Monarda didyma*)
Flowering tobacco (*Nicotiana alata*)
Common garden petunia (*Petunia* × *hybrida*)
Garden phlox, summer phlox, hardy phlox (*Phlox paniculata*)
Rosemary (*Rosmarinus officinalis*)
Black-eyed Susan, coneflowers (*Rudbeckia* spp.)
Pincushion flower (*Scabiosa caucasica*)
Showy stonecrop (*Sedum spectabile*)
Goldenrods (*Solidago* spp.)
French marigolds (*Tagetes patula*)
Common zinnia (*Zinnia elegans*)

*Plant names preceded by an asterisk (*) are cited in the encyclopedia.

Growing Wildflowers and Native Plants

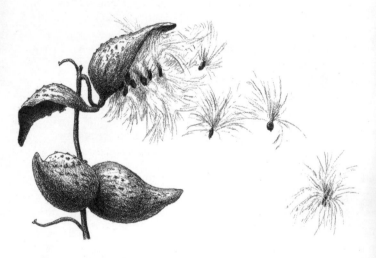

Long admired in their natural habitats, wildflowers and native plants are increasingly being welcomed into gardens. In cultivation, they're prized not only for their beauty and interest but for their performance. Adapted to local conditions — heat, cold, moisture, drought, soil, wind — native plants and wildflowers are survivors. When cultivated in their native regions (or under similar conditions), they usually thrive with little care.

Wildflowers are no more difficult to grow than nonnative plants (called exotics) and, if you've chosen them with your site's conditions in mind, they can be easier. There are drought-tolerant natives and those that prefer wet or boggy spots; there are natives for almost every type of soil as well as those that can withstand searing heat, bone-chilling cold, and gale-force winds. The key to growing native plants, then, is matching the requirements of the plant with the conditions of the site.

Obtaining Native Plants

Digging plants in the wild is unethical, destructive, and unnecessary. It is tempting to stop and dig an admired wildflower on the side of a road or in a meadow, but the increasing encroachment of commercial, industrial, agricultural, and residential development on natural habitats is eliminating whole populations of native plants. These plants may grow elsewhere, even in large numbers, but their disappearance from a particular location impoverishes that landscape and ecosystem.

So, admire wildflowers in the wild, but for your garden buy plants propagated in the nursery or grow them from seed. Many nurseries sell wildflowers and native plants. Be wary, however, of those that offer "nursery-grown" plants. Too often these plants have been dug in the wild and transplanted to a nursery bed or pot before sale. Buying collected plants contributes to habitat destruction; they're also a poor investment, less likely to survive in cultivation than plants propagated in a nursery from seeds or by vegetative means (division, cuttings, and so on). Don't be afraid to ask how the plant was propagated. If the nursery can't or won't tell you, look elsewhere. Many botanical gardens, arboretums, and native plant societies sell native plants or can give you a list of mail-order nurseries that propagate their own plants.

Plants of the same species can vary over a wide geographical range in their tolerance to heat, cold, and drought and even in physical characteristics. Red maple (*Acer rubrum*), for example, is native from Newfoundland to Florida and west to Minnesota, Oklahoma, and Texas. Planted in the North, a seedling from a red maple native to Newfoundland is likely to survive the region's intense cold. Planted in Texas, the same seedling may not be as tolerant of the blistering summer heat as a seedling from a red maple native to Texas. Similar differences occur in herbaceous species. The seed from a particular broom sedge plant may grow to 4 feet in California and only 2 feet in Pennsylvania.

If you're buying natives for their adaptation to a certain area or conditions, try to get seeds collected from plants native to that area or to areas with similar conditions. (If you're buying plants, find out the native region of the parent plants.) You

*Plant names preceded by an asterisk (*) are cited in the encyclopedia.

won't always be able to get this information, but nurseries and seed suppliers specializing in natives are increasingly able to provide it.

Handling mail-order plants

Although more and more nurseries and garden centers are offering native plants, by far the widest selection of natives is available by mail order. Sometimes mail-order plants are shipped with soil intact around their roots, in or out of containers. Others may arrive with no soil, their bare roots wrapped in moistened sphagnum moss or a similar moisture-retentive material. (Some states require that plants be shipped "bare root" to avoid local contamination by insect eggs or larvae hidden in the soil.) If you can't install bare-root mail-order plants immediately in their permanent homes, pot them in suitable containers, then place them, along with those shipped in containers, in a shady spot and keep them watered.

Growing from Seeds

There are a number of reasons to grow native plants from seeds. If nurseries don't sell the plant, seeds may be the only way to get what you want. Seeds are also relatively cheap; buying enough plants to create a meadow or cover a lot of ground can cost a small fortune. Finally, growing native plants from seeds can be both fun and challenging. Like plants, some native seeds are available at local nurseries and garden centers, but mail-order suppliers, native plant societies, botanical gardens, and arboretums offer the largest selections.

The requirements for growing plants from seed vary from plant to plant, and we can't cover them individually here. (See "Further Reading" for books that do.) But a few guidelines on collecting, cleaning, storing, and starting wildflower seeds may be helpful.

Collecting seeds

Growing native plants from seeds you've harvested yourself fosters an intimate connection with the plants and their life cycles and provides a satisfying sense of accomplishment. You can collect seeds from cultivated plants, yours or a friend's, or from the wild. Collecting seeds in the wild avoids the dangers to plants and habitats posed by plant collecting. Don't gather more than 10 percent of the seeds in an area; this helps protect the population's ability to reproduce in the wild.

For best germination, seeds should be allowed to complete their development, or "ripen," before collection. In general, ripe seeds or seed capsules will darken and expand slightly.

(Of course, there are exceptions, such as Jack-in-the-pulpit, *Arisaema triphyllum*, whose seeds are white when ripe.) If the seed capsule has cracked, the enclosed seeds are usually ripe — but they may disperse. Some plants ripen and disperse their seeds over a long period of time; others do it quickly. If you don't think you can collect a capsule just before it cracks, you can cut ripening stalks early and place them in a vase with water or in an envelope to continue to ripen. You can also increase your chances of capturing quickly dispersed seeds by placing a cloth on the ground beneath the plant or by enclosing the developing seed structure in cheesecloth or a bag.

Storing seeds
In the wild, seeds ripen moist or dry. Seeds that ripen dry — coneflowers, black-eyed Susans, butterfly weed (*Asclepias tuberosa*), and columbine, for example — should be air-dried in a garage, basement, or other cool, shady area with low humidity. Place the seed stalks upside down in brown paper bags or spread them on a table covered with newspaper. After 4–7 days, separate the seeds from the debris by rubbing the capsules and stalks over a sieve or strainer resting on a bowl. The openings in the strainer should be large enough for the seeds to pass through. (It isn't necessary to remove the bristlelike appendage or "fluff," called the pappus, that helps some seeds, such as goldenrods, Joe-Pye weed, blazing star, and asters, to disperse.) If you can't sow the seeds immediately, put them in a container in the refrigerator.

Seeds that ripen moist should not be allowed to dry out at any time. These include seeds enclosed in a berry, such as Jack-in-the-pulpit and Solomon's seal (*Polygonatum* spp.), and seeds with a fleshy, enlarged outgrowth called an aril, such as wild bleeding heart (*Dicentra eximia*). For best germination, remove the seeds from the berry or aril and place them in a container in moist sphagnum moss, peat moss, or commercial soil mix before they dry out. (If you can squeeze water from the moss or soil, it is too wet and will encourage fungal growth.) Again, if you can't sow wet seeds immediately, store them in the refrigerator.

Storage containers
Almost any waterproof and airtight container is appropriate. Film canisters, Ziploc freezer bags, empty herb containers, and plastic freezer cartons work well. On two labels, record the botanical name (genus and species), common name, date of collection (include year), source or location of the seed, and any other useful information about the plants from which the seed was collected. Stick one label on the outside of the container and one inside, for insurance.

Starting seeds

You don't need any special talent to start many wildflowers and native plants from seed; depending on the species, direct seeding or starting in containers works as well for natives as for exotics. (For more on starting seeds, see *Taylor's Guide to Gardening Techniques*.)

Some seeds require special treatment, commonly a month or more in cool, moist conditions or exposure to light. In cold-winter areas, it's simplest to sow the seeds outdoors in the fall and let nature provide the requisite cool, moist conditions. If rain is infrequent, water the seed beds or flats; the seeds will germinate in the spring when the soil warms up.

Another way to fulfill this requirement is to place the seeds in a moistened seed-starting mix and refrigerate for 6–8 weeks. This process, called stratification, enhances germination for seeds in general, so if you don't know the requirements of the seeds you are sowing or if the seeds have been stored for a long time, it's advisable to stratify them. Seeds requiring a cool, moist period include Jack-in-the-pulpit, eastern wild columbine (*Aquilegia canadensis*), cardinal flower (*Lobelia cardinalis*), and coneflower (*Echinacea purpurea*).

Coneflowers, cardinal flower, and columbine are also among the seeds that require light to germinate. Rather than covering these seeds with soil, just press them lightly into the surface. A sprinkling of pine needles will prevent them from being washed away by water.

Growing Plants from Plant Parts

Plants have the wonderful capacity to reproduce themselves asexually. This process, also called vegetative reproduction, is familiar to us in plants like daffodils, which produce bulbs, or irises, which grow from rhizomes. But under the right conditions, just part of a stem, root, or leaf can produce a whole new plant.

Vegetative propagation is invaluable to horticulturists and gardeners. It is the only option for increasing the supply of plants that produce few viable seeds or no seeds at all. More important, vegetative propagation is the only way to produce many plants that are prized because they exhibit features unusual to their species. The New England aster (*Aster novae-angliae*), for example, which grows 4–6 feet tall, has a dwarf form, 'Purple Dome', that grows only 2 feet tall. Seed from 'Purple Dome' would produce many tall seedlings, whereas plants grown from stem cuttings will all be dwarfs, exactly like the parent.

Vegetative propagation can be as simple as sticking a shoot in the ground or difficult enough to require a highly controlled environment. Here's a brief summary of several basic techniques; for detailed information consult the books listed in "Further Reading."

Cuttings

Both woody and herbaceous plants are propagated by cuttings from plant stems. Stuck in sand, peat moss, or other suitable rooting media and sometimes treated with growth hormone, the cuttings develop roots and new shoots and are then transplanted and treated as seedlings. For herbaceous plants, softwood or semihardwood cuttings yield the best results. Softwood cuttings are taken from the new, succulent growth that occurs in spring or after the plant has been pruned. Semihardwood cuttings are taken at the next growth stage, when the stems have become firmer but are still pliable. Similar procedures using root cuttings are the only reliable method for reproducing some herbaceous plants.

Division

Not every gardener will want to attempt to propagate by cuttings. But few will garden long without dividing plants. Many plants can be divided. Sometimes a tangled mass of underground stems, called stolons, can be teased apart, as for bee balm (*Monarda didyma*). Others with thicker or more tenacious parts — the thick rhizomes of irises or the dense crowns of native grasses — may require the aid of a knife or sharp spade. It's best to divide plants when they are not in flower. (Generally, divide fall-blooming plants in the spring, spring-blooming plants in the fall.) Cut the foliage back by half, dig the plant, and remove as much soil as possible to see where to divide. Plant the new divisions immediately or pot them into a container and water well.

Gardening with Natives: The Right Plant for the Right Place

Since native plants usually do well in conditions similar to those to which they are accustomed in the wild, if possible, visit their native habitats. What is the soil like? Is it sandy, rocky, lean and infertile, rich in organic matter, clayey or loamy? Is the area dry or wet or somewhere in between? What other plants grow nearby? Are neighboring trees and shrubs predominantly deciduous, so the area is sunny in winter and spring, or are they evergreen, offering winter shade and possible protection from winter winds?

At home, study your property. What direction do the slopes face? Where do the prevailing winds blow from in each season? Are any areas sheltered from sun or wind by trees, fences, or buildings? When and to what extent does sunlight filter through a canopy of trees? Where does frost first accumulate? You'll notice that conditions vary from spot to spot on your property, creating a range of microclimates. The first frost appears earlier on the shaded north side of your house than on the sunny south side; it's windier and drier on the hill behind the garage. These small differences can make a big difference to your plants, delaying or prolonging flowering, perhaps assuring the survival of a plant not ordinarily hardy to your area.

Choosing native plants

Although plants indigenous to your immediate area are safe bets for success, plants native to similar habitats or similar conditions in other regions may also thrive in your garden. Some plants are adapted to a variety of wild habitats. The red maple (*Acer rubrum*), for instance, is found in swampy areas as well as well-drained sites. Others tolerate conditions in cultivation unlike those in their native habitats. Many plants that naturally occur in wet or poorly drained areas, for example, will do well in areas with average drainage. Rose mallow (*Hibiscus moscheutos*) inhabits wet meadows and brackish marshes in the Southeast but adapts readily to sunny, well-drained areas in the garden. Be aware, however, that the opposite is not generally true: plants indigenous to dry areas usually do not tolerate areas with poor drainage.

Growing Native Plants in Traditional Gardens

Most natives take readily to cultivated gardens and coexist harmoniously with exotic perennials, shrubs, and trees. Native wildflowers, shrubs, and trees can be incorporated in flower beds, mixed shrub and perennial borders, and in foundation plantings as well as grown as specimens, in massed plantings, or as privacy hedges or screens.

Most herbaceous native plants do not require the rich soil you've painstakingly created for a flower bed, but they respond very well to it, as well as to mulching and light spot fertilization. Many wildflowers, however, will grow more vigorously in these conditions than in the wild, where they're kept in check by lean soil, sporadic rainfall, and competition with neighboring plants. If plants grow taller, fuller, and faster in the garden, you may need to do more pruning or staking than you'd anticipated.

Some wildflowers increase in the garden by self-sowing. While this may be desirable in a meadow, you may not want such fecundity in a more formal setting. You can cut down on unwanted seedlings by removing, or deadheading, fading flowers, to prevent seeds from forming. Deadheading can also induce fuller growth or more flowers.

Making Meadow and Woodland Gardens

North America provides a treasure trove of native habitats for gardeners interested in naturalistic design. Some are specific to a particular part of a single region; others are more widespread. Two of the most popular ones are meadows and woodlands.

Meadows

It's easy to understand the appeal of meadow gardening — a field of colorful flowers dancing in the breeze is a happy sight. The thought of growing a meadow is seductive indeed, particularly when it is advertised as easy to start and maintain. Unfortunately, the enticing pictures and promises offered by various brands of "meadow in a can" are, at best, simplistic.

True meadows are not a broad sweep of cheerful flowers but a mixture of plants. About half are herbaceous perennials, a little less than half are grasses, and about 10 percent are annuals. In addition, meadows house a wide variety of wildlife. The result is a diverse, constantly changing community.

In North America, meadows are long-lived in the Western Mountains and on the prairies of the Great Plains. Elsewhere they're usually transitory, the first of a succession of stages of regrowth in a disturbed or cleared area. In the Eastern Woodlands, for example, a meadowlike mix of native grasses and herbaceous plants may quickly colonize a cleared area, but in a few years it gives way to honeysuckle and brambles, which in turn are replaced by shrubs and trees.

To maintain a meadow garden in such an area requires regular intervention to forestall the natural course of events. You'll need to mow, burn, apply selected herbicides, or pull out undesirable plants by hand. In addition, the balance of plants will change if the meadow is left to its own devices. Certain grasses and herbaceous plants may crowd out other plants, and these too may need to be controlled. Clearly these meadows are not low-maintenance projects.

Few gardeners have the space, conditions, or energy to establish a true meadow. But many, regardless of where they live, can establish and enjoy a meadowlike mixture of wildflowers and grasses. A few general tips: If this is a first attempt, start small. Mow a strip around the area. Meadow gardening requires an acceptance and appreciation of a "weedy" appearance between the colorful flowering periods. When the meadow is looking unkempt, a mown border will suggest that this is not merely a neglected spot in the landscape.

There are a number of ways to establish a meadow. Here are a few of the most common.

Serendipity

The simplest approach is to just stop mowing a sunny area on your property. You will be surprised at the variety of plants that appear. If you want, plant a few additional wildflowers to achieve more diversity. Not everything that shows up will be a native plant. You may welcome such naturalized exotics as chicory, Queen Anne's lace, and ox-eye daisy; purists may pull them out.

Control

If you want to control the composition of your meadow, you'll need to remove the existing vegetation. You can deep-till the area, as for a flower bed, or shallow-till it, removing the surface vegetation and disturbing the underlying soil as little as possible. Any soil disturbance will bring weed seeds to the surface, requiring one or more subsequent tillings to eradicate the seedlings. If you're not in a hurry, you can till as needed over an entire season, then plant the meadow in the fall or following spring.

You can also destroy existing vegetation by smothering it under black plastic or layers of newspaper. Both these methods work best if extended over a year. After the existing vegetation has been killed, you can till the area (which risks bringing up more weed seeds) or rake away the debris and sow or plant in untilled soil. A meadow does not require heavy fertilization. It is helpful to test the soil, but adding copious amounts of manure or inorganic fertilizers is generally not necessary. If the land is exhausted from extensive farming, you can incorporate organic matter (mulch, compost) to slowly restore the soil.

Seeding a meadow

Sowing seeds on the plot is the simplest and, for large areas, the least costly method of starting a meadow. Make every effort to use seeds from your region; the resulting plants will be better adapted to your conditions. You can sow seeds in the spring or fall. Fall seeding takes advantage of fall and winter rains and provides the cool, moist period many natives need to germinate. The seeds will germinate early in the spring when the soil begins to warm up, and the seedlings will be well established before the arrival of the hot, dry days of summer.

Tiny seeds, such as those of bee balm, can be mixed with sand for more even dispersal. For large areas, sow at a rate of roughly 10 pounds of seed per acre. Sow smaller areas at 4–5 ounces per 1,000 square feet. For very small areas, you can double the rate for more intense color.

After broadcasting the seeds, tamp them in with a roller or the back of a rake. Irrigate regularly; don't let the seeds dry out before germination, and keep the seedlings well watered until they're established. During the first year, water during dry periods.

"Plugging" a meadow

A meadow, like a garden bed or border, can be planted with seedlings grown in trays or containers; you can start the seedlings yourself or buy them from a nursery. This method of "plugging" seedlings into a meadow can be time-consuming or expensive, but it allows you to get the jump on weeds by mulching around the plants. A middle course is to sow native grass seed and plant plugs of wildflower seedlings. Depending on the species and on the look you want, plugs can be spaced as close as 1 foot on center; larger plants need more space — unless you want to mimic the effects of competition in the wild.

Choosing plants for a meadow
Be wary of the "meadow in a can" approach. Many of these mixes are predominantly annuals; after the first year, the meadow declines. Take a little more time and effort to compile your own plant list. If you live in a region with natural meadows, study them; if not, note the plants that colonize roadsides and open spaces.

Remember that some perennial wildflowers (coneflowers, butterfly weed, blazing star) may not flower for three to five years when grown from seed. Consider buying some container-grown perennials and include some native annuals to provide color in the meadow's first years. If you select species that self-seed aggressively and crowd out others, plant them sparingly and be prepared to pull out some of the seedlings to maintain diversity in the planting.

Designing a meadow
It may seem odd to speak of designing a meadow. If you're seeding, it is certainly possible to mix all the seeds together and see what effect broadcasting them creates. But meadows in the wild are seldom, if ever, collections of single plants randomly dotted about the landscape. Competition among plants, grazing, pockets of moisture, fertile soil, and other small-scale differences "organize" the landscape. Some plants grow as individuals; others form drifts, the boundaries of which are indistinct. It takes some effort to capture the essence of a wild meadow in a garden.

In general, plant smaller plants such as butterfly weed (*As-clepias tuberosa*) and blazing star (*Liatris spicata*) in large drifts. Larger plants, such as swamp sunflower (*Helianthus angustifolius*) and swamp milkweed (*Asclepias incarnata*), read well in a meadow when planted in smaller numbers.

Maintenance
As we've noted, in many parts of the country meadows are transitory. The meadow gardener seeks to freeze the natural succession as well as to maintain some control over the mix of plants. Annual mowing can accomplish a great deal; old-fashioned weeding does the rest.

If you mow, start at the end of the second year, sometime

*Plant names preceded by an asterisk (*) are cited in the encyclopedia.

after most of the seeds have ripened. (A meadow is a miniature nursery, providing seeds and seedlings that can be collected and used to fill in bare spots.) Set the mower blades as high as possible to avoid damaging the crowns of plants. Mowing during the growing season can yield interesting results, delaying bloom on some species and giving plants you didn't know were there the opportunity to grow — you might want to experiment.

Woodland Gardens

In contrast to the sunny openness of a meadow, the dappled or deep shade of a woodland garden offers a cool respite and the comfort and mysteries of enclosure. As with any garden, a thorough site analysis is the first step. Observe the pattern of shade in all four seasons, if possible, before planting. Shade is rarely uniform and consistent. Note the differences from one part of the garden to another, one time of day and another. Is the woodland canopy sparse, allowing a dappled light, or heavy, creating deep shade? Is it high, allowing the raking light of morning or evening to penetrate? Morning sun is less intense than that at high noon. In the Southeast, columbine grows well if sunlit for 4 hours in the morning and shaded in the afternoon, but it can scorch if shaded in the morning and sunlit in the afternoon.

Garden structure

If you're gardening on an already wooded site, identify the existing trees and understory shrubs and remove those that are unhealthy or undesirable. Those that remain will be the structure or "bones" of the garden. You may wish to add other trees and shrubs to complete the picture or provide privacy. For high, open shade, remove the lower limbs of existing trees. Similar pruning on some shrubs makes way for plantings of wildflowers beneath.

If large trees and shrubs are the garden's skeleton, paths are its arteries. Use them to set up views of interesting features such as rock formations, a special group of plants, or a handsome tree or shrub. Depending on the size of the garden, you may wish to make a system of main paths that are wide enough for a wheelbarrow and narrower, secondary paths that meander through the woods.

Plants for a woodland garden

Choose plants for their appropriateness to the site and its conditions. Take time to study the woodlands of your region, noting associations and the distribution of plants. As you choose and combine plants, consider form, texture, fragrance, flower color, and leaf color. Flowers can be sparse in woodlands, so the texture and color of leaves are particularly important. Juxtapose bold, coarse textures and fine, feathery textures or create subtle gradations of texture and color. Consider woodland plants for all seasons: spring ephemerals for early flowers, foliage plants for summer interest and fall fireworks. For winter, choose evergreen trees and shrubs or deciduous plants with interesting bark or branching patterns.

Soil preparation

In areas selected for planting wildflowers, dig the soil as deeply as possible. Try not to disturb the roots of established trees or shrubs. If the plants you've chosen prefer soil that differs from yours, you'll have to amend accordingly. Woodland plants that thrive in upstate New York, for example, may not do well in the thinner, warmer, maple-root-infested soil of neighboring Connecticut. As needed, work aged manure, compost, or leaf mold into pockets around existing roots. Don't cover tree roots with large quantities of new soil, which can cut off the supply of oxygen and smother the roots. If you can't use moisture-loving plants where drainage is poor, add coarse sand, fine gravel, or ground granite to improve the drainage. Remember that nestling plants among existing tree roots creates competition for water; choose plants accordingly or be prepared to provide additional water.

Maintenance

Once you've established new plants with extra water and attention, a woodland garden requires policing to encourage desirable plants and eradicate others and occasional pruning to maintain or increase light levels. A woodland mulches itself with fallen leaves, but a heavy covering can hinder the emergence of spring ephemerals or cook seedlings trapped underneath. It helps to rake leaves into the paths and mow them, then spread the shredded leaves in the garden.

Organic Control of Pests and Diseases

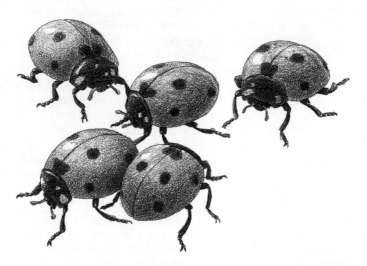

Organic gardening has been around since human beings first scratched up the soil to plant a seed. Until the widespread introduction of petroleum-based, synthetic fertilizers and pesticides, all gardeners used organic techniques. Manures, leaves, and cover crops built up the soil; a well-placed band of materials derived from minerals or plants controlled pests and diseases. More important, these gardeners were keenly aware of the connection between their garden and its environment. They looked closely to nature's ways for guidance.

Why Garden Organically Today?

When synthetic chemical pesticides, such as DDT, first appeared in the 1940s, they offered speedy and long-term relief from many plant pests and diseases. What could be more appealing to a gardener who had watched helplessly as a majestic old tree succumbed to crown gall disease or young seedlings fell prey to a plague of slugs? Gardeners switched to synthetic pesticides in droves.

Over the years, however, it has become evident that these compounds too often create as many problems as they solve. As our awareness of the environmental liabilities of many synthetic pesticides has increased, gardeners have turned once again to an organic approach. At first, concern about pesticide use centered on food plants, but more and more gardeners are turning to organic practices for ornamental plants as well.

The appeal of organic practices is broad and varied. Some gardeners are primarily concerned about the risks of exposing themselves and their families, friends, and pets to toxic compounds. Others want to avoid materials that pollute the environment and kill beneficial insects, fish, and wildlife. Some regard organic gardening as a viable way to sustain our natural resources for future generations. Still others embrace it as part of living in harmony with nature. Whatever their motivation, organic gardeners today can draw upon the best of old practices as well as the newest information and techniques.

Pest and Disease Control: The Choices

To better understand the organic approach to pest and disease control, it will help to look at the other major methods practiced today: the conventional (or "chemical") approach and integrated pest management (IPM).

Chemical controls

The conventional approach relies on synthesized compounds derived from petrochemicals, which range from highly toxic to less toxic in their effect on pests, other living organisms, and the environment. Chemical controls offer a quick knockdown of pests, usually require less time, effort, and thought on the part of the gardener, and often give an initial appearance of complete control.

On the down side, chemical controls can leave toxic residues in the soil, water, and plants. Many compounds are quite toxic to mammals and other organisms, and the long-term effects of exposure to more than one pesticide, or the combined effects of pesticides and other environmental pollutants, are still not clear. Synthetic chemicals have other negative side effects, as well. Once the primary pest is killed, secondary pests that were kept in check by the primary pest increase, creating a new problem that requires another chemical control. Some of the treated pests inevitably develop a resistance to the chemical sprays, requiring stronger control measures. Beneficial insects and other natural controls are often wiped out by broad-spectrum chemicals, and pest populations soar.

Integrated pest management

IPM (also known as least toxic pest management) is a systematic approach that relies on the regular monitoring of pest populations to determine if and when to take action. When control is warranted, nontoxic strategies are used first, including physical, mechanical, cultural, and biological methods. When all else fails, pesticides with the least toxicity, including synthetic chemicals, are selectively applied.

By focusing on a pest in the context of the garden ecosystem rather than as an isolated nuisance to be eliminated, IPM provides the means to carefully target your control efforts. This increases the chances that the actions you do take will be effective. The infrequent use of synthetic pesticides reduces the potential for harming people and the environment but still offers the advantages of these products. IPM does not, however, provide quick fixes. It requires more careful planning and observation, and often more time and effort up front, than the use of synthetic chemicals, but IPM can be less work over the long haul.

Organic Gardening: Basic Principles

Like IPM, an organic approach emphasizes the prevention of problems through careful garden design, sound horticultural practices, and an understanding of pest and disease life cycles. Organic gardeners rely on many of the same tactics employed in IPM, with the exception of synthetic pesticides. They use only naturally occurring or naturally derived materials or organisms for pest control, such as insecticidal soaps, sulfur dust, or beneficial insects. (In the chemist's definition, organic compounds are those that contain carbon. By that standard, some of the accepted organic controls, such as sulfur, would be considered inorganic. But in popular usage, "organic" encompasses a broader view, including the sources of the materials and their processes of breaking down.)

Compared to synthetic chemicals, many organic controls pose little or no risk to you, other creatures, or the environment. This makes it easier for existing predators and parasites to come to your aid. Some pesticides that are derived from plants are highly toxic to mammals or to some beneficial organisms, but they all tend to break down quickly into harmless compounds. (Many organic gardeners, in fact, try to minimize use of the more toxic botanical pesticides.) Naturally derived pesticides do have a few disadvantages. They are sometimes slow to act, and those that break down quickly may require frequent application. As with IPM, your extra work is likely to be rewarded as your garden becomes a more balanced ecosystem.

Organic pest control involves much more than a bag full of environmentally safe remedies. Instead, it's just one part of an overall approach to gardening. Simply put, organic gardeners view the garden as a complete system whose sum is greater than its parts. They model its design and care on natural processes and take action only if it's needed. Myriad gardening practices, from the simple to the sophisticated, continue to evolve from these principles.

This approach, often called holistic, is more than a philosophical preference: it's based on a biological reality. Everything in your garden, living and nonliving, is interrelated in one way or another. Bugs and blight, roots and shoots, sun and soil, water and wind, make up an ecosystem, which is part of still larger ecosystems around it.

Almost anything you do with one part of your garden will eventually cause something to happen in another part of it, for better or worse. Sometimes the connection is simple; in some regions, if you mulch deeply with leaves during the rainy season, you're likely to create a snail haven. At other times, cause and effect may be nearly impossible to pinpoint. The more you learn about how each aspect of your garden fits into the big picture, the better you'll understand when to take action and when to sit back and let nature take its course.

Learning from Nature

Natural systems provide sound guides for maintaining your landscape organically as well as offering aesthetically pleasing ideas for design. With nature as a model, you can design many potential pest and disease problems out of your landscape and design in buffers against future problems, all before you ever put spade to soil. The following practices, basic to an organic approach, will prevent many pest and disease problems and help you establish a landscape that's easier to maintain naturally.

Choose well-adapted plants

First, choose plants that are well adapted to your soil, climate, and any special characteristics of the topography or microclimate, such as a steep hillside, high winds, early frosts, or reflected heat from nearby paving. Native plants and wild-flowers indigenous to your area are usually good choices, but don't overlook plants from other areas that are accustomed to similar conditions. Select disease- and pest-resistant vari-eties or cultivars if they are available.

Provide good growing conditions

Whether you grow native or exotic plants, providing optimal conditions for them can go a long way toward preventing pest and disease problems. Learn about the growing environment preferred by the plants you've chosen, and use it as a guide for planting and caring for them. Group together plants that prefer similar conditions. If you are growing annuals, consider planting them in different locations each year to avoid a po-tential buildup of pests and pathogens (disease-causing or-ganisms).

Gear your soil improvement toward meeting the specific needs of the plants you grow. In general, it's a good idea to enrich the soil with organic matter, such as compost or cover crops, and naturally derived mineral fertilizers. But remember that some natives may not tolerate the rich conditions of a cultivated garden. Cultivate as little as possible except to work up new areas or to control weeds or diseases. Use mulch unless it proves to be an irresistible hangout for pests. Compost your plant debris. All of these practices will help build friable, nu-tritionally balanced soil, encourage an active soil life, and provide growing conditions that will foster stronger, healthier plants. Healthy plants aren't necessarily less appealing to pests and pathogens, but they are usually better able to tolerate the damage.

Encourage diversity

Nature abhors a monoculture and so should you. By in-cluding many different species and avoiding planting all of one kind together, you're more likely to create a stable eco-system with plenty of beneficial organisms that will help keep problems in check. A mixture of plants also greatly reduces the chance that your entire garden will be wiped out by a particular pest. Plant plenty of flowering plants, especially those in the parsley and sunflower families, for they provide food for beneficial insects. Create habitats for other natural predators, such as toads, frogs, and birds.

Diagnosing Pest and Disease Problems

The practices outlined above will help you create a balanced garden system. Even so, you will eventually encounter some pest problem that requires additional action. Find out as much as you can about the pests and diseases that are most common in your area on the plants you're growing. Learn their symptoms and when they're likely to appear. Your nursery supplier, a plant society specializing in natives, or a nearby arboretum or botanical garden may be able to help.

When you see damage to a plant, the first task is to identify the culprit. This is easier said than done, but it is essential if you want to solve the problem with the most environmentally safe and effective techniques. Not every problem is caused by an insect or other pest organism; damage can also be caused by cold, heat, wind, air pollution, too much or too little water or fertilizer, or other environmental and cultural factors, and sometimes this damage looks similar to that caused by pests.

When pests or disease are the problem, they are often misidentified. Many insects look similar to the untrained eye. Sometimes the perpetrator has left the scene before you arrive, and whatever insect is present at that time is blamed. Pests also sometimes hide within the plant or operate underground. Applying controls for the wrong pest often fails to solve the problem or, even worse, aggravates it. Here are some activities to help you figure out who done it.

Be vigilant
Check your garden regularly for damaged plants, insects, and other organisms. Over time, careful observation will help you recognize when something's gone awry and will give you a better sense of local pest and disease cycles. Take a close look: check the top and underside of the leaves, along the stems, where the branches meet the stem, buds and flowers, the base of the plant, and the surrounding soil surface. Note leaves that are munched, covered with webbing, or abnormal in shape or color. Pay attention to whether the damage occurs along the leaf margin, the veins, or throughout the leaf; whether holes or discolored areas are regular or irregular in shape. Look for wilted, blackened, or chewed stems, sticky exudate on branches, withered or browned flower buds, or loose mounds of soil near the plant.

Look for insects — a $10 \times$ hand lens will expose tiny ones. Check for egg masses on or near the plants. Also look at plants in nearby wild areas, where pest species may find a habitat to their liking. Occasional nighttime forays into the garden with a flashlight may reveal critters that are hidden during the day. Collect samples of any insects or damage that you want to identify.

Take notes, keep records
Sometimes casual observation of your plants will give you

all the information you need; at other times, more serious and regular inspection is in order. In either case, you may find it helpful to carry a notebook and record damage or anything else unusual that you observe on your plants. Also record the date you first notice the problem and how it changes over time. Keep track of your garden activities and the environmental conditions. Outbreaks of many pests and pathogens are triggered by changing weather conditions. A prolonged hot, dry spell, for example, will often be followed by an increase in spider mites; weeks of rainy weather may encourage fungal outbreaks. Such records may seem like a lot of trouble, but the information will provide invaluable clues for tracking down the causes of problems.

Identification

One of the best clues to the identity of a pest is the damage it causes. Chewing insects, such as beetles, caterpillars, and grasshoppers, eat holes in leaves or munch away surface leaf tissue, leaving a sort of leaf "skeleton." Cutworms often nip off seedlings at ground level. White, irregularly shaped pathways on the surface of a leaf mark the trails of leaf miners, which tunnel their way between the layers of leaf tissue. Borers burrow into stems and branches, sometimes leaving oozing, sticky sap or sticky sawdust in their wake. Slugs and snails also chomp leaves.

Insects such as aphids, mealybugs, scale, and whiteflies as well as mites (which are more closely related to spiders than insects) all suck the sap from plants. This disruption of normal plant growth causes a variety of symptoms, ranging from wilted, twisted, yellowed, spotted, or curled leaves to stunted or dead plant parts. If aphids or scale insects are causing the damage, there will often be an accumulation of honeydew, a sticky, shiny substance, on leaf surfaces as well.

Plant diseases are most often caused by fungi, bacteria, or viruses. But most pathogens are microscopic and are thus more elusive than insect pests; they are best identified by their typical symptoms or signs. Mildews are recognized by a gray-white powdery coating on leaf surfaces, stems, or fruit, sometimes with yellowed or dead areas beneath. Leaf spots, which can result from fungi or bacteria, appear as discolored lesions on the leaves — yellow, red, brown, tan, gray, or black spots. Sometimes the infected leaves wilt and rot. Blights cause leaves, branches, twigs, or flowers to suddenly wilt or become brown and die. Often the stem appears water-soaked and blackens at the soil line. Rots, caused by fungi or bacteria, can cause similar decay of roots, of the lower part of the stem, or of other succulent plant tissue. Viruses can produce white, yellow, or pale green discolored, patterned, or spotted areas on leaves, less commonly on stems, fruit, or roots. Virus-infected plants often become stunted. While these symptoms are generalizations at best, they should point you in the right direction.

For help in identifying the insects, other organisms, or symptoms you encounter, refer to the books in "Further Reading." Those with good color photographs and/or diagnostic keys are likely to be the most helpful for beginners. The reliable diagnosis of plant problems is often a tricky business, so don't be reluctant to turn to an expert for assistance. Your Cooperative Extension Service (listed in the phone book under Cooperative Extension or in the government offices section) or a nearby nursery or garden center may be able to help or refer you to someone who can.

Before you take action

Learn as much as you can about the pest's life cycle and preferred environment. Find out at which stage in its life cycle the damage occurred; if a caterpillar is chomping your leaves, you'll need to control it, not the butterfly or moth it will become. Monitor the pest population to see if its numbers are increasing, decreasing, or holding steady. Check for insects or other organisms that prey on the pest; given time, they may provide adequate control. Remember that populations of beneficial organisms often build up more slowly than those of the pests; wait a while before taking more drastic action. Even an ill-timed spray of an apparently harmless substance like water can wash off beneficial predators.

Decide if you and your plants can live with the damage. Specific guidelines have been developed to help large-scale growers of commercial crops figure out just how many of a particular insect pest are too many, but home gardeners must rely on their own judgment. Keep in mind that beneficial insects need a supply of pests to maintain their populations. If a pest-covered plant is seriously damaged and going downhill fast, and there are no natural enemies in sight, you need to think seriously about taking action. On the other hand, if you spot a few pests here and there, but they aren't causing much harm and they aren't on the increase, then you can simply wait and see. You should also think about your aesthetic standards and decide just how much damage is acceptable to your eye.

Organic Controls

It is impossible here to address individually the many pests and the controls for each one. Instead we offer an overview of the types of organic controls available. Each particular problem will require some research on your part: consult an experienced neighbor, a nearby professional, or detailed reference books. This research can be interesting, and, with experience, you'll become an expert yourself.

To choose the most appropriate, safest organic control, ask yourself the following questions. Do you need a control with immediate impact or can you wait for a long-term control to take effect? Is this the most specific control for the problem? Is this the right time to take this action? Is this control the least disruptive to beneficial insects and the safest for human beings, other animals, and the environment? If the control requires repeated action, such as handpicking insects off plants, do you have the time and patience to follow through?

Once you decide to take action, start with the most benign controls, ones that you can accomplish with just your own hands (or feet), and move on to other tactics as needed. In the end, a combination of strategies often proves most successful.

Cultural controls

First, change any cultural practices that may make your plants more susceptible to a particular pest. For example, planting earlier may give your plants a chance to establish themselves before the pests that attack them are up and running. Another strategy is to modify the pest's habitat in a way that discourages its survival. For instance, you can remove a thick mulch or clear out adjacent weedy areas where the pests hide when they're not feeding in your garden.

Mechanical and physical controls

Traps, barriers, cages, row covers, and other mechanical devices or barriers can exclude pests before they arrive and create a pest-free zone once you've rid plants of existing problems. Physical controls, such as handpicking pests or crushing them underfoot, are particularly successful for larger types such as beetles, snails, and slugs. Strong water sprays can physically dislodge certain insects. All of these methods pose no risk to people or the environment.

Biological controls

Increasingly, gardeners are making use of their pest's naturally occurring enemies: predators, which are free-living organisms that feed on other organisms; parasitoids, which kill the hosts they live on; and pathogens, microorganisms that release toxins into the insects that ingest them. These beneficial insects, mites, nematodes, and microorganisms are probably already at work naturally in your garden. Under the best of circumstances, you can just sit back and enjoy the fruits of their labor.

If, however, these beneficial organisms haven't appeared yet or are in short supply, you can purchase laboratory-reared populations to release in your garden to control pest insects, mites, or snails. Some, like the larvae of the green lacewing, can be quite effective, while others, like the convergent lady beetle, often fly away before they've adequately controlled their prey. Sometimes the introduced beneficials will establish large enough populations in your garden to provide ongoing control; otherwise you'll need to replenish the supply period-ically.

Microbial insecticides are commercially available as well. These pathogens include bacteria, fungi, and viruses that are effective against insects and, in some cases, against other plant diseases. One of the most common microbial pesticides, *Bacillus thuringiensis* (commonly called Bt), is a toxin-producing bacteria that kills caterpillars and insect larvae after they have eaten leaves or stems sprayed with it. Bt breaks down quickly in sunlight and is sensitive to heat, so it may require reappli-cation and must be stored in cool conditions. Depending on the particular pest you want to control, you can choose among several species and varieties of Bt.

Naturally derived pesticides

A wide range of compounds derived from natural sources can be sprayed or dusted on plants to control pests and dis-eases.

Insecticidal soaps. Made of fatty acids, these compounds penetrate the skin of susceptible insects and dissolve their cell membranes, causing death. They are most effective against soft-bodied insects with sucking mouthparts, such as aphids, mites, whiteflies, and thrips. Fungicidal soap formulations, made of sulfur and fatty acids, are used to control diseases such as mildews, rots, leaf spots, and rust. These soaps, sold as liquid formulations, are sprayed on affected plants. They are very safe to use and break down rapidly in the soil, but they can be poisonous to plants (phytotoxic). Test them on a small portion of the plant first. Thorough coverage and pe-riodic reapplication is needed for good control.

Horticultural oils. Oils are used to smother the adults and eggs of a variety of pests, including certain aphids, scale, cat-erpillars, and mites. Traditionally sprayed when the plant is dormant, newer formulations are safe for spraying on leafed-out plants as well. Follow the label precautions to avoid po-tential phytotoxicity, and wear protective clothing to prevent eye and skin irritation during application. Most of the horticultural oils are derived from petroleum; those extracted from vegetables or animals are preferable for an organic approach. The oils have a low toxicity to human beings and wildlife and biodegrade rapidly.

Diatomaceous earth. An abrasive dust composed of the skeletal remains of microscopic marine creatures, diatomaceous earth is sometimes sprinkled on the ground as a barrier to protect plants from snails and slugs — with varying results. Diatomaceous earth is nontoxic to mammals but can irritate eyes and lungs, so wear goggles and a dust mask when you're applying it.

Botanical pesticides. These are derived from plants that contain substances toxic to insects. Some botanicals, such as pyrethrin, are effective against a wide variety of pests (they're called broad-spectrum pesticides), while others, such as sabadilla, kill a more limited range of pests. Botanicals also vary widely in their toxicity to human beings and other mammals and insects; pyrethrins and sabadilla have low mammalian toxicity, while nicotine and rotenone are highly toxic to mammals. On the other hand, rotenone is not toxic to honeybees, but sabadilla is highly toxic to them. Regardless of their toxicity, botanicals quickly break down into nontoxic compounds in the presence of sunlight or in the soil. They may require frequent reapplication, but their short period of toxicity minimizes potential harm to organisms other than the targeted pests.

Minerals. Sulfur, copper, and lime are used primarily to control fungal and bacterial diseases, including mildews, rots, leaf spots, and blights. Sometimes these minerals are sold in combined formulations, such as copper sulfate or Bordeaux mix, a mix of copper sulfate and hydrated lime. Sulfur dust, lime, and lime sulfur control some plant-sucking pests as well. Both sulfur and copper disrupt the metabolic processes of targeted pathogens and pests. Sulfur is relatively nontoxic to human beings; the toxicity of copper varies, depending on the formulation. Whether you apply minerals as a dust or a spray, protect your eyes, lungs, and skin to avoid irritation.

Safety. It's wise to wear protective clothing when you apply any of the naturally derived pesticides. This includes a long-sleeved shirt and long pants, rubber gloves, boots, goggles, and a mask. Always follow the label directions for use, storage and disposal. Don't spray on windy days.

A Note on Diseases

Diseases can be transmitted to your plants quite rapidly variety of means: air, soil, water, insects, human being propagation tools. They can be carried in seeds, cuttings, and divisions. Since pathogens are rarely visible, it's hard to control them by mechanical or physical means.

Prevention plays a more important role in controlling disease pathogens than insect or animal pests. It's much easier to protect a plant from disease than to cure it. To minimize disease problems in your garden, buy healthy plants, choosing disease-resistant varieties if available. In addition, certain cultural practices can create unfavorable conditions for many pathogens and minimize the spread of existing ones. Space plants far enough apart to allow good air circulation. Don't overwater. Provide adequate drainage. Don't overfertilize, especially with nitrogen. Avoid mechanical damage to your plants; lawn mowers are so frequently rammed into trees that the aftermath has been dubbed "lawn mower blight." Prune out diseased or dead plants. Don't leave long stubs of pruned branches or stems, which can serve as a conduit for disease organisms. Remove plant debris from the garden and compost it. To avoid transmitting disease, discard diseased material rather than composting it.

The Color Plates

Natural gardens and landscapes are as varied as the landscapes nature has created on our vast continent. To give you a taste of the many possibilities, we begin this section with a selection of garden scenes from around the country.

The plant portraits that follow will help you put a "face" to the plant names in the essays and the encyclopedia. The plants represented are all native to North America and are proven garden performers. They are grouped according to plant type: trees, shrubs, wildflowers (herbaceous annuals and perennials), and grasses and vines. A short description accompanies each plate, along with the plant's botanical and common names, its height, its hardiness zone rating, and the page on which you'll find its encyclopedia entry.

A Word about Color

Color, more than many other visual attributes, is in the eye of the beholder. What one person describes as blue, another may call lavender or even purple. And it's not just the names of colors that vary. Light and shade, time of day, other colors nearby, can all affect what we see. A leaf that appears rich red in the midday sun may be a deep lavender in late-afternoon shade.

As you look at the photographs on the following pages, remember that the camera, no less than the eye, captures color as it appears at a certain moment. Add to that the natural variation among plants and the difficulties of printing colors precisely and you'll see why you should not count on your plant having the exact color you see in the photograph.

An Iris Aerie
Lafayette, California

Clusters of assorted Douglas iris cultivars make excellent company for anyone seated beneath this vine maple (background). Like the maple, Douglas irises are western natives. Vigorous, drought-tolerant plants, they are ideal for a region that must use water sparingly. This photo taken in April shows the Coastal Range in the distance.

Treasures of the Forest Floor
Portland, Oregon

Oregon grape, a western native, greets strollers at a bend on this woodland garden path. This informal planting mixes shrubs and perennials, native and exotic plants, including holly, blueberries, arum, primroses, and lungwort.

Mrs. Bancroft's Cactus Garden
Walnut Creek, California

A marvelous creation fashioned of opuntias, agaves, yuccas, aloes, and other cacti and succulent plants, this large garden (only part of which is shown here) represents a lifetime's work. Gardeners with less space or time can create equally pleasing settings with these striking drought-tolerant plants.

A Native Courtyard
Tucson, Arizona

Native plants provide a perfect complement in color, form, and texture for the adobe walls of this southwestern home. Ablaze beneath the distinctive green branches of a palo verde are several species of penstemon; the yellow flowers of a creosotebush and blue salvias complete the palette.

Spring in the Woods
New Hope, Pennsylvania

Warmed by the late spring sun, understory shrubs and wildflowers burst into bloom under a high woodland canopy. The planting artfully mixes exotic plants — wisteria, primrose, and others — with natives, including rhododendron, phlox, columbines, and foamflowers. (This shady, 2-acre garden has moss rather than grass lawns.)

A Backyard Meadow
Minneapolis, Minnesota

Not having a spacious meadow to work with, this midwestern gardener has created a glorious July display by massing many prairie and meadow plants much closer than nature would arrange them. Wildflowers and grasses include liatris, bee balm, black-eyed Susans, prairie smoke, little bluestem, and Indian grass.

A Meadow in Autumn
Pennsylvania

This untamed-looking meadow was a riot of bright blanket
flowers and prairie coreopsis in summer. Now, just before
frost, it presents another face, more subtly colored by
goldenrods and asters.

Random Pleasures
Martha's Vineyard, Massachusetts

One of the many joys of naturalized plantings is their
carefree, unplanned look. Of course, someone chose to mix
these butterfly weeds and black-eyed Susans together, but
the result appears serendipitous, and that's what counts.

Trees

Acer rubrum
Red maple
Zone 3
p. 271

Height: 60–90 ft. A fast-growing tree adaptable to many environments. Small red flowers in early spring. Very colorful foliage in fall.

Amelanchier laevis
Serviceberry
Zones 4–9
p. 276

Height: 15–25 ft. or more. Easy to grow in full or part sun. Year-round interest: early spring flowers, edible fruit in summer, brilliant foliage in fall.

Betula nigra
River birch
Zones 4–9
p. 298

Height: 40–70 ft. A handsome tree
year-round, it is especially useful for
troublesome wet sites and in the South.
Full or partial sun.

*C*ercidium
*f*loridum
*Bl*ue palo verde
*Zo*nes 9–10
*p. 3*08

Height: 20–30 ft. Twiggy limbs provide
light shade for patios and walks. Bears
tiny leaves for a short time in spring.
Flowers in spring, sometimes longer.
Full sun.

Cercis canadensis
Eastern redbud
Zones 4–9
p. 309

Height: 20–35 ft. Offering spring flowers, handsome leaves, and seedpods, redbud meshes easily with formal and informal plantings. Full or partial sun.

Cercocarpus ledifolius
Curl-leaf mountain mahogany
Zones 4–8
p. 311

Height: 10–20 ft. Long-lived, hardy, and trouble-free evergreen good as screen, windbreak, or specimen. Attractive seed heads in late summer and fall. Full or partial sun.

Chilopsis linearis
Desert willow
Zones 6–10
p. 313

Height: 10–30 ft. Heat- and drought-tolerant desert native ideal as an accent specimen or grove planting. Fragrant flowers June to September. Full sun.

Chionanthus virginicus
White fringe tree
Zones 3–9
p. 314

Height: 10–20 ft. or more. Wispy, fragrant flowers in midspring as the leaves expand. Small fruits in late summer. Fall foliage often turns bright yellow. Full or partial sun.

Cladrastis lutea
Yellowwood
Zones 3–8
p. 317

Height: 30–50 ft. A perfect shade tree, especially where space is limited. Sweet-smelling flowers in late spring. Seedpods in late summer. Full sun.

Cornus florida
Flowering
dogwood
Zones 5–8
p. 323

Height: 25 ft. A natural understory tree with year-round appeal: spring flowers, summer shade, fall color, winter form. Sun or partial shade.

**Forestiera
neomexicana**
Desert olive
Zone 4
p. 336

Height: 10–18 ft. Versatile plants grown
as multitrunked specimens and
windbreaks. Fruits attract songbirds to
female plants from late summer into
winter. Full sun or shade.

Halesia carolina
Carolina silverbell
Zones 4–8
p. 342

Height: 30–50 ft. or more. Small trees or
large shrubs with abundant early spring
flowers and attractive bark. Good as
specimens or in small groups. Full or
partial sun.

Ilex opaca
American holly
Zones 6–9
p. 352

Height: 40 ft. A slow-growing tree with interesting spiny leaves and bright red berries. Many cultivars available. Full sun or shade.

Juniperus scopulorum
Rocky Mountain juniper
Zone 4
p. 358

Height: to 30 ft. Reliable plants for dry, exposed areas. Many selections available. Full sun.

**Juniperus
virginiana**
Red cedar
Zones 3–9
p. 358

*Height: to 60 ft. Common along the
Atlantic coast as a windbreak or screen.
Excellent food and shelter for wildlife.
Wide variety of forms. Full sun.*

**Magnolia
grandiflora**
Southern magnolia
Zones 7–9
p. 370

*Height: 60 ft. One of the grandest
broadleaf evergreen trees. Fragrant
flowers from late spring to early summer.
Full or partial sun.*

Magnolia virginiana
Sweet bay
Zones 5–9
p. 371

Height: to 60 ft. A light, airy, slow-growing plant, often grown as a multitrunked shrub or small tree. Blooms late spring to early summer. Full or partial sun.

Nyssa sylvatica
Black gum
Zones 3–9
p. 381

Height: 30–60 ft. Able to withstand harsh conditions, black gum is a handsome specimen or naturalized tree. Fall color begins early and lasts long.

Oxydendrum arboreum
Sourwood
Zones 4–9
p. 388

Height: 30–50 ft. An extraordinary specimen tree with year-round interest: flowers and fruits in summer, colorful leaves in fall, distinctive bark and form in winter. Full or partial sun.

Pinus aristata
Bristlecone pine
Zone 4
p. 401

Height: 20–25 ft. Excellent for western landscapes, it is adaptable to high and low elevations and urban conditions. Slow growing, picturesque with age.

Pinus edulis
Pinyon pine
Zone 5
p. 401

Height: 12–15 ft. An excellent dense screen or picturesque specimen. Slow growing; needs very little water. Full sun.

Pinus flexilis
Limber pine
Zone 4
p. 401

Height: 25–50 ft. A slow-growing tree, it withstands strong winds, hot sun, and dry, alkaline soil. Excellent as a specimen, screen, or windbreak.

Pinus palustris
Longleaf pine
Zones 7–9
p. 402

Height: 80–100 ft. The most distinctive of southern pines. Easily grown, widely adaptable, it makes a fine shade or specimen tree.

Pinus ponderosa
Ponderosa pine
Zone 4
p. 402

Height: 60 ft. or more. Suitable for specimen or group planting. Mature trees have colorful, furrowed bark.

Pinus pungens
Prickly pine
Zones 5–8
p. 402

Height: 40–60 ft. A distinctive specimen tree, it has the look of a huge bonsai when mature. Extremely drought tolerant once established.

Pinus strobus
Eastern white pine
Zones 3–8
p. 403

Height: 80 ft. or more. Soft texture, attractive form, and fast growth make it ideal as a specimen, screen, in groups, or naturalized.

Pinus taeda
Loblolly pine
Zones 7–9
p. 403

Height: 90–100 ft. Fast-growing tree, useful for shade or screening. Endures poor soils and exposed sites.

Populus tremuloides
Quaking aspen
Zone 2
p. 405

Height: 20–30 ft. A lively, striking, small tree that shimmers in the breeze. Effective as a specimen or in groups. Good fall color at higher elevations. Needs moist soil, cool conditions.

Prosopis glandulosa
Honey mesquite
Zones 6–10
p. 405

Height: to 30 ft. Picturesque as specimen, effective grouped for grove or barrier. Flowers in spring and early summer. Highly drought tolerant. Full sun.

Prosopis pubescens
Screwbean mesquite
Zones 6–10
p. 406

Height: to 20 ft. Good barrier, screen, or wildlife habitat. Interesting form, flowers in spring and summer, seedpods used in dried arrangements. Full or partial sun.

Pseudotsuga menziesii
Douglas fir
Zone 4
p. 407

Height: 50–80 ft. A magnificent specimen for a large, formal landscape. Topped and trimmed, it can make an effective tall hedge. Adaptable. Full sun.

Quercus agrifolia
Coast live oak
Zone 9
p. 408

Height: 20–50 ft. or more. Emblematic tree of coastal southern and central California. Provides welcome evergreen shade. Needs dry soil in summer.

Quercus alba
White oak
Zones 3–9
p. 408

Height: 50–100 ft. One of the most beautiful oaks, it is a splendid shade tree, providing food and shelter for many forms of wildlife. Best in moist soils.

Quercus lobata
Valley oak
Zone 9
p. 409

Height: to 70 ft. or more. Highly picturesque deciduous oak with a massive trunk, broad crown, and weeping branches. Full sun.

**Quercus
macrocarpa**
Bur oak
Zones 3–8
p. 410

*Height: 70–80 ft. A slow-growing native
of prairie, savanna, and dry forests.
Provides food and shelter for wildlife.*

Quercus palustris
Pin oak
Zones 4–9
p. 410

*Height: 50–100 ft. Popular, fairly fast
growing, it often provides brilliant
fall color. Very tolerant of wet, clayey,
acid soils.*

Quercus rubra
Northern red oak
Zones 4–8
p. 410

Height: 50–90 ft. A relatively fast growing oak, widely planted as a shade and street tree. Full sun. Adaptable to a variety of conditions.

Quercus virginiana
Live oak
Zones 8–9
p. 411

Height: to 60 ft. or more. A very picturesque tree, typically twice as wide as high. Dominates the maritime forests from North Carolina south. Full sun.

Taxodium distichum
Bald cypress
Zones 6–9
p. 440

Height: 70–100 ft. A long-lived deciduous tree, useful as a specimen, massed, or naturalized. Fertile, moist, well-drained soil. Full sun.

Tsuga canadensis
Hemlock
Zones 3–7
p. 444

Height: 50–100 ft. One of the most graceful conifers, it makes a good specimen, screen, or windbreak. Full sun or shade.

Shrubs

Aesculus californica
California buckeye
Zone 9
p. 272

Height: 10–20 ft. Interesting all year. Flowers from April to June; leaves drop from midsummer on, revealing attractive gray branches. Seeds are large and handsome.

Aesculus parviflora
Bottlebrush buckeye
Zones 5–9
p. 273

Height: to 10 ft. Excellent massed or as a specimen. Blooms for 2–3 weeks in June and July. Large brown seeds are attractive.

Aesculus pavia
Red buckeye
Zones 6–9
p. 273

Height: 5–25 ft. Plant in groups along woodland edges or in shrub borders. Leaves are among the first to appear in spring, followed by dense, eye-catching plumes of flowers.

Agarista populifolia
Leucothoe
Zones 7–9
p. 274

Height: 16 ft. A superior evergreen plant for southern gardens, with arching branches, small leaves, and fragrant flowers in spring. Use as a fast-growing screen or prune heavily as a large foundation plant.

Amelanchier alnifolia
Saskatoon serviceberry
Zone 4
p. 275

Height: 6–15 ft. An excellent shrub border or patio plant. Short-lived, fragrant flowers bloom in spring just before leaves emerge. Small, edible fruit by early summer. Outstanding fall color.

Amorpha fruticosa
False indigo
Zones 3–8
p. 276

Height: 5–20 ft. Fine-textured foliage and dense racemes of deep blue flowers. Thrives in full sun and poor soil with a steady supply of moisture.

Arctostaphylos densiflora 'Howard McMinn'
Sonoma manzanita
Zone 9
p. 281

Height: 4 ft. A dependable, healthy, long-lived evergreen shrub easily pruned to a knee-high ground cover. Profuse bloom in February and March. Full sun.

Arctostaphylos edmundsii
Little Sur manzanita
Zone 9
282

Height: to 4 ft. Fast-growing evergreen with handsome leaves and flowers December–February in southern California. Full sun.

**Arctostaphylos
uva-ursi**
Bearberry
Zone 4
p. 283

Height: 3–4 in. A maintenance-free
evergreen ground cover ideal for rock
gardens and hillsides. Flowers in spring;
leaves turn red in winter. Sun or partial
shade.

Artemisia filifolia
Threadleaf sage
Zones 4–10
p. 286

Height: 3–4 ft. A sweetly pungent plant
with a compact, windswept form. The
semi-evergreen leaves are silver-blue in
summer, silver-gray in winter. Full sun.

Artemisia frigida
Fringed sage
Zones 3–10
p. 286

Height: 18 in. A mat-forming, fine-textured, aromatic ground cover with soft, woolly, semi-evergreen leaves. Sun or partial shade.

Artemisia tridentata
Bigleaf sage
Zones 4–10
p. 287

Height: 1½–15 ft. A picturesque specimen or accent plant. Evergreen leaves are velvety soft and pungent. Full sun.

Atriplex canescens
Saltbush
Zones 4–10
p. 292

Height: to 6 ft. Tolerates saline soil and exposures too harsh for most other plants. Leaves are semi-evergreen. Clusters of gold-tan to brown seed husks are used in dried arrangements. Full sun.

Baccharis halimifolia
Groundsel tree
Zones 4–9
p. 293

Height: to 12 ft. Good for seaside gardens and others in full sun. Leaves persist into winter. Large fruiting clusters on female plants are attractive in fall and winter.

**Baccharis
pilularis**
Coyote brush
Zone 9
p. 294

Height: 3 ft. Excellent evergreen ground
cover, it is drought tolerant but accepts
garden watering and even boggy
conditions. Full sun.

**Calliandra
eriophylla**
Pink fairy duster
Zones 6–10
p. 302

Height: to 3 ft. Extremely drought
tolerant, it is an ideal small shrub or
ground cover for low-water-use gardens
in the warm deserts. Flowers February–
May. Full sun.

Calycanthus floridus
Sweetshrub
Zones 4–9
p. 304

Height: 6–9 ft. Easy to grow and versatile, good for groupings, as informal fence, or as specimen. Fragrant flowers in spring; leaves turn bright yellow or gold in fall. Full sun or shade.

Ceanothus americanus
New Jersey tea
Zones 4–8
p. 306

Height: 3–3½ ft. A wonderful small shrub for dryish, well-drained sites. Blooms for 2–3 weeks from midspring to early summer. Sun or partial shade.

Ceanothus fendleri
Buckbrush
Zone 4
p. 306

Height: 2–5 ft. A hardy, variable plant covered with flowers for 1½–2 weeks in late spring to midsummer. Good as a foundation plant or for naturalizing. Full sun.

Ceanothus griseus
Carmel creeper
Zone 8
p. 307

Height: 8 ft. An evergreen shrub prized for its tremendous display of fragrant flowers from March to May. Full sun.

**Ceanothus
impressus
'Julia Phelps'**
*Santa Barbara
ceanothus*
Zone 8
p. 307

*Height: 6 ft. Fast-growing evergreen
shrub with fragrant flowers in March
and April. Extremely drought tolerant.
This cultivar tolerates some summer
watering. Full sun.*

**Ceanothus
velutinus**
Snowbush
Zone 4
p. 308

*Height: 3–5 ft. An easy-to-grow, hardy,
broadleaf evergreen with fragrant flowers
in late spring to early summer. Sun or
partial shade.*

**Cercis
occidentalis**
Western redbud
Zone 8
p. 310

Height: 20 ft. Dependable, long-lived,
drought tolerant, and attractive all year.
Flowers February–April; fall color.
Good patio tree. Full sun.

**Chamaebatieria
millefolium**
Fernbush
Zones 4–8
p. 311

Height: 4–6 ft. Undemanding semi-
evergreen shrub effective as a backdrop,
filler, or specimen. Flowers in summer.
Sun or partial shade.

Chrysothamnus nauseosus
Chamisa
Zones 4–8
p. 316

Height: 3–6 ft. Easy-to-grow plants effective as background plantings, soil stabilizers, and accent groupings. Fragrant flowers in autumn attract butterflies. Interesting in winter. Full sun.

Clethra alnifolia
Sweet pepper bush
Zones 5–9
p. 320

Height: 9 ft. Excellent for damp areas and the seaside, it is attractive in screens, massed, or as a specimen. Fragrant flowers in summer. Sun or partial shade.

Dalea greggii
Prostrate
indigobush
Zones 6–10
p. 324

*Height: 6–10 in. Grown mostly as a
ground cover, it is awash with flowers in
spring and early summer. Bees love it.
Sun or partial shade.*

**Encelia
californica**
Bush sunflower
Zone 9
p. 327

*Height: 5 ft. Drought-tolerant evergreen
shrub produces masses of golden daisies
March–June. Full sun.*

Encelia farinosa
Brittlebush
Zones 8–10
p. 328

Height: 2–3 ft. Drought-tolerant plant with evergreen foliage that goes well with desert wildflowers. Blooms most heavily in early spring. Full sun.

Eriogonum giganteum
Giant buckwheat
Zones 9–10
p. 330

Height: 6–10 ft. A bold, evergreen accent plant. Flowers from April to October turn russet-red as seeds mature. Full sun.

Euonymus americanus
Strawberry bush
Zones 6–9
p. 333

Height: 4–6 ft. Trouble-free, easy to grow, and versatile, with showy fruit and often colorful fall foliage. Full sun or shade.

Fallugia paradoxa
Apache plume
Zones 5–10
p. 335

Height: 4–6 ft. An easy-to-grow, semi-evergreen shrub graced by flowers and attractive seed heads May–September. Good natural hedge. Sun or partial shade.

Fothergilla major
Witch alder
Zones 4–8
p. 336

Height: 5–10 ft. Excellent when massed in shrub border, as a specimen, or in a small group. Sun or partial shade. Acid soil essential.

Fremontodendron
'California Glory'
Flannel bush
Zone 9
p. 338

Height: 15–20 ft. The showiest of California's spring-blooming shrubs, it is perfect for dry landscapes. Full sun. Must have dry soil.

**Garrya elliptica
'James Roof'**
Silk-tassel bush
Zone 8
p. 340

Height: 10 ft. or more. Striking catkins December–February make this evergreen shrub ideal for the winter garden. Sun or partial shade.

**Gordonia
lasianthus**
Loblolly bay
Zones 7–9
p. 341

Height: 40 ft. This slender evergreen Coastal Plain wetland native is effective in groups of 3–5. Blooms from June to frost. Full sun.

Hamamelis
virginiana
Witch hazel
Zones 3–8
p. 343

Height: 15–30 ft. Small tree or shrub good for informal screens or naturalized groups. Fall color. Blooms sporadically from fall to spring. Sun or partial shade.

Hesperaloe
parviflora
Red yucca
Zones 6–10
p. 346

Height: 2 ft. (Flower stalks to 5 ft.) Effective in formal or natural gardens as a specimen, in groups, or as a ground cover. Flowers March–September in sun or shade.

**Heteromeles
arbutifolia**
Toyon
Zone 8
p. 347

Height: 30 ft. Adaptable, drought-
tolerant evergreen shrub or small tree.
Effective as a screen or specimen.
Flowers in June and July. Attractive
berries November–February. Sun or
partial shade.

**Hydrangea
quercifolia**
Oakleaf hydrangea
Zones 5–9
p. 350

Height: 5–6 ft. A large shrub offering
flowers in spring, handsome leaves
in summer, and colorful bark in
winter. Excellent for massing. Partial
sun or shade.

Ilex cassine
Dahoon
Zones 7–10
p. 351

Height: 20–30 ft. A good plant for
southern gardens as a hedge or informal
barrier. Berries fall and winter. Sun or
partial shade.

Ilex glabra
Inkberry
Zones 5–9
p. 351

Height: 6 ft. A good hedge or foundation
plant with fine-textured leaves and dark
black fruit in fall. Sun or partial shade.

Ilex verticillata
Common
winterberry
Zones 3–9
p. 352

Height: 5–10 ft. Berries superb in winter
after deciduous leaves drop. Ideal for wet
soils. Sun or partial shade.

Ilex vomitoria
Yaupon
Zones 7–9
p. 353

Height: 20 ft. An easy-to-grow plant
whose cultivars make good hedges or
foundation plantings, screens, or
graceful, free-standing specimens. Sun or
partial shade.

Itea virginica
Virginia sweetspire
Zones 5–9
p. 356

Height: 3–6 ft. or more. Fine plant for a shrub border or naturalizing on damp or wet sites. Fragrant flowers in early spring. Foliage colorful in fall. Sun or partial shade.

Juniperus communis
'Calgary Carpet'
Common juniper
Zone 2
p. 357

Height: 2–15 ft. The hardiest of all junipers. Low-growing forms are excellent for foundations, informal plantings, or rock gardens. Many cultivars. Sun or partial shade.

Juniperus horizontalis
Creeping juniper
Zones 3–9
p. 357

Height: 1–1½ ft. One of the most popular junipers for low ground cover, especially in poor soils and all-day sun.

Kalmia latifolia
Mountain laurel
Zones 4–9
p. 359

Height: 8–20 ft. Long-lived and tough evergreen plant for full sun or shade. Good in masses or as specimen. Blooms for 1–3 weeks in late spring. Needs acid soil.

Larrea tridentata
Creosotebush
Zones 6–10
p. 361

Height: 3–10 ft. This evergreen shrub
grows in the hottest, driest desert
conditions. Good as specimen, massed,
or as informal hedge. Blooms
intermittently spring–fall. Sun or
partial shade.

**Leucophyllum
frutescens**
Texas sage
Zones 7–10
p. 362

Height: 4–8 ft. A versatile evergreen
shrub excellent for warm-desert gardens.
Blooms intermittently spring–fall in
response to rain. Full sun, poor soil.

Mahonia aquifolium
Oregon grape
Zone 4
p. 372

Height: 6–8 ft. All-year interest.
Evergreen leaflets turn reddish in fall.
Fragrant flowers for 1½–2 weeks in
midspring. Fruit in late summer.
Full sun or shade.

Mahonia repens
Creeping holly
grape
Zone 4
p. 372

Height: 2–3 ft. An excellent ground
cover for sun or shade, clay or loam
soils. It withstands cold, dry weather.
Leaflets are bronze in winter.
Fragrant flowers for 2–3 weeks from
April to June.

Myrica cerifera
Wax myrtle
Zones 6–9
p. 378

Height: to 30 ft. A good low-maintenance shrub for much of the South. Ideal for screening. Leaves are fragrant; fruits in fall and winter attract birds. Sun or partial shade.

Myrica pensylvanica
Bayberry
Zones 4–9
p. 378

Height: 8–10 ft. Hardier than M. cerifera, it is useful as a border or screening plant. Fragrant leaves, attractive fruit. Full sun.

Opuntia bigelovii
Teddy bear cholla
Zones 7–10
p. 384

Height: 2–5 ft. Effective singly as accents or massed in a hedge or barrier. Flowers are inconspicuous. Full sun.

Opuntia humifusa
Prickly pear
Zones 4–9
p. 385

Height: 1 ft. A low-growing cactus effective in dry, sandy habitats as a specimen or barrier. Flowers bloom May–June, followed by late summer fruit.

Opuntia
polycantha
Plains prickly pear
Zones 3–6
p. 385

Height: 4 in. The waxy flowers are
spectacular in late June. Native to the
driest sites, this is a tough ground cover
where all else fails.

Osmanthus
americanus
Devilwood
Zones 6–8
p. 387

Height: to 30 ft. An evergreen shrub or
small tree, grown as a specimen, in
hedges, screens, or naturalized
landscapes. Flowers will perfume a wide
area around the plant. Partial shade.

Paxistima canbyi
Mountain lover
Zones 3–8
p. 391

Height: 1 ft. A good evergreen ground
cover or low hedge, border edging, rock
garden specimen, or underplanting
in a naturalized garden. Flowers
inconspicuous. Very cold hardy. Sun or
partial shade.

**Paxistima
myrsinites**
Oregon boxwood
Zone 4
p. 391

Height: 1–3 ft. Can be used in the same
ways as mountain lover, its eastern
relative, but often more upright. Full sun
or shade.

Rhododendron austrinum
Yellow wild azalea
Zones 7–9
p. 413

Height: 12 ft. A good choice for the South. Clusters of fragrant flowers appear in spring before or as the leaves develop. Deciduous.

Rhododendron canescens
Wild azalea
Zones 7–8
p. 414

Height: 10–15 ft. A southern deciduous azalea producing abundant fragrant flowers from March to early April.

Rhododendron maximum
Rosebay rhododendron
Zones 4–8
p. 414

Height: 8–15 ft. or more. One of the largest and hardiest of the evergreen species. Flowers in late spring.

Rhododendron periclymenoides
Pinxterbloom azalea
Zones 3–9
p. 415

Height: 4–10 ft. Hardy, luxuriously fragrant, it gradually colonizes an area. Tolerates dry sites and drought once established. Blooms in midspring for 1–3 weeks.

Rhododendron prunifolium
Plumleaf azalea
Zones 7–9
p. 415

Height: 15–20 ft. The most distinctive of the southern deciduous azaleas. Adds color to a shade garden in July and August.

Rhododendron viscosum
Swamp azalea
Zones 3–9
p. 416

Height: 3–15 ft. One of the hardiest deciduous natives. Richly fragrant flowers bloom 1–3 weeks from late spring to midsummer.

Rhus aromatica
Aromatic sumac
Zones 3–7
p. 417

Height: 4–6 ft. A good candidate for a screen or windbreak, especially in poor, dry soils where few other shrubs prosper. Colorful fall foliage. Full or partial sun.

Rhus copallina
Winged sumac
Zones 4–9
p. 417

Height: 10–30 ft. Forms beautiful domed colonies with fiery fall color and attractive seed heads. Easily established in all but wet or poorly drained soils.

Rhus microphylla
Littleleaf sumac
Zones 6–10
p. 417

Height: 6–12 ft. An excellent screen or informal hedge. Foliage turns deep burgundy-red in fall. Full sun. Likes poor, dry soil and heat.

Ribes odoratum
Buffalo currant
Zones 4–6
p. 420

Height: 3–6 ft. Low-growing and thicket-forming, valuable in windbreak plantings. Clove-scented flowers in May, edible fruit in July. Full sun.

**Ribes
sanguineum**
Flowering currant
Zone 6
p. 420

*Height: to 12 ft. An adaptable shrub
offering very early (January–March)
bloom. The cultivar 'King Edward VII',
shown here, is well suited to cool, wet
climates. Sun or shade.*

Ribes speciosum
Fuchsia-flowered
gooseberry
Zone 7
p. 420

*Height: to 10 ft. Bristly branches thickly
hung with flowers enliven the garden in
winter. Excellent for planting in the dry
shade of native oaks. Tolerates dry or
poor soil and heat.*

Rosa arkansana
Prairie rose
Zone 3
p. 422

Height: 12–18 in. This freely spreading rose gives spring color to a natural planting, shrubby border, or mixed windbreak. Full sun. Does well in poor or dry soil and heat.

Rosa palustris
Swamp rose
Zones 5–9
p. 423

Height: 5–8 ft. Ideal plant for the edge of a pond or a garden with drainage problems. Fragrant flowers May–June, followed by red hips from July to October. Full sun.

Rosa woodsii
Wood's rose
Zone 4
p. 423

Height: 3–5 ft. A versatile rose, effective in formal or naturalized settings. Blooms in spring, then sporadically through the summer. Sun or partial shade.

Salvia clevelandii
Cleveland sage
Zone 10
p. 426

Height: 4 ft. Good plant for dry, sunny hillsides. Blooms May–August. Leaves can be used in cooking.

Salvia greggii
Cherry sage
Zones 6–10
p. 428

Height: 1–2 ft. Repeated as an accent, it unifies a border. Blooms from May to November. Evergreen in warm climates (zone 8). Adaptable to many conditions as long as soil is well drained.

Tecoma stans
Yellow bells
Zones 7–10
p. 441

Height: 3–24 ft. Fast-growing, long-flowering shrubs or small trees have a variety of landscape uses. Blooms intermittently from April to November. Sun or partial shade.

**Vaccinium
arboreum**
Sparkleberry
Zones 7–9
p. 444

Height: 20–26 ft. Good for naturalizing
as a multitrunked shrub or small tree
or in screens or shrub borders. Leaves
are semi-evergreen. Grows well in dry,
acid soil in sun or partial shade.

**Vaccinium
corymbosum**
Highbush
blueberry
Zones 4–9
p. 444

Height: 6–15 ft. Excellent for
naturalizing in moist, acid soil. Blooms
in early spring. Deciduous leaves have
good fall color. Fruit is delicious.

**Viburnum
acerifolium**
Maple-leaved
viburnum
Zones 3–8
p. 446

Height: 4–6 ft. Ideal for naturalizing,
these shrubs slowly form a multistemmed
colony. Attractive flowers in late spring,
early summer. Spectacular fall color.
Full sun or shade.

**Viburnum
lentago**
Nannyberry
Zones 2–8
p. 446

Height: 15–20 ft. or more. A hardy,
durable shrub for informal borders and
natural plantings. Blooms 1–3 weeks
in spring. Fruit and form are interesting
in fall and winter.

Viburnum nudum
Possum haw
Zones 5–9
p. 446

Height: 5–9 ft. Good choice as specimen, for borders, or naturalized. Blooms in late spring; colorful fruit and fall foliage. Full sun.

Yucca brevifolia
Joshua tree
Zones 6–10
p. 450

Height: to 25 ft. or more. A striking addition to a naturalized southwestern landscape. Blooms April–May.

Yucca elata
Soaptree
Zones 6–10
p. 451

Height: 5–20 ft. An effective foil for lush desert tree and shrub plantings. Flowers May–June. Seed capsules are used in flower arrangements.

Yucca filamentosa
Beargrass
Zones 5–9
p. 451

Height: 5–6 ft. A southeastern native with flowers in June. Several cultivars with variegated leaves are available.

Yucca glauca
Spanish bayonet
Zones 3–8
p. 451

Height: 3–6 ft. Makes sharp contrast with fine-textured plants in a prairie meadow. Blooms around June.

Yucca whipplei
Whipple's yucca
Zones 7–9
p. 452

Height: to 12 ft. Perfect accent for a drought-tolerant planting with Matilija poppies and Cleveland sage. Blooms May–June.

Wildflowers

Achillea
millefolium
Western yarrow
Zones 4–9
p. 271

Height: 6–24 in. At home in traditional
or natural landscapes. Flowers
throughout the summer. Excellent in
fresh or dried arrangements. Full sun.

Allium cernuum
Nodding wild
onion
Zone 4
p. 274

Height: 8–12 in. Combines well with
other small plants. Blooms from May
through early July. Flowers good for
cutting. Full sun.

**Amsonia
tabernaemontana**
Blue star
Zones 3–9
p. 277

*Height: 2–3 ft. Tough, attractive plant
for the perennial bed or moist meadow.
Early spring bloom; leaves provide
great fall color. Seedpods are handsome
all season.*

**Anaphalis
margaritacea**
Pearly everlasting
Zone 3
p. 278

*Height: 1–3 ft. Flower and seed heads
provide color and interest from late
summer to late fall. An excellent plant
for high-elevation gardens. Sun.*

Anemone patens
Pasque flower
Zone 4
p. 279

Height: 8 in. Reliable, hardy, early bloomer, with fernlike, ground-hugging foliage. Attractive in beds, borders, containers, or naturalized areas.

Aquilegia caerulea
Rocky Mountain columbine
Zones 3–8
p. 280

Height: 1–2 ft. Excellent for mountain gardens, beds and borders, or naturalized in a woodland garden. Striking flowers in spring or early summer and delicate, fernlike foliage.

Aquilegia canadensis
Canadian columbine
Zones 3–8
p. 280

Height: 2–3 ft. Tolerant of wide range of conditions, including sun and shade. Flowers, early to late spring, attract hummingbirds.

Aquilegia chrysantha
Golden columbine
Zones 3–9
p. 281

Height: 2½–3½ ft. Native to moist ravines in the southern Rockies, but adaptable to many conditions. Blooms from late spring through midsummer.

Arisaema triphyllum
Jack-in-the-pulpit
Zones 4–9
p. 284

Height: 1–2 ft. A curious, spring-flowering woodland native prized for shade gardens. Plant as specimens, in groups, or naturalize.

Artemisia ludoviciana
White sage
Zones 3–8
p. 287

Height: 1–3 ft. Ideal for dry gardens. Aromatic foliage provides a backdrop for other flowering plants. Full sun.

Aruncus dioicus
Goatsbeard
Zone 5
p. 288

Height: 4–6 ft. A streamside native useful as a background plant or hedge. Flowers in early to mid summer. Partial sun or shade; accepts ordinary moisture.

epias
nata
milkweed
–8

Height: 4–5 ft. Native to moist spots, this plant will grow in all but the driest garden soils. Flowers in summer. Full sun.

Asclepias tuberosa
Butterfly weed
Zones 3–8
p. 289

Height: 1–1½ ft. Spectacular flowers last about 2 weeks in June and July, followed by a beige seedpod. Full sun.

Aster alpinus
Alpine aster
Zone 3
p. 290

Height: 6–12 in. Compact plant, per for small gardens. One of the few asters to bloom in late spring. Sun partial shade.

Aster divaricatus
White wood aster
Zones 4–8
p. 290

Height: 2–3 ft. Adds color to shady spots in late summer and fall. Plants spread to fill gaps in the summer garden. Partial sun or shade.

Aster linariifolius
Stiff-leaved aster
Zones 3–8
291

Height: 2–3 ft. Rounded clumps of stiff foliage form backdrop for early fall daisies. Full sun.

Aster novae-angliae
New England aster
Zones 3–8
p. 291

Height: 3–5 ft. Easy to grow, with long-lasting flowers in August. Excellent for damp areas in sun or partial shade.

Aster oblongifolius
Aromatic aster
Zones 3–6
p. 292

Height: 16 in. A delightful plant for harsh, dry conditions. Flowers bloom well into autumn, even after heavy frosts. Foliage is pungent when crushed. Full sun.

**Baileya
multiradiata**
Desert marigold
Zones 6–10
p. 294

Height: 12–18 in. Excellent for very
hot, dry desert gardens, this biennial or
short-lived perennial blooms for several
months between April and October.
Full sun.

**Baptisia australis
var. australis**
Wild blue indigo
Zones 3–9
296

Height: 3–4 ft. A durable, drought-
tolerant plant whose spectacular
midspring flowers and striking, shrubby
foliage are ideal for borders or meadows,
singly or in groups. Sun or partial shade.

Baptisia alba
var. **alba**
White wild indigo
Zones 5–8
p. 296

Height: 2–3½ ft. A white-flowered baptisia offering the same qualities as B. australis. Durable, drought tolerant, and handsome from spring to fall. Sun or partial shade.

Berlandiera lyrata
Chocolateflower
Zones 5–6
p. 297

Height: 12–24 in. An easy-to-grow plant that flowers profusely from April to September. Good for massed plantings, beds and borders, meadows, and other naturalized plantings. Full sun.

Boltonia asteroides
White boltonia
Zones 4–9
p. 300

Height: 3–5 ft. Good for moist, open natural plantings, where it blends nicely with brighter fall colors.

Callirhoe involucrata
Purple poppy mallow
Zones 4–8
303

Height: 6–12 in. These easy-to-grow, drought-tolerant plants are spectacular as individuals or massed, in borders or naturalized. Blooms spring–early summer or longer. Full sun.

**Campanula
rotundifolia**
Bluebell
Zones 2–7
p. 305

Height: 4–12 in. A remarkably hardy
plant, good for rockeries, meadows,
beds, and borders. Flowers throughout
the summer. Sun or partial shade.

Chelone glabra
Turtlehead
Zones 3–8
p. 313

Height: 3 ft. Attractive foliage and
unusual flowers from late August to
frost. Ideal for cooler parts of the
garden. Sun or partial shade.

Chrysopsis mariana
Maryland golden aster
Zones 4–9
p. 315

Height: 1–3 ft. Perfect for borders, meadows, or rock gardens in dry, sunny sites. Flowers in late summer and early fall.

Chrysopsis villosa
Golden aster
Zones 3–7
p. 315

Height: 1–2½ ft. Attractive foliage and butterfly-attracting flowers from July to September. Full sun.

Cimicifuga racemosa
Black cohosh
Zones 3–8
p. 317

Height: 6–8 ft. Long-lived, easy-to-grow plants with handsome foliage and flowers that brighten shady spots in midsummer.

Clarkia amoena
Farewell-to-spring
Annual
p. 318

Height: 1½–2½ ft. A California native that blooms from May to August. Seed strains vary in color and from low and spreading to tall and erect. Full sun.

Coreopsis auriculata
Eared coreopsis
Zones 4–9
p. 321

Height: 1–2 ft. 'Nana', shown here, is the dwarf form (6–9 in.) of the species. An excellent evergreen ground cover for light shade. Blooms in late spring.

Coreopsis lanceolata
Lance-leaved coreopsis
Zones 3–8
p. 321

Height: 1½–2½ ft. Fast growing and useful in many situations. Blooms from late spring to early summer. May need support. ('Baby Sun' shown here.) Sun or partial shade.

**Coreopsis
maritima**
Sea dahlia
Grow as annual
p. 322

*Height: 1–3 ft. A native of cool coastal
California, it will not survive cold
winters. A choice cut flower that blooms
February and March. Full sun.*

**Coreopsis
tinctoria**
Plains coreopsis
Annual
p. 322

*Height: 1–3 ft. Valuable "quick cover"
for new prairie planting or meadow.
Blooms June–September. Full sun.*

Coreopsis verticillata
Thread-leaved coreopsis
Zones 3–9
p. 322

Height: 2½ ft. Forms dense patches that add a distinctive texture to the middle border or meadow. Blooms in midsummer. Full sun.

Cornus canadensis
Bunchberry
Zone 2
p. 323

Height: 4–10 in. Low-growing relative of the familiar dogwood trees and shrubs. Forms a carpet in moist, cool areas. Flowers June–August. Colorful fruits and foliage in fall. Partial sun or shade.

Dalea purpurea
Purple prairie
clover
Zones 3–8
p. 324

Height: 1–2 ft. A good choice where space is limited. Flowers in July and August. Full sun.

Dicentra eximia
Bleeding heart
Zones 3–8
p. 325

Height: 1–1½ ft. Unusual for a shade-loving perennial, bleeding heart blooms from spring to frost. Numerous cultivars in a variety of flower colors.

Echinacea angustifolia
Purple coneflower
Zones 3–7
p. 327

Height: 12–20 in. *Early summer flowers, dried stems, and seed heads later are striking in a border or prairie planting. Full sun.*

...hinacea
...purea
...le coneflower
...s 4–8
...7

Height: 1½–3 ft. *The eastern relative of E. angustifolia. Large flowers from summer into early fall. Full sun.*

**Eriogonum
flavum**
Sulfur flower
Zone 4
p. 330

Height: 4–12 in. Fine for the front of the border or the rock garden. Flowers, late May–June, are good for drying. Full sun, dry soil.

**Eriogonum
umbellatum**
Sulfur buckwheat
Zones 7–9
p. 330

Height: 1 ft. A choice rock garden plan Flowers bloom June–September, turnir rusty red as they mature. Sun or parti shade.

Eriophyllum lanatum
Woolly sunflower
Zone 5
p. 331

Height: 4–16 in. Good plant for dry gardens with sandy soil. Enlivens borders, rock gardens, or naturalized plantings. Full sun.

*schscholzia
lifornica
ifornia poppy
ual
2*

Height: 9–24 in. Easy to grow, perfect for naturalizing with other wildflowers in a drought-tolerant garden. In cultivation, can bloom throughout the year where hardy. Full sun.

Eschscholzia mexicana
Mexican gold poppy
Annual
p. 332

Height: 8 in. Broad sweeps of these plants blaze with color from February to May when moisture and temperature are right. Full sun.

Eupatorium coelestinum
Wild ageratum
Zones 6–10
p. 333

Height: 2–2½ ft. Flowers brighten the garden in late summer and fall. Ideal f[e] moist, sunny spots. Sun or partial sha[de]

**Eupatorium
purpureum**
Joe-Pye weed
Zones 4–9
p. 334

Height: 5–9 ft. A bold contribution to
the rear of a border or a damp meadow.
Blooms 3–4 weeks in late summer.
Full sun.

*ustoma
ndiflora
ip gentian
e 4
4*

Height: 18–24 in. Adds color to moist
borders or naturalized plantings in
moist areas from June to September.
Cultivars are excellent cut flowers.
Sun or partial shade.

Fragaria virginiana
Wild strawberry
Zone 5
p. 337

Height: 4–16 in. Excellent ground cover suitable for naturalizing among trees and shrubs. Blooms 2–3 weeks from midspring to early summer. Sun or partial shade.

Gaillardia aristata
Blanket flower
Zones 5–10
p. 339

Height: to 12 in. Easy to grow, drought and heat tolerant. The showy flowers brighten gardens and meadows from April to October. Sun or partial shade.

Gaillardia pulchella
Indian blanket
Annual (most areas)
p. 339

Height: 1–2 ft. Easy, drought- and heat-tolerant plant blooms June–October. Also tolerates sea spray, ideal for coastal garden. Full sun.

Helenium autumnale
Sneezeweed
Zones 3–8
. 343

Height: 4–5 ft. Easy-to-grow, highly adaptable plant for borders or naturalized areas. Blooms for up to 10 weeks from mid to late summer. Full sun.

Helenium hoopesii
Sneezeweed
Zones 4–8
p. 344

Height: 2–3 ft. A great accent plant for perennial beds or among shrubs in an informal garden. Flowers borne on long stems July–September are excellent for cutting. Full sun.

Helianthus angustifolius
Swamp sunflower
Zones 6–9
p. 344

Height: 5–10 ft. Excellent for large borders or for naturalizing in damp meadows. Abundant flowers 2–4 weeks in late summer and fall. Seeds attract birds. Full sun.

**Helianthus
maximiliani**
Maximilian
sunflower
Zones 5–10
p. 345

*Height: 6–8 ft. Long-lived plant makes
a spectacular display August–October.
Sun or partial shade, tolerates dry soil.*

**Heuchera
sanguinea**
Coral bells
Zone 5
348

*Height: leaves 6 in., flower stalks 2 ft.
An old favorite for edging beds of roses
and borders. Great for woodland
gardens with summer rain. Flowers
April–August. Partial sun or shade.*

***Hibiscus
coccineus***
Wild red mallow
Zones 6–9
p. 349

Height: 6 ft. A handsome plant for large
borders or as a specimen. Handsome
foliage; blooms from midsummer into
September. Full sun.

***Hibiscus
moscheutos***
Rose mallow
Zones 6–9
p. 349

Height: 5–6 ft. A vigorous plant with
huge flowers in midsummer. Full sun.

**Ipomopsis
aggregata**
Skyrocket gilia
Zone 4
p. 353

Height: 1–3 ft. A biennial with eye-
catching flowers June–August. Best in
natural meadows or open woodlands.
Sun or partial shade.

Iris cristata
Dwarf crested iris
Zones 3–9
p. 354

Height: 4–7 in. Delightful, spring-
blooming miniature that spreads easily
to form a ground cover. Ideal for
woodlands or rock garden. Sun or
light shade.

Iris douglasiana
Douglas iris
Zone 9
p. 355

Height: to 3 ft. A vigorous plant tolerant
of shade, constant moisture, or dry soil
and heat. Flowers March–May. Sun or
partial shade.

Iris missouriensis
Western blue flag
Zones 3–6
p. 355

Height: 1–2 ft. An extremely drought-
tolerant native of the Plains and Western
Mountains, it requires moisture in spring
and early summer. Flowers in June.
Full sun.

Iris versicolor
Blue flag
Zones 3–7
p. 355

Height: 3 ft. A vigorous aquatic iris for
a water or bog garden. Blooms for
3 weeks in the spring. The leaves are
attractive all season. Full sun.

**Kosteletzkya
virginica**
Seashore mallow
Zone 5
p. 360

Height: 5 ft. This coastal salt marsh
native also does well inland with
ordinary moisture. Blooms heavily for
6–8 weeks in August and September.
Full sun.

Layia platyglossa
Tidy-tips
Annual
p. 361

Height: 12–18 in. Dependable and easy to grow, ideal for naturalizing or in more formal gardens. Prolific bloom March to June. Full sun. Tolerates dry soil.

Liatris punctata
Gayfeather
Zones 4–8
p. 363

Height: 18–24 in. Easy to grow and very long lived, it produces tall flower spikes for 2–3 weeks in September. Attracts butterflies. Full sun.

**Liatris
pycnostachya**
Gayfeather
Zones 3–8
p. 364

Height: 2–4½ ft. A prairie native
requiring uniformly moist soil. Blooms
for several weeks in midsummer. Good
for naturalizing. Attracts butterflies.
Full sun.

Liatris spicata
Blazing star
Zones 4–9
p. 364

Height: 3–4 ft. Good choice for beds
and borders, where it provides interesting
texture. Larger plants may require
support. Full sun.

Lilium canadense
Canada lily
Zones 4–9
p. 365

Height: 4–7 ft. A good plant for moist beds and borders and a real treat in a naturalized setting. Sweet-smelling flowers for 1–3 weeks in mid to late summer. Partial sun.

Lilium superbum
Turk's cap lily
Zones 4–9
p. 365

Height: 4–7 ft. Mature plant bears up to 50 flowers in a candelabra pattern 1–3 weeks in mid to late summer. Full sun.

Linum perenne lewisii
Lewis flax
Zones 5–8
p. 366

Height: 1–2 ft. Excellent in meadows or grouped in informal beds. Flowers from midspring to early summer. Sun or partial shade. Well-drained soil.

Lobelia cardinalis
Cardinal flower
Zones 2–9
p. 367

Height: 4–6 ft. Hummingbirds love the flowers, which appear for 4–8 weeks in midsummer. Sun or partial shade. Needs moist, fertile soil.

**Lobelia
siphilitica**
Great blue lobelia
Zones 4–9
p. 367

*Height: 2–3 ft. More tolerant of dry
conditions than L.* cardinalis, *this lobelia
is also popular with hummingbirds.
Blooms 4–8 weeks in midsummer.*

**Lupinus
argenteus**
Silvery lupine
Zones 3–6
p. 369

*Height: 1½–3 ft. Spectacular naturalized
in a meadow, effective in more formal
plantings. Blooms in June and July.
Attracts butterflies. Full sun.*

Lupinus latifolius
Canyon lupine
Zone 9
p. 369

Height: 3–6 ft. Easy to grow, it has fragrant flowers that are excellent for cutting. Blooms April–August. Sun or partial shade.

Lupinus polyphyllus
Washington lupine
Zone 5
p. 369

Height: 3–5 ft. This robust plant blooms 2–3 weeks in May. Flower spikes are good for cutting. Sun or partial shade. Tolerates poor soil.

Melampodium leucanthum
Blackfoot daisy
Zones 5–10
p. 373

Height: 12–18 in. Crisp, tidy plants are effective in many garden settings, from formal to naturalized. Flowers from spring to fall. Sun or partial shade.

Mertensia virginica
Virginia bluebells
Zones 3–9
p. 374

Height: 1–2 ft. A longtime favorite for spring gardens, flowering 1–4 weeks. Goes dormant in summer. Partial sun or shade.

Mimulus guttatus
Common monkey
flower
Zones 9–10
p. 374

Height: 3 ft. Grow as annual in colder areas. Cheerful flowers March–August. Blooms first year from seed. Full sun, moist soil.

**Mirabilis
multiflora**
Giant four-o'clock
Zones 5–10
p. 375

Height: to 18 in. A long-lived, undemanding ground cover that will bloom all season if deep-watered every few weeks. Must have well-drained soil. Sun or partial shade.

Monarda didyma
Bee balm
Zones 4–9
p. 376

Height: 2–4 ft. A flamboyant plant for wild or tame gardens. Flowers bloom 3–5 weeks early to mid summer, attract hummingbirds. Sun or partial shade. Prefers moist soil.

Monarda fistulosa
Bergamot
Zones 3–9
p. 377

Height: 2–4 ft. A native of prairies, open woodlands, and savannas, bergamot tolerates drier conditions and poorer soil than M. didyma. Blooms in midsummer. Sun or partial shade.

Nelumbo lutea
American lotus
Zones 4–9
p. 229

Height: 1–4 ft. A bold plant, suitable for naturalizing in a pond or growing singly in a tub. Flowers 6–8 weeks in midsummer. The fruiting receptacle is excellent for dried arrangements. Full sun.

Nemophila menziesii
Baby blue eyes
Annual
p. 380

Height: 6 in. This western native is great for cool, moist sites, naturalized, or in beds and borders. Blooms in early spring. Full sun or shade.

Nymphaea odorata
Water lily
All zones
p. 380

Height: 6 in. The large leaves and fragrant flowers impart tranquillity to a pond or barrel planting all summer. Full sun.

Oenothera berlandiera
Mexican evening primrose
Zones 5–10
p. 382

Height: 12–18 in. A good ground cover in natural landscapes, it can be invasive in beds and borders. Blooms during daylight in spring. Full sun or shade.

Oenothera fruticosa
Sundrops
Zones 4–9
p. 383

Height: 2–3 ft. Bright, sunny flowers cheer up an open border or meadow 2–4 weeks or more from midspring to early summer. Daylight bloom. Full sun.

Oenothera missouriensis
Missouri evening primrose
Zones 4–8
p. 383

Height: 8–10 in. A low-growing plant with exceptional drought tolerance. Flowers open in the evening from late spring to early fall. Full sun.

**Oenothera
speciosa**
Showy primrose
Zones 5–9
p. 382

Height: 1½ ft. Slightly scented flowers
bloom prolifically in midsummer
for 4–8 weeks. Ideal for dry, infertile
conditions, it can be extremely invasive
in richer, moister soils. Full sun.

**Orthocarpus
purpurascens**
Owl's clover
Annual
p. 386

Height: 4–14 in. Beautiful when
naturalized alone or with other native
annuals in any sunny, open area. Blooms
March–May. Full sun.

Penstemon ambiguus
Sand penstemon
Zones 5–10
p. 392

Height: 1–2 ft. A long-lived plant that produces billows of flowers in hot, dry conditions. Blooms most heavily in May, continuing until October depending on water. Sun or partial shade.

Penstemon digitalis
White beardtongue
Zones 3–9
p. 392

Height: 3–5 ft. One of the larger, more robust penstemons, it blooms 2–5 weeks in early summer. Tolerant of less than perfect drainage. Sun or partial shade.

**Penstemon
grandiflorus**
Large-flowered
beardtongue
Zones 3–5
p. 393

Height: 12–40 in. Flowers bloom in late
spring and attract hummingbirds. Ideal
for a sandy site or well-drained garden
soil. Full sun.

**Penstemon
heterophyllus**
Foothill penstemon
Zones 7–8
p. 393

Height: 1–1½ ft. More adaptable to
garden conditions than most dry-land
penstemons. Blooms April–July. Sun or
partial shade.

Penstemon pinifolius
Pineleaf penstemon
Zones 5–10
p. 394

Height: 1 ft. A versatile plant, useful as a ground cover, specimen, or edging plant. Blooms most heavily May–June, recurring through September. Foliage is evergreen. Tolerates considerable shade.

Penstemon smallii
Small's beardtongue
Zones 6–8
p. 394

Height: 1–2½ ft. Effective naturalized on dry banks or meadows or in dry soils around tree roots. Foliage is usually evergreen. Flowers 3–6 weeks from late spring through early summer.

Penstemon strictus
Rocky Mountain penstemon
Zones 5–10
p. 395

Height: to 3 ft. A Western Mountain native with evergreen foliage. Blooms May–June.

Phlox carolina
Thick-leaf phlox
Zones 3–9
p. 396

Height: 1–4 ft. Useful for a sunny border or naturalizing in open woodlands or moist meadows. Lightly scented flowers in early summer and sporadically through late summer.

Phlox divaricata
Wild sweet
William
Zones 3–9
p. 396

Height: 8–12 in. An ideal ground cover
or fill-in plant for a shade garden.
Blooms early–mid spring. Partial sun
or shade.

**Phlox
drummondi**
Drummond's
phlox
Annual
p. 397

Height: 4–20 in. A good garden plant
and quick cover for poor, bare soils.
Blooms from spring to frost if faded
flowers are removed. Full sun.

Phlox glaberrima
Smooth phlox
Zones 3–8
p. 397

Height: 2½–5 ft. Similar to P. carolina *and* P. maculata *and equally useful for sunny borders or naturalizing at the edge of a woodland. Slightly fragrant flowers mid to late spring.*

Phlox paniculata
Summer phlox
Zones 4–8
p. 397

Height: 4–6 ft. One of the best of the tall phlox, it is an essential member of a sunny or lightly shaded border and a welcome addition to a naturalized area. Fragrant flowers mid to late summer.

Phlox pilosa
Prairie phlox
Zones 3–9
p. 398

Height: 1–2 ft. A cheerful addition to a sunny bank or border or woodland edge. Blooms for 3–6 weeks from midspring into midsummer. Tolerates poor or dry soil and heat.

Phlox stolonifera
Creeping phlox
Zones 2–9
p. 398

Height: 6–10 in. Loose mats of medium green foliage and clusters of large, highly scented flowers add soft texture to a shade garden. Blooms in midspring. Partial sun or shade.

Physostegia virginiana
Obedient plant
Zones 2–9
p. 399

Height: 3–4 ft. A fine addition to sunny beds or naturalized plantings in moist or wet soils. Blooms in late summer and fall. Invasive in ideal conditions. Full sun.

Ratibida columnifera
Coneflower
Zones 4–10
p. 412

Height: 12–18 in. An eye-catcher whether naturalized in a meadow or massed in a border. Blooms May to September. Full sun.

Ratibida pinnata
Prairie coneflower
Zones 6–8
p. 412

Height: 3–5 ft. One of the most striking wildflowers, it blooms profusely in midsummer. Full sun. Does well in dry or clay soils.

Romneya coulteri
Matilija poppy
Zones 8–10
p. 421

Height: 8 ft. One of California's most famous wildflowers. Blooms May–July. Spreads widely; suitable for naturalizing on dry flats and slopes. Full sun.

Rudbeckia fulgida
Black-eyed Susan
Zones 6–9
p. 424

Height: 24–30 in. A cheerful plant for beds, borders, and naturalized sites. 'Goldsturm' is the most widely grown cultivar. Full sun.

Rudbeckia hirta
Black-eyed Susan
Zones 3–9
p. 425

Height: 12–20 in. Extremely easy to grow from seed, it self-sows readily. Blooms from June until hard frost. Full sun. Tolerates poor or dry soil and heat.

Salvia azurea
Pitcher sage
Zones 5–10
p. 426

Height: 3–5 ft. A good meadow plant,
it flowers in August and September.
Bees and butterflies love it. Sun or
partial shade.

Salvia coccineus
Scarlet sage
Zones 8–10
p. 427

Height: 3 ft. Most often grown as an
annual, it blooms from summer through
the first hard frost. A drought-tolerant
favorite of hummingbirds and butterflies.
Full sun.

Salvia farinacea
Mealy blue sage
Zones 6–8
p. 427

Height: 2–3 ft. Grown as an annual in colder climates, it provides an attractive mass of color in beds and borders, as a foundation planting, or naturalized. Blooms April–November.

Sedum lanceolatum
Lance-leaved stonecrop
Zone 5
p. 429

Height: 3–7 in. Ideal for tucking among rocks or planting in containers. Blooms for several weeks from midspring to midsummer. Full sun.

Sedum ternatum
Stonecrop
Zones 4–8
p. 430

Height: 2–6 in. A quickly spreading ground cover for shady spots and a good container plant, it blooms for 2–3 weeks in spring.

Silphium laciniatum
Compass plant
Zones 3–8
p. 431

Height: 3–12 ft. A large plant best used in meadow or prairie plantings. Flowers in early summer. Leaves orient along a north-south axis. Attracts birds and butterflies. Full sun.

**Sisyrinchium
angustifolium**
Blue-eyed grass
Zone 5
p. 432

*Height: 1–1½ ft. Effective in meadows
or around ponds and pools. Blooms
4–5 weeks from May to July. Prefers
moist soil.*

**Sisyrinchium
bellum**
Blue-eyed grass
Zone 8
p. 432

*Height: 3–18 in. Good for naturalizing
on summer-dry sites. Blooms March to
May. Sun or partial shade. Easy to grow
from seeds.*

Smilacina racemosa
False Solomon's seal
Zones 3–7
p. 433

Height: 2–3 ft. A year-round focal point in the woodland garden. Fragrant flowers bloom 2–3 weeks in early to mid spring. Red berries in fall.

Solidago canadensis
Goldenrod
Zone 4
p. 434

Height: 1½–4 ft. Enhances formal beds or natural plantings. Blooms August to September. Spreads by underground stems. Full sun.

Solidago sempervirens
Seaside goldenrod
Zones 3–10
p. 436

Height: 4–6 ft. Flowers brighten the fall border. Basal leaves are evergreen. Tolerates salty conditions and can hold eroding soils. Full sun.

Stokesia laevis
Stoke's aster
Zones 5–10
p. 439

Height: 1–2 ft. An old favorite in perennial borders, with evergreen basal leaves. Blooms 3–5 weeks in summer. Does well in light shade.

**Stylomecon
heterophylla**
Wind poppy
Annual
p. 439

Height: 6–18 in. An exquisitely delicate
annual grown in beds and borders and
naturalized under the light shade of
high-branched trees.

**Stylophorum
diphyllum**
Celandine poppy
Zones 4–9
p. 440

Height: 1–2½ ft. One of the most useful
plants for the shade garden. In bloom
for much of spring and sporadically
through summer.

Thermopsis montana
Golden banner
Zone 4
p. 442

Height: 3–4 ft. Good for sunny borders or naturalized along a stream or in a woodland. Blooms mid to late spring, sometimes through the summer. Full or partial sun.

Thermopsis villosa
Carolina bush pea
Zones 4–8
p. 443

Height: 4–7 ft. Dramatic plants for large borders or naturalized plantings. Blooms for 1–3 weeks in late spring. Full sun.

Viola canadensis
Canada violet
Zones 3–8
p. 447

Height: 6–12 in. Best when massed on a shady woodland bank or border. Blooms for 2–3 weeks in spring. Prefers fertile, moist, well-drained soil.

Viola pedata
Birdfoot violet
Zones 4–9
p. 448

Height: 2–6 in. One of the showiest native violets. Blooms in spring, 1–3 weeks. Best in very well drained soil and lots of sun.

Viola pubescens
Downy yellow
violet
Zones 3–7
p. 449

Height: 6–8 in. An outstanding ground
cover for shaded, windless sites with
moist soil. Blooms in early spring.

Viola sororia
complex
Blue woods violet
Zones 3–8
p. 449

Height: 6–8 in. The most widespread
viola species group in the eastern U.S.
Blooms in early spring.

**Zauschneria
californica**
California fuchsia
Zones 8–10
p. 453

*Height: 1–2 ft. Good candidate for
casual woodland gardens or informal
borders. Spreads quickly. Blooms July
to October; hummingbird favorite. Full
sun or light shade.*

**Zinnia
grandiflora**
Desert zinnia
Zones 5–10
p. 454

*Height: 6–8 in. Possibly the toughest
low ground cover in the West. Blooms
June–October. Flowers dry to a straw
color. Needs dry soil and full sun.*

Grasses

Andropogon gerardii
Big bluestem
Zones 3–8
p. 279

Height: 3–8 ft. A must for any prairie planting. The tall, narrow leaves turn bronze in fall. Plant as specimen, massed, as ground cover, or naturalized.

Bouteloua curtipendula
Sideoats grama
Zones 4–10
p. 301

Height: 18–36 in. A favorite bunchgrass for tall meadows. Blue-green in the growing season, the blades cure to a golden tan. Sun or partial shade.

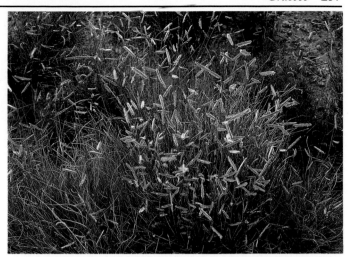

Bouteloua gracilis
Blue grama
Zones 5–8
p. 301

Height: 6–24 in. This fine, low-growing
bunchgrass makes an attractive water-
saving lawn or meadow grass. Very
adaptable and easy to grow in full sun.

**Buchloe
dactyloides**
Buffalo grass
Zones 5–10
p. 302

Height: 3–5 in. An excellent lawn grass
for hot, dry climates, it is an attractive
ground cover when not mowed. Sun or
partial shade.

Chasmanthium latifolium
River oats
Zones 5–9
p. 312

Height: 1½–3½ ft. Easy to grow, this shade-tolerant, clump-forming grass makes an excellent ground cover on slopes or open woodland; smaller clumps can accent a pathway. Full sun or shade.

Eragrostis trichoides
Sand lovegrass
Zones 5–9
p. 329

Height: 2½–4 ft. An easy-to-grow, graceful bunchgrass, attractive in large sweeps or as a lone specimen. Sun or partial shade.

**Muhlenbergia
dumosa**
Bamboo muhly
Zones 8–10
p. 377

Height: to 5 ft. A desert grass grown for
its foliage and form rather than for
flowers or seed heads. Effective in mass
plantings or as individual clumps. Sun or
partial shade.

**Oryzopsis
hymenoides**
Indian ricegrass
Zones 5–10
p. 386

Height: 18 in. A heat- and drought-
tolerant cool-season bunchgrass effective
in beds and borders or naturalized
plantings. Good for wildlife forage and
dried arrangements. Full sun. Needs
dry soil.

**Schizachyrium
scoparium**
Little bluestem
Zones 3–8
p. 428

*Height: 1½–2½ ft. One of the most
widespread and most beautiful of native
grasses. Plant clumps as specimens or
grow as ground cover. Full sun.*

**Sorghastrum
nutans**
Indian grass
Zones 3–9
p. 436

*Height: 3–6 ft. One of the premier
elements of the tallgrass prairie, Indian
grass can be grown as a specimen in a
bed or border, as a ground cover, screen,
or naturalized. Full sun.*

Sporobolus heterolepis
Northern dropseed
Zone 4
p. 437

Height: 1–2 ft. An ideal grass for making a transition from a traditional planting to a more natural one. Flowers inconspicuous but aromatic. Full sun.

Sporobolus wrightii
Giant sacaton
Zones 6–10
p. 261

Height: 4–6 ft. Well adapted to desert heat, it makes an impressive accent planting or a naturalized ground cover in runoff catchments. Full sun.

Vines

Aristolochia durior
Dutchman's pipe vine
Zones 4–8
p. 285

Height: 30 ft. or more. Spring flowers, summer leaves, and fall seed capsules provide three seasons of interest. Sun or partial shade.

Bignonia capreolata
Cross vine
Zones 6–8
p. 299

Height: 60 ft. Colorful flowers in spring. Evergreen foliage turns purplish in winter. Large seed capsules are attractive. Full sun or shade.

**Clematis
ligusticifolia**
*Western virgin's
bower*
Zone 4
p. 319

Height: 18–30 ft. Train on trellis or
fence, naturalize among shrubs.
Attractive flowers and fruit in summer.
Widely adaptable, tough, and disease
resistant. Sun or partial shade.

**Gelsemium
sempervirens**
Yellow jasmine
Zones 8–9
p. 341

Height: 10–20 ft. This evergreen vine
does well as a climber or ground cover.
Fragrant flowers in early spring. Sun or
partial shade.

**Lonicera
sempervirens**
Coral honeysuckle
Zones 3–9
p. 368

Height: 10–20 ft. An easy, rewarding
vine that flowers heavily for 3–5 weeks
in early summer, then intermittently
through the fall. Evergreen to
semi-evergreen in the South. Sun or
partial shade.

**Parthenocissus
quinquefolia**
Virginia creeper
Zones 3–9
p. 389

Height: grows up to 10 ft. per year.
An easy, well-behaved vine for almost
any situation needing leafy cover.
Flowers and fruit inconspicuous. Sun
or partial shade.

Passiflora incarnata
Passionflower
Zones 5–10
p. 390

Height: 20 ft. or more. Perfect for a trellis or rambling over a fence or hedgerow. Blooms from late spring through summer. Edible fruits late summer to fall. Attracts butterflies. Sun or partial shade.

Encyclopedia of Plants

The plants described in this section are among the best North American natives for gardeners, giving character and beauty to a range of landscapes from traditional borders to naturalized meadows or woodlands. The entries are organized alphabetically by genus. A short description of the genus is followed by individual entries for featured species and cultivars. These entries pack a lot of information into a small space. Here are a few comments to help you make the best use of them.

Names. Plant taxonomists are continually reclassifying plants and renaming the groupings to which the plants are assigned, making any book outdated almost before it appears. We have tried to use widely accepted names and classifications here, even if they are not the most recent versions. For example, we have retained the family name Compositae rather than the newer Asteraceae because readers are more likely to be familiar with the older term.

Where appropriate, synonymous botanical names are listed, designated by a.k.a. ("also known as").

Regions. You'll find the plant's native regions listed after the common name, using these abbreviations:

CA: California Floristic Province
CP: Coastal Plain
EW: Eastern Woodlands
GP: Great Plains
WD: Western Deserts
WM: Western Mountains and Pacific Northwest

These are the same regions discussed in the essays and shown on the map on p. xiv. Remember, if conditions are favorable, many of these plants can be successfully grown outside their native regions.

How to grow. Unless otherwise indicated, the plant will grow in ordinary garden soil and moisture. Of course, what is ordinary in one region might be unusual in another, so consider the plant's native region and its natural habitat if you are in doubt.

We have provided information on starting some of the plants from seeds, but if you purchase seeds, follow the detailed instructions many suppliers provide. If you collect your own seeds, consult one of the reference books in "Further Reading" to find out what special measures, if any, are required for germination.

Native plants are generally a sturdy lot. Nevertheless, seedlings and young plants often require extra care — protection from heat, cold, or wind and regular watering, even if the mature plant is drought tolerant. Very few of the plants listed here have pest or disease problems, and we've mentioned only those problems that can be serious.

Acer
A'ser. Maple
Aceraceae. Maple family

Description
Attractive deciduous foliage, a wide variety of sizes and forms, and outstanding fall color make maples important plants in the landscape, useful for shade, screening, background, and specimens. The numerous tree and shrub cultivars are derived from a selected few species.

glabrum
Rocky Mountain maple
WM CA. Deciduous tree/shrub. Zone 4
Height: 20–25 ft. Spread: 10–15 ft.
This small tree or large shrub is well suited to the small urban landscape. It offers inconspicuous but fragrant flowers in early spring; medium-size, lobed, shiny green leaves in summer, turning yellow to reddish orange in fall. The gray bark contrasts with smooth red twigs and buds and reddish winged seeds, adding color to the winter landscape. Native to streamsides and canyons, foothills to the montane zone, it is one of the few maples that does well at both low and high altitudes. *A. glabrum douglasii* and *A. g. rhodocarpum* are similar.

How to Grow
Sun or partial shade. Prefers fertile, organic soil; tolerates ample moisture if well drained. Doesn't tolerate heat. Sold in containers and balled-and-burlapped. Plant in spring. Leaves may scorch if grown in open, hot, dry, and windy sites.

rubrum *p. 120*
Red maple, swamp maple
CP EW. Deciduous tree. Zone 3
Height: 60–90 ft. Spread: 30–40 ft.
A rapid-growing tree often found in damp conditions in the wild but adaptable to many environments. Clusters of small red flowers appear before leaves emerge in early spring. Very colorful foliage in fall. 'Red Sunset', 'October Glory', and 'Autumn Flame' are among many good cultivars. A densely rooted tree inhospitable to plants within its dripline.

How to Grow
Full sun. Needs fertile, organic soil. Tolerates constant moisture and heat. Sold in containers, bare root, and balled-and-burlapped. Prone to fungal leaf spots in late summer.

Achillea
Ak-i-le′a. Yarrow
Compositae. Daisy family

Description
Yarrows bring attractive, finely divided leaves and dense clusters of small flowers to beds and borders, rock gardens, and meadows. Some of the many species are weedy; those cultivated are effective in groups. Dwarf varieties make excellent ground covers.

millefolium *p. 188   Pictured above*
Western yarrow, common yarrow. (a.k.a. *A. lanulosa*)
WM CA. Perennial. Zones 4–9
Height: 6–24 in. Spread: 6–18 in.
Equally at home in traditional or natural landscapes. Flat-topped clusters of small, white, aromatic flowers bloom

throughout the summer, rising above fernlike grayish foliage. Use in fresh or dried arrangements. 'Floral King' has red flowers.

How to Grow
Full sun. Well-drained soil; tolerates poor or dry soil and heat. Sold as seeds and in containers. Increase by division in spring or early fall. Plant 8–18 in. apart. Remove spent flowers regularly.

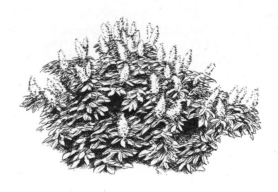

Aesculus
Es'ku-lus. Horse chestnut, buckeye
Hippocastanaceae. Horse chestnut family

Description
This small genus provides some useful shade and street trees as well as shrubs for specimens or borders. Noteworthy for large palmately compound leaves, long, showy, upright panicles of flowers, and attractive (but inedible) fruit. Groups of shrubs described below provide visual anchors in the landscape.

californica p. 142
California buckeye
CA. Deciduous shrub. Zone 9
Height: 10–20 ft. Spread: equal to height
Interesting all year. In spring, fans of smooth, 3–6-in.-long dark green leaflets appear, followed from April to June by dense clusters of 1-in.-wide white or pale pink flowers with orange anthers. Leaves drop in midsummer if not irrigated, late summer or early autumn otherwise. Attractive gray branches, good structure, and large, handsome seeds provide

interest through dormant period. *A. parryi* is a dwarf form (3–12 ft. tall).

How to Grow
Full sun. Tolerates poor or dry soil and heat. Sold in containers. Easy to grow from seed; sow in fall. Needs plenty of room.

parviflora p. 142   Pictured on facing page
Bottlebrush buckeye
EW CP. Deciduous shrub. Zones 5–9
Height: to 10 ft. Spread: to 15 ft.
Graceful, dense shrub, excellent for massing or as specimens. The cylindrical clusters of white flowers make a pleasant addition to the landscape for 2–3 weeks in June and July. Moundlike form; coarse, light green leaflets, 4–8 in. long; large, smooth, brown seeds are also attractive.

How to Grow
Sun or partial shade. Ordinary or fertile soil; tolerates heat. Sold in containers or grow from seed. Root-prune suckers in fall for early spring transplanting. Plant 18 ft. apart. Prune to control size.

pavia p. 143
Red buckeye (a.k.a. *A. splendens*)
EW CP. Deciduous shrub/tree. Zones 6–9
Height: 5–25 ft. Spread: 10 ft.
Masses of this large, open shrub are attractive along woodland edges or in shrub borders. Leaves (coarse, dark green leaflets, 2½–6 in. long) are among the first to appear in spring, followed by dense, eye-catching plumes of red flowers. *A. sylvatica,* painted or Georgia buckeye, is similar with yellow flowers.

How to Grow
As for *A. parviflora,* but plant 10 ft. apart. Susceptible to leaf spot disease.

Agarista
A-ga-ris′ta
Ericaceae. Heath family

Description
Shrubs or small trees with fragrant flowers used in mass plantings, as hedges and screens, as large foundation plants, or naturalized.

populifolia p. 143
Leucothoe, fetterbush (a.k.a. *Leucothoe populifolia*)
CP. Evergreen shrub. Zones 7–9
Height: 16 ft. Spread: 10 ft.
A superior plant for southern gardens, with arching branches, small, narrow, bright green leaves, and, in spring, loose racemes of small white flowers with honeylike fragrance. Terrific as a fast-growing screen or, pruned heavily, as a large foundation plant.

How to Grow
Sun or partial shade. Native to moist or wet areas, it accepts ordinary moisture and soil. Tolerates heat. Sold in containers; propagate by cuttings in summer. Plant 6–8 ft. apart. Prune to restrict growth.

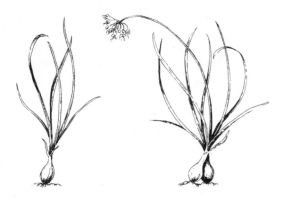

Allium
Al'ee-um. Flowering onion.
Liliaceae. Lily family.

Description
A large genus familiar for its culinary onions, garlic, and chives. The striking flowers and pungent foliage of some species serve as underplantings for ground covers and in beds and borders, rock gardens, and naturalized plantings.

cernuum p. 188   *Pictured above*
Nodding wild onion
EW GP WM. Perennial. Zone 4
Height: 8–12 in. Spread: 2–3 in.
Its delicate leaves and decorative flowers combine well with other small plants. Stalks bear nodding clusters of pink to

purple starlike flowers from May through early July. Use for cut flowers. *A. geyeri* has upright clusters of pink flowers.

How to Grow
Full sun. Well-drained soil; tolerates dry soil and heat. Sold as seeds and bulbs. (Flowers in 2–3 years from seed.) Increase by division of bulbs. Plant in early fall or spring in groups of 8–12 or more bulbs, 2–3 in. deep. Deadhead after flowering; design companion plantings to hide spent foliage.

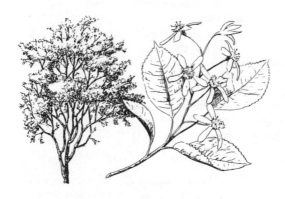

Amelanchier
Am-e-lan'ki-er. Shadbush, serviceberry
Rosaceae. Rose family

Description
A small genus (6 species) of deciduous shrubs or small trees, often with multiple trunks, these plants are grown for their spring flowers, summer fruit, and fall color. Grouped or as specimens, they are well suited for informal or naturalized landscapes. A perfect understory tree in woodlands and for blending areas and calming abrupt contrasts.

alnifolia p. 144
Saskatoon serviceberry, Juneberry
WM. Deciduous shrub. Zone 4
Height: 6–15 ft. Spread: 5–8 ft. or more
One of the finest native shrubs of the western mountain ranges, it makes an excellent shrub border or patio plant. Short-lived, fragrant white flowers emerge in spring just before small, oval, light green leaves appear. Small, sweet, juicy fruits taste like blueberries, ripen by early summer. Outstanding orange to red fall color. The semidwarf 'Regent' grows 4–5 ft. tall.

How to Grow
Sun or partial shade. Adapts to a variety of soil and moisture
conditions; will tolerate poor or dry soil and heat. Sold in
containers, bare root, and balled-and-burlapped. Plant anytime; easy to grow. Will sucker at its base; pruning suckers is
optional.

laevis p. 120   Pictured on p. 275
Serviceberry, shadbush, sarvisbush
EW. Deciduous shrub/tree. Zones 4–9
Height: 15–25 ft. or more. Spread: variable, depending on
number of trunks
Easy to grow, provides year-round interest as a specimen or
naturalized. Pendulous clusters of white and occasionally pinkish flowers are a delight in early spring. Clusters of berrylike,
red to purplish fruit are tasty in June or July. The small leaves
turn superb yellows, oranges, and reds in fall. A perfect size
for most gardens, filling the often-overlooked gap between
shrubs and tall trees. *A. arborea* is similar; *A. canadensis* is a
bit more shrubby.

How to Grow
Sun or partial shade. Well-drained acid soil; tolerates dry soil
and heat. Sold in containers and balled-and-burlapped. Plant
in fall or early spring. Prune to single trunk if desired; rarely
needs other pruning. Although susceptible to leaf rusts, mildews, and borers, as in apple and pear trees, these are usually
not threatening.

Amorpha
A-mor′fa
Leguminosae. Pea family

Description
A small genus (15 species) of shrubs and small trees, wide-
spread in North America with many regional variations.
Grown as specimens, in masses, as hedges, or naturalized.

fruticosa p. 144
False indigo
GP CP EW WD. Deciduous shrub. Zones 3–8
Height: 5–20 ft. Spread: 12–15 ft.
Fine-textured foliage (numerous small leaflets on long stems)
gives a cloudlike appearance. For 2 weeks in late spring, dense
racemes of deep blue flowers with showy orange anthers are
showcased against the bright green leaflets. The foliage is

borne on the upper third of the plant, making it ideal for underplanting with shade-tolerant plants. *A. nana* (fragrant false indigo) and *A. canescens* (leadplant) have similar flowers and foliage but tolerate drier conditions and are low-growing and more suitable for small gardens.

How to Grow
Full sun. Steady supply of moisture. Nutrient-poor soil restricts legginess, enhances floral display. Tolerates heat. Sold as seeds, in containers, bare root, and balled-and-burlapped. Plant no closer than 4 ft. Obtain locally adapted stock; subject to dieback in zones 3 and 4. Prune every few years to renew. Occasionally susceptible to leaf blight.

Amsonia
Am-so'ni-a
Apocynaceae. Dogbane family

Description
Long-lived, low-maintenance perennial plants that adapt easily to most gardens, this small genus includes a number of species grown for their handsome foliage and early spring flowers. Best used in small groups, the foliage is an excellent foil for the middle or back of a border.

tabernaemontana *p. 189*
Blue star, willow herb
EW CP. Perennial. Zones 3–9
Height: 2–3 ft. Spread: 3 ft.
One of the toughest and most attractive plants for the perennial bed or moist meadow. In early spring, long-lasting (3–4 weeks) clusters of small, pale, steel-blue flowers force a closer look. Smooth, neat, light green leaves also provide great fall color; long, thin seedpods are handsome all season. *A. t. salicifolia* has glossier, narrow leaves; *A. angustifolia* has hairy, slightly narrower leaves; *A. hubrectii* is an excellent dwarf version, about 2 ft. tall.

How to Grow
Sun or partial shade. Tolerates constant moisture. Sold in containers. Plant in fall or spring in permanent location, 3–4 ft. apart. Increase by division in fall or early spring; cuttings, spring to early summer. To plant seeds, clip end to allow moisture in, sow after frost. Cut back after bloom, especially in shade, to help keep plants erect.

Anaphalis
A-naf'a-lis. Pearly everlasting
Compositae. Daisy family

Description
Perennials grown for their prolific late summer flowers and handsome foliage. Can be naturalized in meadow gardens or, in more formal styles, mass planted or grown in borders. Dried flowers make excellent arrangements.

margaritacea p. 189
Pearly everlasting (a.k.a. *A. subalpina*)
WM GP EW CA. Perennial. Zone 3
Height: 1–3 ft. Spread: to 4 ft.
Clouds of small (¼-in.), crisp, white papery blossoms followed by fluffy seed heads provide color and interest from late summer to late fall. Narrow grayish white leaves are attractive throughout growing season. Found on rocky, high-elevation slopes and in dry, open locations, it is an excellent plant for high-elevation gardens. *A. m. yedoensis* is more refined and compact.

How to Grow
Full sun. Will tolerate poor or dry soil and heat. Sold as seeds and in containers. Increase by division in spring. Plant 12 in. apart. Keep soil slightly on the dry side; fertilize in spring.

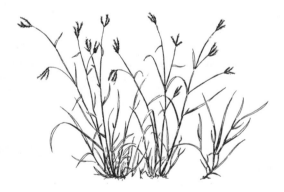

Andropogon
An-dro-po'gon
Gramineae. Grass family

Description
Best known in the great North American prairies, these grasses are unforgettable for the windblown dance of their long flow-

ering stems. In fall, the leaves turn a rich bronze. Valuable also for erosion control and wildlife forage and shelter.

gerardii p. 256   *Pictured on facing page*
Big bluestem, turkey foot
CP GP EW. Perennial grass. Zones 3–8
Height: 3–8 ft. Spread: 2–3 ft.
Big bluestem, the essence of the tallgrass prairie, is a must for any prairie planting. Tall, narrow leaves are blue-green in spring and summer, a statuary bronze in fall. The flower cluster, shaped like a turkey's foot, tops long stems in July and August. Plant as specimen, massed, as ground cover, or naturalized. Use sparingly; it takes a lot of space once established and admits no interplanting.

How to Grow
Full sun. Tolerates both wet and dry conditions, poor soil, and heat. Sold as seeds and in containers. Sow or plant in spring. Mow or burn in spring.

Anemone
A-nem′oh-nee. Windflower
Ranunculaceae. Buttercup family

Description
A diverse group of plants with large, attractive flowers and foliage that provide interesting texture. Use in beds, borders, containers, or naturalized areas. Anemones have a wide range of bloom times (early spring to fall), hardiness, and flower colors.

patens p. 190
Pasque flower (a.k.a. *Pulsatilla patens*)
GP WM. Perennial. Zone 4
Height: 8 in. Spread: 8 in.
These reliable, hardy, early bloomers push their way through the snow in early spring. Pale blue, lavender, and white cup-shaped flowers (2 in. wide) with gold centers unfold from silky bracts. Fernlike, whitish green foliage hugs the ground. In late summer, feathery fruits make the plant appear to bloom again.

How to Grow
Sun or partial shade. Well-drained soil; tolerates dry soil and heat. Sold as seeds and in containers. Plant 6–8 in. apart in early spring through summer. Increase by seed or division (can be difficult to transplant).

Aquilegia
Ak-wi-lee′gee-a. Columbine
Ranunculaceae. Buttercup family

Description
Outstanding garden plants, equally at home in beds and borders or naturalized in a woodland garden. Striking spring or early summer flowers resemble crowns with distinctive backward-projecting spurs. Foliage is fernlike and delicate. Some species are short-lived; several reseed freely.

caerulea p. 190
Rocky Mountain columbine
WM. Perennial. Zones 3–8
Height: 1–2 ft. Spread: 1–2 ft.
Large upright blue and white flowers with long spurs (about 2 in.) rise above deeply cut, light green foliage. Excellent for mountain gardens; its wild habitat is in aspen groves and on moist, rocky slopes. Most selections are hybrids in which this species is one parent. May live 4–5 years.

How to Grow
Sun or partial shade. Prefers moist, well-drained soil. Keep moist if planted in full sun. Doesn't tolerate heat. Sold as seeds and in containers. Sow seeds outside in fall. Divide mature plants in late summer or early fall. Plant 12–15 in. apart. Susceptible to aphids when grown in an open area.

canadensis p. 191 *Pictured above*
Columbine, Canadian columbine
EW GP CP. Perennial. Zones 3–8
Height: 2–3 ft. Spread: 1 ft.
Attractive to humans and hummingbirds alike, red and yellow nodding flowers bloom in early to late spring for about 6

weeks. Delicate, lacy foliage may survive southern winters. At home in wide range of habitats.

How to Grow
Sun or shade. Tolerant of many soil and moisture conditions; does best with assured supply of moisture. Tolerates heat if shaded. Sold as seeds, in containers, and bare root. Easy to grow from seed (usually blooms in second season). Stands up well to leaf miner infestations.

chrysantha p. 191
Golden columbine
WM. Perennial. Zones 3–9
Height: 2½–3½ ft. Spread: 1 ft.
Large (2–3-in.), fragrant yellow flowers bloom from late spring through midsummer. Native to moist ravines in the southern Rockies, it adapts to many garden conditions. Of the many cultivars, 'Yellow Queen' has large lemon-yellow flowers, 'Alba Plena' has pale yellow flowers, and 'Nana' is a dwarf form (1½ ft. tall).

How to Grow
Sun or partial shade. Tolerates dry soil and some heat. Sold as seeds and in containers. Sow in late fall; divide mature plants in late summer. Plant 12 in. apart. In hot, arid conditions it is susceptible to spider mites and aphids.

Arctostaphylos
Ark-to-staf'i-los. Manzanita
Ericaceae. Heath family

Description
From ground covers to large shrubs and small trees, this diverse group of broadleaf evergreens deserves greater attention. Their attractive urn-shaped flowers and red berries, thick, leathery leaves, smooth red bark, and sinuous, picturesque branches enhance the landscape year-round. The berries attract wildlife.

densiflora 'Howard McMinn' p. 145
Sonoma manzanita, Vine Hill manzanita
CA. Evergreen shrub. Zone 9
Height: 4 ft. Spread: 7 ft.
The most dependable, healthy, and long-lived of the cultivated manzanitas. A spreading plant, when tip-pruned it forms a knee-high ground cover. Small white flowers tinged with pink

clustered in panicles bloom profusely in February and March, followed by tiny, glossy red berries in spring and summer. 'Harmony' and 'Sentinel' are more upright; *A. manzanita* 'Dr. Hurd' is a popular, large (15-ft.), multistemmed specimen with large clusters of white flowers, hardy to zones 7–8.

How to Grow
Full sun. Tolerates poor or dry soil and heat. Sold in containers; increase by cuttings taken in cool weather. Plant in fall (4 ft. apart for ground cover).

edmundsii p. 145   *Pictured above*
Little Sur manzanita
CA. Evergreen shrub. Zone 9
Height: to 4 ft. Spread: 6 ft.
Fast-growing plants whose small, bright green leaves are tinged with red. Compact clusters of pink flowers bloom from December through February (in Southern California). Native to a tiny area near the ocean, they adapt well to hot summers of the interior and tolerate summer watering. 'Carmel Sur' is less than 1 ft. tall and ideal for ground cover.

How to Grow
As for *A. densiflora*. Plant 'Carmel Sur' 24 in. apart for ground cover; shear or tip-prune after bloom to increase denseness. Overhead watering can encourage fungal diseases, causing branches to die back.

nevadensis
Pinemat manzanita
WM. Evergreen shrub. Zone 5
Height: 10–18 in. Spread: 3–5 ft.
An excellent, low-maintenance ground cover with rich ever-

green foliage, pendulous pale pink to light rose flowers in spring.

How to Grow
Sun or partial shade. Prefers well-drained, slightly acid soil. Tolerates dry soil and heat. Sold in containers. Increase by tip cuttings taken November–March. Plant 3 ft. apart.

patula
Greenleaf manzanita
WM. Evergreen shrub. Zone 5
Height: 4–6 ft. Spread: 3–5 ft.
A stately, slow-growing shrub, its rigid, leathery foliage contrasts with polished mahogany-colored stems. Pendulous clusters of delicate pink flowers for 2–3 weeks in early to late spring; berries in late summer. Good as specimen, foundation plant, or ground cover.

How to Grow
As for *A. nevadensis.*

uva-ursi p. 146
Bearberry, kinnikinick
EW WM GP CA. Evergreen shrub. Zone 4
Height: 3–4 in. Spread: 3–5 ft. or more
A maintenance-free ground cover ideal for rock gardens and hillsides. The glossy green leaves turn red in winter. Spring flowers are white, tipped with pink; berries in late summer. 'Point Reyes' is more vigorous but less hardy than the species; 'Big Bear' has larger leaves and fruit.

How to Grow
As for *A. nevadensis.* Plant in spring, 1½ ft. apart. Pinch back growing tips in spring for compact growth.

Arisaema
Ar-i-se'ma. Jack-in-the-pulpit
Araceae. Arum family

Description
Woodland natives prized by adults and children alike for their curious spring flowers and brilliant red fall berries. Suitable as specimens or small groups in beds and borders or naturalized; effective among creeping ground covers. Best viewed in elevated planting or near a path. Only a few of the 150 species in the genus are cultivated.

triphyllum *p. 192   Pictured above*
Jack-in-the-pulpit
EW CP. Perennial. Zones 4–9
Height: 1–2 ft. Spread: 2 ft.
Adds interest to the shade garden. The leaves are large (1–1½ ft. long) and medium green, divided into 3, sometimes 5 parts. The peculiar flower, consisting of a spadix (Jack) surrounded and shaded by a spathe (his pulpit), lasts 2–4 weeks in spring. In ideal conditions it is carefree and long lived and will spread readily throughout the garden. Green dragon (*A. dracontium*) is equally exotic; its spathe has a long tip. Native species are extremely variable; many worthy Asian species are also available.

How to Grow
Shade. Prefers rich, moist soil, well drained to avoid rot. Sold as corms, in containers, and bare root. Plant in fall or anytime they're dormant. Increase by transplanting offshoots of the corm or clean seeds and sow in late fall. Both methods take several years to provide a flowering plant.

Aristolochia
A-ris-toe-low′kee-a
Aristolochiaceae. Birthwort family

Description
A large genus of perennial vines whose cultivated members are most often valued for creating shade with the help of a trellis or arbor. There are many tropical species, and all parts of the plant have a refreshing tropical appearance.

durior *p. 264*
Dutchman's pipe vine (a.k.a. *A. macrophylla*)
EW GP. Deciduous vine. Zones 4–8
Height: 30 ft. plus. Spread: as allowed
This vine provides 3-season interest and is easy to maintain. Fast-growing green stems bear large (12-in.), heart-shaped green leaves and readily twine over trellis or other support. Intriguing 3-in.-long, pipe-shaped flowers of mottled green and burgundy bloom for 2–3 weeks in mid to late spring. Cylindrical, ridged capsules, 3–4 in. long, ripen to dark gray or black in early fall. It is the host plant for the pipevine swallowtail butterfly.

How to Grow
Sun or partial shade. Prefers organic, well-drained soil. Tolerates heat fairly well. Sold in containers. Increase by layering, division, July cuttings, or by seed sown outdoors in fall. If a screen is desired, plant 1–2 ft. apart and provide support (tie stems at first). Pinch growing tips to encourage branching. Prune as needed when dormant.

Artemisia
Ar-te-meez'i-a, Ar-tem-is'i-a. Sage
Compositae. Daisy family

Description
Many species in this large genus of annuals, perennials, and shrubs are grown for their foliage and interesting windswept or gnarled forms. (Annual species are not cultivated.) The fine-textured silver leaves, often evergreen or semi-evergreen and aromatic, complement plants with dark green foliage or brightly colored flowers. Attractive year-round, they can be

used in numerous ways: as specimens and mass plantings and in beds, borders, and naturalized plantings. Some grow tall enough to serve as hedges and windbreaks. Highly drought resistant. Where well adapted, these tough plants are easy to grow.

californica 'Canyon Gray' *Pictured on p. 285*
California sagebrush
CA. Evergreen shrub. Zone 9
Height: 1–2 ft. Spread: 6 ft.
The species is a ubiquitous upright shrub of the coastal California scrublands. The prostrate form, 'Canyon Gray', has much greater landscape value. At its best on banks and hillsides, it forms a dense, fragrant, mounding and spreading ground cover, its fine-textured gray-green leaves pleasing to the eye and soft to the touch. (The blossoms are insignificant.) 'Montana' is a similarly low-spreading clone.

How to Grow
Full sun. Tolerates poor or dry soil and heat. Sold in containers. Increase by cuttings taken in cool weather. Plant in fall, singly or 3–4 ft. apart for ground cover. After bloom, cut back stems several inches for neat appearance.

filifolia *p. 146*
Threadleaf sage, sand sage
WD GP. Semi-evergreen shrub. Zones 4–10
Height: 3–4 ft. Spread: 3–4 ft.
The very fine, threadlike semi-evergreen leaves are silver-blue in summer, silver-gray in winter. The graceful, windswept form is compact. Whole plant is sweetly pungent. Flowers and fruit are inconspicuous.

How to Grow
Full sun. Prefers sand, but grows well in any well-drained soil. Tolerates poor soil and heat. Sold in containers; may self-sow in preferred conditions. Transplant anytime. Space irregularly, 3–5 ft. apart for natural look. With little supplemental water will grow moderately fast. Remove oldest stems every 3–4 years. Too much water or fertilizer induces rank growth, which will need pruning each year.

frigida *p. 147*
Fringed sage
WD GP WM. Semi-evergreen shrub. Zones 3–10
Height: 18 in. Spread: 18 in.
A mat-forming, fine-textured, aromatic ground cover, with tiny, finely segmented leaves that are soft and woolly. Flowers and fruit are inconspicuous.

How to Grow

Sun or partial shade. Does well in poor, dry soil. Sold as seeds and in containers. Increase by division or layering. Transplant anytime, best when soil is cool. Space 18 in. apart for solid ground cover. Shear flower stems off to basal foliage to induce new growth and keep plant in its prime.

ludoviciana p. 192
White sage
GP WD WM. Deciduous perennial. Zones 3–8
Height: 1–3 ft. Spread: rapidly forms colonies
Ideally suited for dry conditions, its aromatic, fine gray foliage provides a backdrop for other flowering plants. Mixed with blue grama grass in a prairie planting, it can produce an ethereal, cloudlike effect.

How to Grow

Full sun. Does best in poor or dry soils (becomes leggy in fertile, moist soils). Tolerates heat. Sold as seeds, in containers, and bare root. Increase by sowing seeds or dividing the rhizomes in spring or fall.

tridentata p. 147   *Pictured above*
Bigleaf sage, Basin big sage, sagebrush
WD WM CA. Evergreen shrub. Zones 4–10
Height: 1½–15 ft. Spread: somewhat less than height
A picturesque specimen or accent plant with small, velvety soft, silvery evergreen leaves and a sweet pungent aroma. Its "big" leaves are only ¾ in. long and ⅕ in. wide. Inconspicuous flowers. Black sage (*A. tridentata* subsp. *nova*) is more compact and lower growing, often only 2 ft. tall and wide. Low sagebrush (*A. arbuscula*) grows to 3 ft. Silver sagebrush (*A. cana*) has a more uniform growth habit than bigleaf sage; in masses, it imparts a graceful, wispy appearance to the landscape.

How to Grow
Full sun. Tolerates poor soil if well drained and heat if not
overwatered. Sold in containers. Transplants best when soil is
cool in spring or fall. Space 4–8 ft. apart depending on desired
effect. Periodic heavy pruning to remove old stems rejuvenates
plants. Susceptible to root rot if too wet in summer, especially
in heavier soils.

Aruncus
A-run'kus
Rosaceae. Rose family

Description
A small group of tall perennial plants resembling large astilbes.
Excellent for shady areas, they can be massed as background
plants or as hedges, naturalized among shrubs, or used to
accent a dull corner.

dioicus p. 193
Goatsbeard
EW WM. Perennial. Zone 5
Height: 4–6 ft. Spread: 3 ft.
This impressive streamside perennial produces long spikes of
tiny white flowers in early to mid summer. Its height and
coarse-textured foliage make it useful as a background plant
for shady, moist spots or as a perennial hedge. A smaller cultivar, 'Kneiffii', is good for small gardens.

How to Grow
Partial sun or shade. Easy to grow in most garden soils with
ordinary moisture. Sold as seeds and in containers. Increase
by division in early spring or fall; sow seeds in spring. Plant
18–24 in. apart.

Asclepias
Ass-klee'pi-as. Milkweed
Asclepiadaceae. Milkweed family

Description
Milkweeds inhabit open woodlands and sunlit areas from dry
prairies to marshes. Their beautiful and unusual flower clusters
resemble chalices or candlestick holders. Colors range from
pure white through pinks, brilliant reds and oranges, to deep
purple. A major source of food for monarch butterflies, milkweeds can be grown as specimen plants, in massed plantings,

beds and borders, and naturalized plantings. Several of the 120 species in the genus are cultivated, though some can be weedy.

incarnata p. 193
Swamp milkweed, marsh milkweed, red milkweed
EW GP. Perennial. Zones 3–8
Height: 4–5 ft. Spread: 1 ft.
Native to marshes, wet prairies, and sedge meadows, this plant will grow in all but the driest garden soils. Red to pink flowers are borne in July in flat-topped umbels above darkish green foliage. Produces typical milkweed pods in fall. Handsome as a specimen or in massed planting.

How to Grow
Full sun. Tolerates constant moisture and heat. Sold as seeds, in containers, and bare root. Easy to grow from seed; provide 2 months cool/moist stratification.

tuberosa p. 194 *Pictured above*
Butterfly weed, pleurisy root
EW GP CP WD. Perennial. Zones 3–8
Height: 1–1½ ft. Spread: 1–2 ft.
Spectacular flat clusters, 2–5 in. across, of yellow, orange, or occasionally bright red flowers adorn these perennials for about 2 weeks in June and July. A beige seedpod follows in autumn. Leaves are narrow, green, and alternate.

How to Grow
Full sun; will tolerate poor or dry soil and heat. Sold in containers, bare root, and as seeds. Sow seeds in fall (they need cool/moist stratification) or root divisions in spring. Occasionally defoliated by butterfly larvae; doesn't permanently damage most plants. Susceptible to aphids and powdery mildew.

Aster
As'ter
Compositae. Daisy family

Description
Many members of this large and complex genus of herbaceous annuals and perennials are known for the variety of their daisylike flowers. There are asters for almost every habitat and garden situation, from formal borders to meadows. Hard to beat for late summer and fall color.

Most asters are susceptible to foliar mildews. To control mildew, keep the soil moist, thin stems to increase air circulation, and, if necessary, treat with sulfur or other fungicides.

alpinus p. 194
Alpine aster
WM. Perennial. Zone 3
Height: 6–12 in. Spread: 12 in.
These compact plants with single, 1–2-in.-wide daisies in lavender and blue with yellow centers are perfect for small gardens. One of the few asters to bloom in late spring, blossoms last 2–3 weeks. *A. a.* var. *albus* has white rays; *A. a.* var. *rubra* has red rays.

How to Grow
Sun or partial shade. Prefers well-drained alkaline soil; will grow in ordinary soils. Tolerates some heat. Sold as seeds and in containers. Increase by division in spring or fall. Plant 6 in. apart.

divaricatus p. 195
White wood aster
EW CP. Perennial. Zones 4–8
Height: 2–3 ft. Spread: 2–3 ft.

Unlike most asters, this one prefers shady spots, where it adds welcome color in late summer and fall. Dense clusters of small white flowers with yellow centers last for 2–4 weeks. The handsome green leaves, often burgundy underneath, alternate on dark burgundy to black stems. The plants spread by rhizomes, filling gaps in the summer garden and hiding the foliage of early bloomers.

How to Grow

Partial sun or shade. Tolerates dry soil (when established) and some heat. Sold as seeds and in containers. Increase by division or stem cuttings in spring. Sow seed outdoors in fall or spring. Plant 2–3 ft. apart. Can pinch back to 1 ft. in late spring to limit height and promote bushier growth.

linariifolius p. 195

Stiff-leaved aster, bristly aster
EW CP. Perennial. Zones 3–8
Height: 2–3 ft. Spread: 2–2½ ft.
Growing in distinct, rounded clumps of stiff, deep green, glossy foliage, this aster looks like a small evergreen. Blooms for 3–4 weeks in early fall, with clusters of daisylike flowers, blue to violet, rarely white to pink, all with yellow or reddish centers. 'Albus' has white petals, 'Purpureus' has purple petals, and 'Roseus' has pink petals.

How to Grow

Tolerates sun, partial shade, sandy or rocky soils, dry conditions, and heat. Avoid poorly drained soil. Sold as seeds and in containers. Sow seeds outdoors in fall or spring. Increase by division or tip cuttings in spring. Plant 2½–3 ft. apart. Pinch back in late spring for bushier growth.

novae-angliae p. 196   *Pictured on facing page*

New England aster, Michaelmas daisy
EW CP GP. Perennial. Zones 3–8
Height: 3–5 ft. Spread: 3 ft.
Long-lasting, large, showy flowers and ease of culture make this one of the most desired native asters for all types of gardening, particularly in damp areas. Flowers in blue, violet, purple, or pink, 1½–2 in. wide, appear in August for 2–4 weeks. The many cultivars vary in flower size and color.

How to Grow

Sun or partial shade. Needs moist, fertile, organic soil. Tolerates heat if kept moist. Sold as seeds and in containers. Sow seeds outside in late fall or spring. Increase by tip cuttings in spring. Divide outside sections of the plant every 2 or 3 years

in early spring or fall. (The center of the plant becomes bare
in 1–2 years.) Plant 3–3½ ft. apart. Does well if fertilized.
Stake to prevent floppiness or shear stems by a third in late
spring for more compact form.

oblongifolius p. 196
Aromatic aster, savory-leaved aster
EW GP. Perennial. Zones 3–6
Height: 16 in. Spread: about 12 in.
A delightful plant for small dry-prairie plantings. Borne at the
ends of stems, the small sky-blue flowers (blue ray, yellow disk)
bloom well into autumn, even after heavy frosts. Fine green-
blue foliage exudes pungent odor when crushed.

How to Grow
Full sun. Tolerates poor or dry soil, heat, cold, and harsh
winds. Sold as seeds, in containers, and bare root. Gather seed
in autumn for spring planting; divide plants in spring. Plant
on 1-ft. centers for ground cover, randomly in dry prairie.

Atriplex
At'ri-pleks
Chenopodiaceae. Goosefoot family

Description
Only a few of the species in this genus of shrubs are cultivated.
The one below is valuable for stabilizing soil and providing
wildlife habitat in dry climates (6–10 in. annual rainfall) where
all else fails.

canescens p. 148
Saltbush, fourwing saltbush
WD CA. Semi-evergreen shrub. Zones 4–10
Height: to 6 ft. Spread: 4–8 ft.
This mounded shrub is recommended for its tolerance of saline
soil and durability in exposures too harsh for most other plants
rather than for its beauty. The small, narrow, semi-evergreen
leaves are silver-green; some selections turn purple-pink in
winter. Flowers are insignificant, but the clusters of gold-tan
to brown papery winged seed husks are used in dried flower
arrangements. Fire retardant, it provides cover and food for
wildlife. However, its windborne pollen can cause allergies,
and it can be invasive and difficult to eradicate. *A. oborata,*
A. confertifolia, and *A. cuneata* are compact and mounded,
12–18 in. tall and wide.

How to Grow
Full sun. Dry soil. Tolerates poor soil and heat. Sold as seeds and in containers. Transplant anytime, water consistently for a few months to establish, then limit water. Severe pruning produces best specimens. Too much water, too little sun, or too fertile soil makes plant scraggly, increases susceptibility to scale insects and gall midges.

Baccharis
Bak'a-ris
Compositae. Daisy family

Description
A few species in this large group of tough, undemanding shrubs are cultivated. Their deep, soil-holding root systems provide erosion control on streambanks and hillsides. The snowy white fruiting heads of some species add color in fall and winter.

halimifolia p. 148 *Pictured above*
Groundsel tree, silverling, sea myrtle
CP. Deciduous shrub. Zones 4–9
Height: to 12 ft. Spread: somewhat less than height
Its tolerance for salt spray makes this shrub a good candidate for seaside gardens. Also does well elsewhere if in full sun. Light gray-green leaves persist into winter. Large clusters of white fruiting heads on female plants are attractive in fall and winter.

How to Grow
Full sun. Prefers moist soil. Tolerates heat. Sold in containers. Increase by cuttings taken in summer. Plant 6 ft. apart. Prune yearly to maintain size.

pilularis p. 149
Coyote brush
CA. Evergreen shrub. Zone 9
Height: 3 ft. Spread: 10 ft.
Selected male forms (which form no seed heads) are extremely drought tolerant and make excellent evergreen ground covers. Leaves are small, thick, and resinous, dark green or gray-green. (Flowers and fruit are unimportant on cultivated varieties.) Their tolerance of garden watering and even boggy conditions makes them acceptable for a wide range of gardens; native to coastal California, they thrive in interior valleys and on the high desert. 'Twin Peaks #2' is a low, compact form; 'Pigeon Point', with light green leaves, is fast growing.

How to Grow
Full sun. Tolerates poor or dry soil and heat. Sold in containers. Plant in fall, 3–4 ft. apart. Prune or shear as often as once a year to shape or control height. Overgrown plants can be cut back by half to rejuvenate. Susceptible to spider mites, lace-bugs, and whitefly.

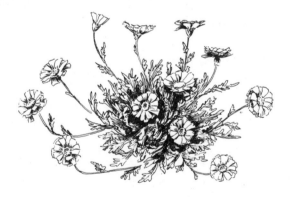

Baileya
Bay-lay′a
Compositae. Daisy family

Description
The species below is the only cultivated member of this small genus (4 species) of southwestern desert natives.

multiradiata p. 197   *Pictured above*
Desert marigold
WD. Biennial or short-lived perennial. Zones 6–10
Height: 12–18 in. Spread: 12–18 in.

An excellent addition to very hot, dry desert gardens, suitable for borders, massed plantings, or naturalized. Clear, bright yellow daisylike flowers, about 1½ in. in diameter, rise on nearly leafless stems above mounds of woolly, white foliage. Depending on when seeds germinate, plants may flower from April to October; individual plants flower for several months.

How to Grow
Full sun. Tolerates poor or dry soil and heat. Sold as seeds and in containers. (Seeding is more reliable.) Germination is erratic, so sow a lot of seeds (1 oz. per 2,500–5,000 sq. ft.). Sow fresh seeds in fall; moist, chilled seeds in spring. A stand will self-seed, but the surface of the soil must be repeatedly disturbed to ensure adequate germination. (Dogs running regularly through a patch will do the trick.) Rosettes require a period of cold-weather dormancy to set buds.

Baptisia
Bap-tizh′i-a. Wild indigo
Leguminosae. Pea family

Description
A small genus of North American natives with spectacular racemes of pealike flowers and striking, shrubby foliage. Among the best perennials for the garden, they're suited to the middle to rear of a border, prominently sited in a meadow or in a naturalized landscape. Groups are particularly handsome, though a single well-placed specimen can make a garden. Early June flowers fill the gap between spring- and summer-flowering plants.

alba var. *alba* p. 198
White wild indigo (a.k.a. *B. pendula, B. leucantha, B. lactea*)
EW. Perennial. Zones 5–8
Height: 2–3½ ft. Spread: 3½–5 ft.
A white-flowered baptisia offering the same qualities as *B. australis.* Eggshell-white to bright white flowers are often supported by attractive gray bracts. Many of the white species have recently been reclassified under *B. alba.* One of these, which was called *B. pendula,* has beautiful gray stems.

How to Grow
As for *B. australis.*

australis var. *australis* p. 197   *Pictured on p. 295*
Wild blue indigo
EW. Perennial. Zones 3–9
Height: 3–4 ft. Spread: 4–6 ft. or more
For show, durability, and drought tolerance, this is a perfect plant. Foot-long racemes of small (1-in.), indigo-blue flowers appear in midspring and last for 3–5 weeks. The shrubby, light blue-green foliage is a perfect backdrop all summer. From midsummer into winter the plant displays large, woody, charcoal-colored pods. *B. a.* var. *minor,* a smaller version of var. *australis,* is the only other blue-flowered baptisia.

How to Grow
Sun or partial shade. Prefers fertile, organic soil. Tolerates poor or dry soil and heat. Sold as seeds, in containers, and balled-and-burlapped. (Purchase plants 2–3 years old for easier establishment.) Plant 3–6 ft. apart in deeply prepared soil in fall or spring. Increase by sowing fresh seeds in early summer, by dividing in fall or spring, or by stem cuttings.

leucophaea
Plains wild indigo
GP. Perennial. Zones 4–7
Height: 15 in. Spread: 3 ft.
An exquisite plant. In June, clusters of clear, light yellow flowers terminate cascading stems that rise from gray-green foliage. Slow to bloom (5 years), but worth the wait.

How to Grow
Full sun. Tolerates poor or dry soil and heat. Sold as seeds, in containers, and bare root. Plant 3–4 ft. apart. Seeds germinate best when scarified and wet stratified.

Berlandiera
Ber-lan'dee-era
Compositae. Daisy family

Description
The four species in this genus of flowering perennials are native to the southern U.S. and Mexico, where large stands naturalize along roadsides.

lyrata p. 198   *Pictured above*
Chocolateflower, greeneyes
WD. Perennial. Zones 5–6
Height: 12–24 in. Spread: 12–24 in.
These easy-to-grow plants bloom profusely from April to September. The daisylike blossoms (yellow rays, maroon center) and mounded coarse, gray-green foliage have a pleasant chocolate aroma. The cuplike seed heads are also attractive. Flowers open in morning, droop in heat of day. In the garden, they can be used in massed plantings, beds and borders, meadows, and other naturalized plantings.

How to Grow
Full sun. Well-drained soil; susceptible to root rot in heavy soils that are too wet. Tolerates poor or dry soil and heat. Sold as seeds and in containers. Seeds germinate well outdoors April through summer. Transplants best when soil is warm. Space 12–24 in. for solid masses. Deadhead for continuous bloom.

Betula
Bet'you-la. Birch
Betulaceae. Birch family

Description
This genus of trees and shrubs is popular for many reasons: graceful form, handsome bark, and attractive leaves that dance in the wind and, in many species, turn bright yellow in the fall. Birches are effective as specimens, in groups, or naturalized.

fontinalis
Western river birch (a.k.a. *B. occidentalis*)
WM. Deciduous shrub/small tree. Zone 4
Height: to 25 ft. Spread: somewhat less than height
A shrubby, often multistemmed tree, it usually forms graceful clumps. Ideal for small properties, it doesn't cast heavy shade, thus permitting underplanting. The small leaves are bright green above and yellow-green beneath. The bark is a shiny, reddish brown. Catkins aren't ornamental.

How to Grow
Sun or partial shade. Native to moist, streamside sites, it won't tolerate dry soil. Will stand some heat if kept moist. Sold in containers and balled-and-burlapped. Plant in spring. Susceptible to borers, aphids, and other problems if grown in dry soil.

nigra   p. 121   *Pictured above*
River birch, red birch, black birch
EW CP. Deciduous tree. Zones 4–9
Height: 40–70 ft. Spread: 40–60 ft.
Its shimmering leaves and light, shredding bark on single or multiple trunks make river birch handsome year-round. Es-

pecially useful for troublesome wet sites and in the South, where other birches may not adapt. 'Heritage', with much lighter bark, is a good substitute for paper birch in warmer regions.

How to Grow
Sun or partial shade. Prefers fertile, organic, acidic soil. Tolerates constant moisture and heat. Sold in containers and balled-and-burlapped. Plant when dormant. Space 8–10 ft. apart; 20 ft. or more if multitrunked. Roots are shallow; plan walks and fences accordingly. Crotches of multiple trunks can weaken with age.

Bignonia
Big-no'nee-a
Bignoniaceae. Bignonia family

Description
The single species in this genus is described below.

capreolata p. 264   *Pictured above*
Cross vine, trumpet flower (a.k.a. *Anisostichus capreolata*)
EW CP. Evergreen vine. Zones 6–8
Height: 60 ft.
Climbing on masonry walls, fences, trees, arbors, and trellises, this vine is grown for its handsome, evergreen foliage and distinctive flowers. Coarse leaflets, 3–6 in. long, turn purplish in winter. Clusters of 2-in.-long flowers, orange to reddish outside, yellow to red inside, appear in spring. Large seed capsules (5–8 in. long) turn from green to brown. 'Atrosanguinea' has dark purple flowers.

How to Grow
Sun or shade. Prefers fertile, organic soil and regular moisture.
Tolerates heat. Sold in containers. Increase by seeds or cuttings
taken in summer. Prune to train on support.

Boltonia
Bol-toe'nee-a
Compositae. Daisy family

Description
Grown in borders or naturalized for their profuse, long-lasting,
daisylike flowers on erect, leafy stems. Generally easy to grow,
most members of this small genus are native to the eastern
half of North America.

asteroides *p. 199*
White boltonia
EW CP. Perennial. Zones 4–9
Height: 3–5 ft. Spread: 4–5 ft.
This large, open plant with fine blue-green leaves is covered
for 3–5 weeks in late summer with clusters of 1-in. white ray
flowers surrounding yellow centers. Best for moist, open natural plantings where it can freely spread among and blend
with brighter fall colors. 'Snowbank', an erect cultivar that
doesn't need staking, is best for borders. The variety *latis-
quama* is similar to *B. asteroides,* but with pink to violet
flowers; 'Nana' is its dwarf form (2–3 ft.).

How to Grow
Sun or partial shade. Prefers fertile, organic soil. Tolerates heat.
Sold as seeds and in containers. Increase by seeds sown in late
fall or spring, cuttings in spring. Divide every 2–3 years in
fall or early spring. Plant 3 ft. or more apart. Prune in late
spring to reduce height.

Bouteloua
Boo-tel-oo'ah
Gramineae. Grass family

Description
Attractive, easy to grow, and vigorous under adverse conditions, several of the 39 species in this genus of perennial grasses
are gaining in popularity for use in meadows, as ground covers,
and in water-saving lawns. Use the seed heads in dried flower
arrangements.

curtipendula *p. 256   Pictured above*
Sideoats grama
WD GP EW. Perennial grass. Zones 4–10
Height: 18–36 in. Spread: to 12 in.
The upright form and handsome drooping heads of small,
oatlike seeds make this bunchgrass a favorite for tall meadows.
Blue-green in the growing season, the blades cure to a golden
tan. Vigorous enough to be a larval forage plant in a butterfly
meadow. Noteworthy cultivars include 'El Reno', for central
Kansas, Oklahoma, and Texas; 'Haskell', a rhizomatous form
adapted to central and south Texas; 'Niner', for New Mexico
and Colorado. 'Premier' is adapted farthest south.

How to Grow
Sun or partial shade. Tolerates poor or dry soil and heat. Sold
as seeds; sow in spring or early summer when soil is warm.
Mow to 8 in. high in winter or early spring. Can be fertilized
in spring.

gracilis *p. 257*
Blue grama
WD GP. Perennial grass. Zones 5–8
Height: 6–24 in. Spread: 18 in.
A fine, wiry, low-growing bunchgrass, blue-gray curing to tan
when dormant. The seed head, an eyebrow-shaped flag, seems
to float above the foliage. Makes an attractive water-saving
lawn or meadow grass. Very adaptable and easy to grow.
'Hachita' is a drought-tolerant cultivar recommended for New
Mexico, southern Colorado, and the Texas-Oklahoma pan-
handle.

How to Grow
Full sun. Tolerates poor or dry soil and heat. Sold as seeds and
in containers. Sow seeds in autumn when soil is warm, at least

8 weeks before frost. For lawn, mow 4–6 in. high to encourage sod formation.

Buchloe
Bu-kloh'ee
Gramineae. Grass family

Description
The single species in this genus is described below.

dactyloides p. 257
Buffalo grass
WD GP. Perennial grass. Zones 5–10
Height: 3–5 in. Spread: 2 ft. (by stolons)
This is an excellent lawn grass for hot, dry climates, requiring deep, infrequent watering, one annual fertilizing, and monthly (or less) mowing May–September. Sage-green, fine and soft bladed when growing, straw-tan and stiffer when dormant, it is an attractive ground cover when not mowed. 'Prairie', a very low growing selection, is available as sod. 'Texoka' is well adapted to northwestern Texas, western Kansas, Oklahoma, and eastern New Mexico.

How to Grow
Sun or partial shade. Tolerates poor or dry soil and heat. Sold as seeds, sod, and plugs. Sow seeds treated to enhance germination May–August, 3–6 lb. per 1,000 sq. ft. Plant plugs 1 ft. apart. Fertilize mowed, trafficked areas in spring; no-mow areas may not need fertilizing once established. Excessive watering or fertilization can lead to pest and disease problems.

Calliandra
Kal-i-an'dra
Leguminosae. Pea family

Description
A large genus of tropical and subtropical shrubs and trees, a few of which are grown in gardens for their drought tolerance and showy flowers.

eriophylla p. 149   *Pictured on facing page*
Pink fairy duster
WD. Shrub. Zones 6–10

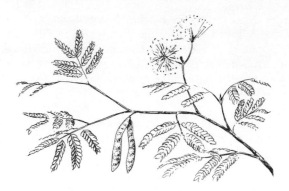

Height: to 3 ft. Spread: to 2½ ft.
An extremely drought-tolerant plant, pink fairy duster is an ideal small shrub or ground cover for low-water-use gardens in the warm deserts. Its tiny gray-green leaves, very fine and hairy, may be deciduous or evergreen depending on available moisture. From February to May, its 2-in.-wide, rose-pink to white flowers become the focus of the garden. Slender, tapered seedpods lure quail in mid to late summer. *C. californica* is larger (to 6 ft.) but more frost tender.

How to Grow
Full sun. Tolerates poor or dry soil and heat. Sold as seeds and in containers. Sow seeds when soil is warm. Plant from containers anytime. For ground cover, plant 3 ft. apart. Slow growing. Appreciates monthly deep watering. Tip-prune to increase density.

Callirhoe
Ka-lir'oh-ee
Malvaceae. Mallow family

Description
Members of this small genus of North American herbaceous annuals and perennials are prized for their large pink, white, and reddish purple flowers, their drought tolerance, and ease of cultivation.

involucrata p. 199
Purple poppy mallow, wine cup
GP WD. Perennial. Zones 4–8
Height: 6–12 in. or more. Spread: 6–12 in. or more

Large (to 2½ in. wide) wine-colored, cup-shaped flowers rise above deeply lobed green foliage from spring to early summer (through fall with moisture). Spectacular as individuals or massed, in borders or naturalized. Self-sows without becoming weedy. *C. triangulata* is a larger plant.

How to Grow
Full sun. Tolerates poor or dry soils and heat. Sold as seeds. Sow in fall; scarification aids germination. Increase by division. Highly drought resistant.

Calycanthus
Kal-i-kan'thus
Calycanthaceae. Calycanthus family

Description
Two species of shrub or small tree grown by generations of gardeners for their fragrant flowers and leaves.

floridus p. 150   Pictured above
Sweetshrub, Carolina allspice
EW CP. Deciduous shrub or small tree. Zones 4–9
Height: 6–9 ft. Spread: 6–10 ft. or more
One of the easiest and most versatile native shrubs, sweetshrub serves as an understory shrub for shade, a transition plant along a woodland edge or building, or a specimen clump along a path. The large, oblong, glossy leaves turn bright yellow or gold in fall. Unusual maroon flowers with numerous ribbon-like petals appear midspring for 3–4 weeks and sporadically through early summer. Spreads slowly to form dense clumps; ideal for informal fence. Floral fragrance is highly variable from plant to plant; other parts of the plant have a spicy scent

when crushed. *C. occidentalis,* a California native, grows 4–12 ft. tall and is hardy to zone 8.

How to Grow
Sun or shade. Best in fertile, organic soils with even moisture but adapts to most soils. Tolerates heat. Sold in containers and balled-and-burlapped. Increase by division in fall or early spring; by seed sown when fresh or in late fall; or by layering or softwood cuttings. Plant 8–10 ft. apart. Prune off sprouts to maintain as small, multitrunked tree.

Campanula
Kam-pan'you-la
Campanulaceae. Bellflower family

Description
A large, diverse group including many long-lived ornamental plants ranging from small, matted tufts to large sprawling or erect plants. Grown in rock gardens and perennial beds for their deep blue, bell-shaped flowers and tidy foliage.

rotundifolia p. 200
Bluebell, bellflower, harebell
WM GP. Perennial. Zones 2–7
Height: 4–12 in. Spread: 8 in.
Dainty and delicate in appearance, this little plant is remarkably hardy and tolerates windy, exposed sites. Throughout the summer, numerous small, nodding, bell-shaped blue flowers dangle from slender stalks above narrow, light green, grasslike foliage. A good plant for rockeries, meadows, and traditional beds and borders. Can be sprawling and weedlike in the South. 'Olympia' has intense blue flowers July–August; var. *alba* has white flowers.

How to Grow
Sun or partial shade. Prefers fertile soil; tolerates dry soil and heat. Sold as seeds and in containers. Sow seeds in spring (leave them uncovered). Increase by division in spring. Plant 6–8 in. apart. Water in dry weather, fertilize in spring.

Ceanothus
See-a-no′thus
Rhamnaceae. Buckthorn family

Description
Ceanothus are among the favorite flowering shrubs of almost every North American region. They offer dense panicles of blue, pink, purple, or white flowers and a neat appearance. The majority of species are native to the West; some of these are evergreen. Low-growing species make good ground covers. Larger plants serve as specimens or screens.

americanus p. 150
New Jersey tea, red root, mountain sweet
EW CP. Deciduous shrub. Zones 4–8
Height: 3–3½ ft. Spread: 3–4 ft.
Often admired along roadsides but too seldom found in gardens, New Jersey tea is a wonderful small shrub for dryish, well-drained sites. Small, fluffy racemes of creamy white flowers bloom for 2–3 weeks from midspring to early summer. Flowers attract butterflies. *C. ovatus* (a.k.a. *C. herbaceous* var. *pubescens*), a native of the Great Plains and Eastern Woodlands, is a similar, closely related, and desirable species.

How to Grow
Sun or partial shade. Tolerates poor or dry soil and heat. Well-drained, light acid soil is essential. Sold in containers. Increase by sowing seed outdoors in late fall, by softwood and hardwood cuttings. Plant 4–5 ft. apart. For denser appearance, in spring prune back ½ to ⅔ previous year's growth.

fendleri p. 151
Buckbrush, Fendler ceanothus

WM. Deciduous shrub. Zone 4
Height: 2–5 ft. Spread: 2–5 ft.
The hardiest of the western species, buckbrush varies from an upright, refined shrub to a low, sprawling plant. Covered with small clusters of white flowers for 1½–2 weeks in late spring to midsummer. Serves as foundation plant or for naturalizing.

How to Grow
Full sun. Tolerates dry soil and heat. Sold as seeds and in containers. Shear for compact growth. Susceptible to root rot if overwatered.

griseus *p. 151 Pictured on facing page*
Carmel ceanothus, Carmel creeper
CA. Evergreen shrub. Zone 8
Height: 8 ft. Spread: 10 ft.
Prized for its tremendous display of fragrant, tiny blue flowers, borne in dense, 2-in.-long panicles from March to May. Small, evergreen leaves are dark green above, gray-green underneath. A coastal native, it does well in California's interior valleys. Numerous hybrids and cultivars include 'Louis Edmonds', 6 ft. tall, up to 20 ft. wide, with medium-blue flowers; 'Santa Ana', to 14 ft. tall and greater spread, with deep purplish blue flowers. The prostrate 'Yankee Point', 2–3 ft. tall and 6 ft. wide, is a good ground cover.

How to Grow
Full sun. Tolerates dry soil on the coast, needs moisture inland. Tolerates poor soil and heat (provide afternoon shade in hotter areas). Sold in containers. Plant in fall; fast growing, give specimens plenty of room. Plant 'Yankee Point' 6 ft. apart for ground cover. Prune flexible growth to control size; avoid cutting older, woody growth. Avoid frequent watering.

impressus *p. 152*
Santa Barbara ceanothus
CA. Evergreen shrub. Zone 8
Height: 6 ft. Spread: 8 ft.
A fast-growing shrub with dark green evergreen foliage, spectacular in March and April when covered with small clusters of tiny blue fragrant flowers. Extremely drought tolerant. Plant with *Fremontodendron* 'California Glory' on an unirrigated hillside for a blue and gold combination. The species doesn't tolerate summer watering well. Hybrid offspring are more water tolerant; they include 'Concha', 'Dark Star', and 'Julia Phelps'.

How to Grow
See *C. griseus.*

velutinus p. 152
Snowbush
WM. Evergreen shrub. Zone 4
Height: 3–5 ft. Spread: 3–5 ft.
An easy-to-grow plant that is one of the few hardy native broadleaf evergreens. In late spring to early summer, clusters of fragrant, creamy white flowers contrast nicely with the dark, balsam-scented foliage.

How to Grow
Sun or partial shade. Well-drained soil. Tolerates heat. Sold as seeds and in containers. Sow seeds in fall. Protect transplants from drying winds. Susceptible to root rot in wet soil.

Cercidium
Ser-sid'i-um. Palo verde
Leguminosae. Pea family

Description
Leafless most of the year, palo verdes provide light shade on hot, dry sites with poor soil. The rounded crown, gnarled branches, striking bark, and spectacular bloom of these trees add character to a landscape.

floridum p. 121   Pictured above
Blue palo verde
WD. Deciduous tree. Zones 9–10; marginal in 8
Height: 20–30 ft. Spread: 20–30 ft.
Provides mass and form in the garden; the smooth green bark and billows of yellow flowers add color. Noninvasive roots

make it ideal for shading patios and walks and make under-planting easy. Thorny branches harbor small birds; plant bears tiny leaves for only a short time in spring. Small flowers in clusters 2–4 in. long in spring, sometimes repeatedly through the summer, depending on rainfall. Flat, thin pods, 2–3 in. long, ripen yellow-brown in summer. Yellow foothills palo verde (*C. microphyllum*) is the most drought tolerant; Sonoran palo verde (*C. praecox*) is more open and "clean" looking but less cold-hardy.

How to Grow
Full sun. Dry soil; tolerates poor soil and heat. Sold in con-tainers and balled-and-burlapped. Container plants can be transplanted year-round. Space specimens 30 ft. or more apart; plant 12–15 ft. apart for groves. Deep but infrequent watering is best. Leave twiggy growth on major limbs to protect from sunscald. Trees weakened by sunscald, too much water, and fertilizer are prone to borers.

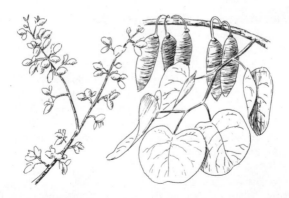

Cercis
Ser'sis
Leguminosae. Pea family

Description
Almost all of the species in this small genus of native American trees and shrubs are cultivated for their prolific early spring displays of showy flowers. Adapted to dry, sunny sites, they are small enough to fit easily in courtyards and are spectacular when massed. Multitrunked specimens make nice shade trees.

canadensis p. 122
Eastern redbud, Judas tree
EW CP. Deciduous tree. Zones 4–9

Height: 20–35 ft. Spread: 25–35 ft.
Redbuds are a staple of the eastern landscape. A heavy bloom of small, pealike flowers in bright rose to lavender shades appear for 2–3 weeks in spring before the leaves. (Makes a handsome combination with dogwood, which usually flowers at same time.) Dark green leaves often have a maroon cast. Flat pods are interesting later in season. Redbuds mesh easily with formal and informal plantings. 'Royal' and *C. c.* var. *alba* have white flowers; 'Flame', double flowers; 'Withers Pink Charm', delicate pink flowers; 'Pink Bud', true pink flowers; 'Forest Pansy', purple leaves.

How to Grow
Sun or partial shade. Prefers fertile, organic soil; tolerates poor or dry soil and heat. Avoid poorly drained sites. Sold in containers and balled-and-burlapped. Plant 20–30 ft. apart. Cankers appearing as elongate fissures on trunk and branches can kill affected part; consult a tree specialist. Redbud leafspot and verticillium wilt can be treated with fungicides.

occidentalis *p. 153* *Pictured on p. 311*
Western redbud
CA WD. Deciduous tree/shrub. Zone 8
Height: 20 ft. Spread: 20 ft.
This large shrub or small tree is dependable, long-lived, drought tolerant, and attractive all year. Clusters of small magenta, rose-red, or white flowers appear in February and continue through April as large bluish green leaves develop. Reddish seedpods and golden or red leaves in fall (especially in colder areas) make it a good patio tree.

How to Grow
Full sun. Tolerates poor or dry soil. Sold in containers. Plant in fall; give plenty of room. Prune to thin or shape. Highly resistant to oak-root fungus.

Cercocarpus
Ser-koh-kar′pus
Rosaceae. Rose family

Description
Several species of this small genus of trees and shrubs are cultivated for their attractive, upright, vase-shaped form, sometimes evergreen foliage, and silver seed plumes. Effective as specimens or closely planted for screening or wildlife habitat.

ledifolius p. 122
Curl-leaf mountain mahogany
WM WD. Evergreen shrub. Zones 4–8
Height: 10–20 ft. Spread: 10–30 ft.
A long-lived, hardy, and troublefree evergreen equally useful as a neutral backdrop (screen or windbreak) or, pruned to tree form, as a specimen. The small leathery leaves, stiff and slightly hairy, are dark green on top, silver underneath. Flowers are inconspicuous. In late summer and fall, the seed heads, short spiral plumes with fine silver hairs, are eye-catching, particularly when backlit. Whole plant has a spicy aroma. *C. montanus, C. brevifolius, C. intricatus,* and *C. betuloides* are equally valuable, not as large as C. *ledifolius,* and may not be evergreen.

How to Grow
Sun or partial shade. Tolerates poor or dry soil and heat. Sold as seeds and in containers. Slow growing from seeds; they require 3 months moist chilling, sow in cool soil. Plant container-grown plants anytime except midwinter. Periodic deep watering maintains density of foliage.

Chamaebatieria
Kam-ee-ba-tea-air′ee-a
Rosaceae. Rose family

Description
The single species in this genus is described below.

millefolium p. 153
Fernbush
WD. Semi-evergreen shrub. Zones 4–8, possibly 10
Height: 4–6 ft. Spread: 4–6 ft.
A handsome, undemanding shrub effective as a backdrop, filler, or specimen. Its leaves and flowers are clustered at the ends of the branches. Leaves are downy, fernlike, and gray-green; most of the older leaves drop during the winter, revealing smooth russet bark. In the heat of summer (June, July, sometimes into September), clusters of small white flowers appear.

How to Grow
Sun or partial shade. Does well in poor, dry soil and heat. Sold as seeds or in containers. Seeds require 3 months moist chilling; sow on soil surface. Plant container-grown plants 4–8 ft. apart. Deep-water monthly for best appearance.

Chasmanthium
Kas-man'thee-um. River oats
Gramineae. Grass family

Description
River oats are medium-size grasses whose unique, showy seed heads provide fall and winter interest and are used in dried arrangements. A tendency to spread makes them best for natural landscapes. (Also classed in the genus *Uniola*.)

latifolium p. 258 *Pictured above*
River oats
EW CP. Perennial grass. Zones 5–9
Height: 1½–3½ ft. Spread: 2 ft. or more
Easy to grow and shade tolerant, this clump-forming grass makes an excellent ground cover on slopes or open woodland; smaller clumps can accent a path. Narrow green leaves, 5–9 in. tall, turn tan in fall and winter. Drooping panicles of oatlike seeds (green turning tan-bronze in fall) sway above the leaves in the slightest breeze. Spreads readily in wet sites, less invasive in dry conditions.

How to Grow
Sun or shade. Looks best in full sun and fertile, moist soil; tolerates poor or dry soils and heat. Sold as seeds and in containers. Sow seeds in spring; increase by division anytime. Remove seed heads to control spread.

Chelone
Key-low'nee
Scrophulariaceae. Figwort family

Description
Members of this small genus of streambank natives are grown for their unique, showy flowers and lush foliage. Perfect for the edge of a water garden or other damp spot, they add color in late summer and fall.

glabra p. 200
Turtlehead, white turtlehead (a.k.a. *C. obliqua* var. *alba*, *C. chlorantha*, *C. montana*)
EW. Perennial. Zones 3–8
Height: 3 ft. Spread: 2½ ft.
Tightly clustered spikes of unusual creamy white flowers, sometimes brushed with pink, draw the eye into the cooler reaches of the garden from late August until frost. Large, lance-shaped green leaves are lush and full all season. *C. lyonii* flowers are pink, *C. obliqua*'s are rose to deep pink, *C. obliqua* 'Bethelii' offers brighter color and heavier bloom.

How to Grow
Sun or partial shade. Prefers moist, fertile organic soil. Tolerates ordinary soil and moisture. Tolerates heat if kept moist. Sold as seeds and in containers. Sow seeds in late fall or stratify 6 weeks before spring sowing. Increase by division in late fall or stem cuttings in spring or summer. Plant 2½–3 ft. apart. If desired, prune in early summer to reduce height.

Chilopsis
Ky-lop'sis. Desert willow
Bignoniaceae. Bignonia family

Description
The single species in this genus is described below.

linearis p. 123
Desert willow
WD. Deciduous tree. Zones 6–10
Height: 10–30 ft. Spread: 10–30 ft.
Sculptural form, fine-textured foliage, and long season of showy bloom make this heat- and drought-tolerant desert native ideal as an accent specimen or grove planting. Deep, little-branched root system permits siting close to buildings or paving as well as underplanting with flowers or ground covers.

Clusters of fragrant, orchidlike pale pink to red-purple and white flowers bloom heaviest in June and sporadically until September. Long, pencil-thin seedpods. Of the many selections, 'Hope' has white flowers, 'Marfa Lace', double pink flowers. × *Chitalpa*, a rare cross between two genera (*Catalpa* and *Chilopsis*), has coarser leaves and larger clusters of pale pink flowers and no seedpods.

How to Grow
Full sun. Tolerates poor or dry soil. At its best in hot conditions. Sold as seeds or in containers. Sow fresh seeds in spring in warm soil (seedlings are very cold-tender). Transplant during warm weather. Roots easily from semisoft tip cuttings in mid to late summer. Prune suckers in early summer to enhance form.

Chionanthus
Ki-oh-nan'thus. Fringe tree
Oleaceae. Olive family

Description
Spectacular in flower, these large shrubs or small trees add elegance to any landscape as a specimen, in groups, or in a border.

virginicus *p. 123   Pictured above*
White fringe tree, old-man's beard
EW CP. Deciduous shrub/tree. Zones 3–9
Height: 10–20 ft. or more. Spread: 10–20 ft.
In midspring, as the leaves expand, panicles of fragrant, wispy, lacy white flowers begin to flutter in the breeze. (Male plants are most attractive.) Small, dark blue fruits appear in late

summer and attract birds. Foliage often turns bright yellow in fall.

How to Grow
Sun or partial shade. Prefers fertile, organic, acid soil but tolerates poor or dry soil and heat. Sold in containers and balled-and-burlapped. Plant 10–15 ft. apart. Slow growing. Occasional trouble with scale, leaf spots, powdery mildew, or canker — rarely serious.

Chrysopsis
Kris-op'sis. Golden aster
Compositae. Daisy family

Description
Blooming in late summer and early fall, golden asters are perfect for tough sites, such as steep, dry banks, but equally at home in a sunny border, meadow, or rock garden. Members of this small genus readily reseed and can make good ground covers.

mariana p. 201
Maryland golden aster (a.k.a. *Heterotheca mariana*)
EW CP. Perennial. Zones 4–9
Height: 1–3 ft. Spread: 6–18 in.
A roadside weed in the wild, this plant does well in dry, sunny sites where few perennials will grow. Given rich, well-drained soil, it produces lush foliage and many flowers. Foliage is dark green with hairs of a silvery cast. Clusters of bright yellow daisies, 1–1½ in. wide, appear in late summer and fall for 3–4 weeks. Seeds ripen to attractive fluffy heads. Silkgrass (*C. graminifolia*) has silvery grasslike foliage.

How to Grow
Full sun. Tolerates poor or dry soil and heat. Avoid poorly drained soil. Sold as seeds and in containers. Sow seeds after last frost. Increase by dividing in early spring. Plant 12–18 in. apart. Raise crown slightly when transplanting to avoid rot. Water and mulch sparingly.

villosa p. 201
Golden aster (a.k.a. *C. camporum, Heterotheca villosa*)
GP CP WD WM. Perennial. Zones 3–7
Height: 1–2½ ft. Spread: 2 ft.
Fine grayish green foliage. Bright yellow daisies July–Septem-

ber attract butterflies. Highly variable species; if possible, get seeds or plants indigenous to your area.

How to Grow
See *C. mariana.*

Chrysothamnus
Kris-oh-tham'nus
Compositae. Daisy family

Description
A few species of this small genus of western shrubs make effective background plantings, soil stabilizers, and accent groupings.

nauseosus p. 154   Pictured above
Chamisa, rabbitbush.
WD WM. Deciduous shrub. Zones 4–8
Height: 3–6 ft. Spread: 3–6 ft.
An easy plant to grow, chamisa has narrow, densely hairy leaves, silver-blue to green. When grown in relatively dry, well-drained soil it takes a soft, mounded form. Dense clusters of fragrant, large, velvety yellow flowers appear in autumn for a month or so and attract butterflies. In winter, the white stems and dry seed heads are interesting. *C. nauseosus* subsp. *nauseosus* is a dwarf form, only 18–24 in. high, flowering mid-summer to early autumn.

How to Grow
Full sun. Tolerates poor or dry soil and heat. Sold as seeds and in containers. (Species is extremely variable; if possible, collect seeds yourself from desirable plants.) Plant moist, chilled seeds

in cool soil. Plant container-grown plants anytime. Space 4–8 ft. apart. Every few years, cut back severely at bud break in spring to rejuvenate. Water infrequently and deeply; overwatering produces rank, floppy growth, shortens lifespan.

Cimicifuga
Sim-i-sif'you-ga. Bugbane
Ranunculaceae. Buttercup family

Description
The deep green foliage of the bugbanes is often the foundation of a woodland garden. Tall, feathery wands of bright white flowers add color to shady spots late in the season.

racemosa p. 202
Black cohosh, bugbane, black snakeroot
EW. Perennial. Zones 3–8
Height: 6–8 ft. Spread: 2–4 ft.
A long-lived, easy-to-grow perennial that covers acres of woodland understory in the East. Stalks rise high above large, coarse, deep green foliage, culminating in a wandlike raceme, 3–4 ft. long, covered with tiny white flowers for 3–4 weeks in midsummer. Mature plants have more stalks. Best effect in groups. Seedpods dry in late summer; can be used for decoration.

How to Grow
Partial sun or shade. Needs acidic soil, fertile and organic. Sold as seeds and in containers. Plant 1½–3 ft. apart. Increase by division; include large section of crown with a bud.

Cladrastis
Kla-dras'tis
Leguminosae. Pea family

Description
The only North American native in this small genus of trees is described below.

lutea p. 124   Pictured on p. 318
Yellowwood, virgilia (a.k.a. *C. kentuckea*)
EW. Deciduous tree. Zones 3–8
Height: 30–50 ft. Spread: 40–50 ft.
Its medium size, broad rounded crown, and spreading branches make yellowwood a perfect shade tree, especially

where space is limited. Bright green compound leaves are often glossy. Long, pendant clusters of sweet-smelling, white "pea" flowers appear for 3–4 weeks in late spring. Brown pods, 3–4 in. long, ripen in late summer.

How to Grow
Full sun. Prefers well-drained, fertile, organic soil. Tolerates some heat. Sold in containers and balled-and-burlapped. Plant 25–40 ft. apart. Fairly slow growing. Prune in summer. Prone to weak crotches that break with age.

Clarkia
Klar'ki-a
Onagraceae. Evening primrose family

Description
One of the most important genera of western wildflowers, with 15–20 cultivated species. Some are shade tolerant, but most prefer the sun.

amoena p. 202
Farewell-to-spring, herald of summer (a.k.a. *Godetia amoena, G. grandiflora*)
CA. Annual.
Height: 1½–2½ ft. Spread: 2 ft.
The showiest of the California native clarkias, its cup-shaped flowers, lavender-pink with a splash of bright red on each petal, bloom from May to August, later than most native wildflowers. It is pretty with blue-flowered gilias, nigellas, and

centaureas. Seed strains vary in color and habit: some are low
(5–10 in.) and spreading, others tall and erect.

How to Grow

Full sun. Tolerates poor soil and some heat. Sold as seeds and
in containers. Sow seeds after frost in cold-winter zones, in
fall elsewhere. Pinch out central leader to encourage branching
and heavy bloom.

Clematis

Klem′a-tis
Ranunculaceae. Buttercup family

Description

This large genus includes many vigorous climbing vines with
handsome flowers and fruits. Excellent on trellises or fences,
meandering through shrubs, or cascading down slopes.

ligusticifolia p. 265   *Pictured above*

Western virgin's bower
WM WD. Deciduous vine. Zone 4
Height: 18–30 ft. Spread: 5 ft.
This western native is not as flamboyant as the hybrid clematis.
Its mass display of clustered small white flowers in summer
and its large, plumelike fruits are nevertheless exciting. Widely
adaptable, tough, and disease resistant.

How to Grow

Sun or partial shade. Prefers rich, well-drained, neutral pH
soil. Tolerates dry soil and heat (once established). Sold as

seeds and in containers. Sow seeds in fall (slow to germinate). Increase by late spring cuttings. Every 3–5 years, cut back to 1 ft. above ground to rejuvenate. Provide afternoon shade in arid and semiarid areas. Mulch with organic matter to keep roots cool.

Clethra
Kleth'ra
Clethraceae. White alder family

Description
The several North American natives in this genus of flowering shrubs and small trees are grown as screens, specimens, and in masses.

alnifolia p. 154
Sweet pepper bush, summersweet (a.k.a. *C. tomentosa*)
EW CP. Deciduous shrub. Zones 5–9
Height: 9 ft. Spread: 12 ft.
An excellent shrub for damp areas, sweet pepper bush will grow in any reasonably moist soil. Erect clusters of small flowers, white and fragrant, bloom in summer for 2–3 weeks.

How to Grow
Sun or partial shade. Prefers moist, fertile soil. Tolerates heat and seaside conditions. Sold in containers. Increase by cuttings taken in midsummer. Plant 5–6 ft. apart. Needs little pruning. Susceptible to spider mites.

Coreopsis
Koh-ree-op'sis. Tickseed
Compositae. Daisy family

Description
Long a staple of perennial beds and open, natural landscapes, coreopsis are easy-to-grow plants that produce prolific displays of colorful, daisylike flowers. Small to large groupings are effective, often from great distances. They are common in seed mixes for "naturalizing."

auriculata p. 203 *Pictured above*
Eared coreopsis
EW CP. Perennial. Zones 4–9
Height: 1–2 ft. Spread: 1 ft. or more
Unusual for coreopsis, this species of the woodland and forest edge is best in light shade and blooms in spring. The 1–2-in. golden yellow flowers top long, sometimes branched, stems. Dark green lobed foliage is effective as an evergreen ground cover in a woodland garden. 'Nana' is a dwarf form.

How to Grow
Light shade. Prefers well-drained, fertile, organic soil. Tolerates heat. Sold as seeds and in containers. Raise crown slightly when transplanting. Divide every several years for increased vigor.

lanceolata p. 203
Lance-leaved coreopsis
EW GP. Perennial. Zones 3–8
Height: 1½–2½ ft. Spread: 2–3 ft.
A classic coreopsis, fast growing and useful in many situations. Several large golden yellow daisies top each long stem from late spring to early summer. May need support. 'Flore-pleno' is double flowered; 'Sunburst' is semidouble. 'Brown eyes' has maroon center.

How to Grow
Sun or partial shade. Tolerates poor or dry soil and heat. Sold as seeds and in containers. Deadheading increases flowering period. Plant is short-lived; divide regularly or cultivate plentiful self-sown seedlings.

maritima p. 204

Sea dahlia, seashore daisy
CA. Perennial. Zone: grow as annual in cold-winter areas
Height: 1–3 ft. Spread: 1–3 ft.
A native of cool coastal California, it thrives in mixed perennial plantings. Large (2½–4-in.-wide), bright yellow flowers sway on long stems above long, fleshy, somewhat succulent, bright green leaves. An excellent early-blooming (February and March) companion for early annual wildflowers and a choice cut flower. *C. gigantea* has unusual 3-ft.-tall, leafless, fleshy stem; leaves and flowers are similar to those of *C. maritima*.

How to Grow

Full sun. Tolerates poor soil. Goes dormant during hot summer weather. Sold as seeds and in containers. In fall, sow seeds or transplant 18 in. apart. Deadhead to prolong bloom. Tuberlike root liable to rot in warm, wet conditions.

tinctoria p. 204

Plains coreopsis (a.k.a. *Calliopsis tinctoria*)
GP EW. Annual
Height: 1–3 ft. Spread: 6 in.
Probably the most commonly grown annual coreopsis, this tall, narrow plant has glossy, dark green, lance-shaped leaves. Blooms June–September. Yellow ray flowers are deep red at the base; the disk flowers are maroon. A valuable "quick cover" for the initial stages of a prairie planting.

How to Grow

Full sun. Tolerates poor or dry soil and heat. Easy to grow from seeds sown in fall or spring. Self-sows readily.

verticillata p. 205

Thread-leaved coreopsis
EW. Perennial. Zones 3–9
Height: 2½ ft. Spread: 2–3 ft.
Valued for its deeply divided, fine, feathery foliage and pale, golden yellow flowers, 1–2 in. wide, for 4–6 weeks in midsummer. Spreads by thin stolons to form dense patches that add a distinctive texture to the mid-border or meadow. 'Moonbeam' forms a dense clump with long-lasting lemon-yellow flowers. 'Zagreb' grows 8–12 in. high.

How to Grow

Full sun. Tolerates dry or poor soil and heat. Avoid overly wet soils. Sold as seeds and in containers. Sow seeds in spring or late fall. Increase by division in spring. Deadhead to encourage second bloom.

Cornus
Kor'nus
Cornaceae. Dogwood family

Description
Dogwoods are hardy plants with handsome foliage, often brilliantly colored in fall, and attractive flowers and fruit. Used as specimens, as border accents, or naturalized.

canadensis p. 205
Bunchberry
WM EW. Perennial. Zone 2
Height: 4–10 in. Spread: 8 in. or more
This low-growing herbaceous plant spreads by growth of its woody rhizomes, forming a carpet in moist, cool areas. Small clusters of flowers with prominent, pure white bracts contrast with the dark green foliage from June through August. Red fruits and yellow or red foliage brighten the plant from August to October. Leaves deciduous.

How to Grow
Partial sun or shade. Needs well-drained, acidic, fertile, organic soil. Sold as seeds and in containers. Sow seeds in fall (sow collected ripe seeds immediately). Increase by division in spring. Plant 6–8 in. apart.

florida p. 124   Pictured above
Flowering dogwood
CP EW. Deciduous tree. Zones 5–8
Height: 25 ft. Spread: often wider than height
Beloved in the eastern U.S., flowering dogwood is a natural understory tree with year-round appeal: in spring, clusters of flowers with snow-white or pink to red bracts; in summer, welcome shade; in fall, bright red fruit and foliage; in winter,

a handsome silhouette. Numerous cultivars offer a range of leaf and bract colors. Pacific dogwood, *C. nuttalli,* is a similar tree, native from British Columbia to California. The shrub dogwood, *C. amomum,* has showy blue fruit; *C. alternifolia,* a shrub or small tree, has handsome foliage and interesting greenish stems.

How to Grow
Partial sun or shade. Tolerates heat. Sold in containers, bare root, and balled-and-burlapped. Plant 12–15 ft. apart. Prune lightly to develop shape. Susceptible to borers and fungus disease in Northeast and southeastern mountains. Leaves may "burn" in hot, dry situations.

Dalea
Day-lee′a
Leguminosae. Pea family

Description
A large group of herbaceous perennials and woody shrubs with fine-textured leaves and masses of tiny flowers. Mostly native to desert or dry conditions, they are excellent for dry, hot, and exposed sites with gravelly or sandy soils.

greggii p. 155
Prostrate indigobush, mat dalea
WD. Deciduous shrub. Zones 6–10
Height: 6–10 in. Spread: 2–4 ft.
Grown mostly as a ground cover for its fine-textured, silvery blue-green foliage, mat dalea is awash with clusters of tiny, pea-shaped purple flowers in spring and early summer. Bees love it; rabbits avoid it. Several other native species are available locally; check with a native-plant nursery in your area.

How to Grow
Sun or partial shade. Tolerates poor or dry soil and heat. Sold in containers. Increase by layering. Plant in warm weather, 3 ft. apart, for dense cover. Fills in more quickly when watered deeply every 2 weeks during summer. Prune back to the main stem annually, in early winter after frost has killed top growth or in spring before growth begins. Too much water when dormant can result in rot.

purpurea p. 206
Purple prairie clover (a.k.a. *Petalostemum purpurea*)
GP WD. Perennial. Zones 3–8

Height: 1–2 ft. Spread: 6–12 in.
A good plant where space is limited. Fine-textured green foliage is a backdrop for small, cylindrical clusters of dark purple, occasionally crimson or pink, flowers in July and August.

How to Grow
Full sun. Tolerates poor or dry soil and heat. Sold as seeds, in containers, and bare root. Plant scarified, innoculated seeds in spring, 1 ft. apart or randomly spaced.

Dicentra
Die-sen'tra. Bleeding heart
Fumariaceae. Fumitory family

Description
Bleeding hearts are old garden favorites for their nodding, curiously shaped flowers and delicate, lacy foliage. They are at home in perennial borders or naturalized in woodland gardens. Nearly every region of the country has at least one charming native species.

eximia p. 206   *Pictured above*
Bleeding heart, fringed bleeding heart
EW. Perennial. Zones 3–8
Height: 1–1½ ft. Spread: 1–1½ ft.
A nearly ever-blooming shade perennial, bleeding heart's panicles of heart-shaped, rosy pink flowers begin as early as March, hesitate slightly in the summer heat, then continue until frost. Numerous cultivars offer flowers in a variety of white, pink, red, and crimson shades.

How to Grow
Partial sun. Prefers well-drained, fertile, organic soil. Avoid afternoon sun in southern gardens. Sold as seeds and in con-

tainers. Sow fresh seeds in summer; don't allow it to dry before sowing. Increase by division in fall or spring or cultivate self-sown seedlings. Deadhead to encourage more bloom.

formosa
Western or Pacific bleeding heart
CA WM. Perennial. Zones 4–8
Height: 18 in. Spread: 18 in. (more with age)
This delightful, casual ground cover grows under redwoods and oaks in the Western Mountains. Offers long blue-green leaves and small, nodding, heart-shaped flowers, rose-purple, pink, and white, on long leafless stems from March to July. A tough, persistent plant despite its delicate appearance. 'Sweetheart' produces white flowers from summer into fall; *D. f. oregana* has pale yellow or cream-colored flowers tipped with pink.

How to Grow
Partial sun or shade. Prefers moist, fertile, organic soil. Tolerates heat surprisingly well in southern California valleys. Sold in containers and bare root. Increase by division anytime. Plant in fall or spring; one plant will spread widely over time. Susceptible to root rot in poorly drained soil.

Echinacea
Ek-i-nay'see-a
Compositae. Daisy family

Description
A small genus of sun-loving North American perennials grown for their striking flowers.

angustifolia p. 207
Purple coneflower
GP. Perennial. Zones 3–7
Height: 12–20 in. Spread: 6–12 in.
Whorls of drooping pink ray flowers clustered about a but-terfly-luring central cone of deep mahogany give a prairie planting or border a special dynamism in early summer. Stems and seed heads dry to matte black and are a vivid sight among prairie grasses. Another prairie native, pale coneflower (*E. pallida*) has creamy white ray flowers.

How to Grow
Full sun. Tolerates poor or dry soil and heat. Sold as seeds, in containers, and bare root. Increase by division or root cuttings.

purpurea p. 207 *Pictured on facing page*
Purple coneflower
EW CP. Perennial. Zones 4–8
Height: 1½–3 ft. Spread: 2 ft.
Large (4–6-in.-wide) flowers with rose to pink rays and brown central cone bloom from summer into early fall. Coarse, dark green leaves are 4–6 in. long. Popular stop for butterflies. 'Bright Star' has deep pink rays and maroon cone. 'White Lustre' has white rays with bronze disk.

How to Grow
Same as *E. angustifolia*. Space 18–25 in. apart.

Encelia
En-see'lee-a
Compositae. Daisy family

Description
A small genus of drought-tolerant evergreen shrubs that pro-duce masses of golden daisies in winter and spring. Easy and fast growing, they're at home on dry slopes or in water-con-serving gardens.

californica p. 155
Bush sunflower
CA. Evergreen shrub. Zone 9
Height: 5 ft. Spread: 8 ft.
A native of coastal bluffs and brushy slopes, bush sunflower combines well with larger ceonothus or smaller flowering shrubs and perennials. Large blooms appear March–June on

long leafless stalks; yellow ray flowers surround reddish purple disk flowers.

How to Grow

Full sun. Tolerates poor or dry soils and heat. Sold as seeds and in containers. Plant seeds or container-grown plants in fall. Space 4–6 ft. apart. Cut back by half in fall before new growth begins.

farinosa p. 156
Brittlebush, incienso
WD. Evergreen shrub. Zones 8–10
Height: 2–3 ft. Spread: 2–3 ft.
Clusters of large (2-in.-wide), daisylike yellow flowers hover several inches above the woolly white foliage. Heaviest bloom is in early spring. Goes dormant in very dry conditions, but may bloom subsequently in response to water. The foliage is an effective foil for colorful desert wildflowers.

How to Grow

Full sun. Tolerates poor or dry soils and heat. Sold as seeds and in containers. Plant in spring or summer, 2–4 ft. apart. Increase by cultivating self-sown seedlings or by tip cuttings. Water deeply once a month for best display of flowers and foliage. Will die if severely water stressed. Avoid fall watering.

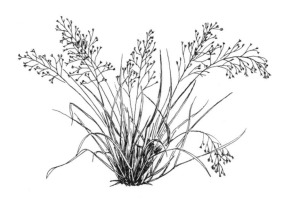

Eragrostis

Er-a-gros'tis
Gramineae. Grass family

Description

A large genus of annual and perennial grasses, a few of which are cultivated. Grown for their gracefully airy flower spikes, which are used in dried flower arrangements. Coarse, extensive root system binds the soil, checking erosion. Height and form vary greatly from less than 1 ft. and rather stiff to 5 ft. and arching.

trichoides p. 258   *Pictured on facing page*
Sand lovegrass
WD. Perennial bunchgrass. Zones 5–9
Height: 2½–4 ft. Spread: 2 ft.
An easy-to-grow, graceful arching grass, attractive in large sweeps or as a specimen. Softly pliant bright green leaves rise to 2 ft. and turn rusty tan when dormant. Loose open flower spikes appear in late summer.

How to Grow
Sun or partial shade. Tolerates poor or dry soil and heat. Sold as seeds or in containers. Sow tiny seeds close to surface in spring or summer (1 oz./2,500 sq. ft.). Set container-grown plants 2 ft. apart. Increase by dividing clumps in spring; also self-sows on sandy soils. Mow high (8–12 in.) in late winter; closer cropping can reduce vigor.

Eriogonum
E-ri-og′oh-num. Buckwheat
Polygonaceae. Buckwheat family

Description
Every area of the West has its own buckwheats, a large genus of annuals, perennials, and shrubs, many with appealing flowers. The best known are the shrubs of the California coast and islands, which are grown as ground covers or specimen plants. Those below are excellent plants for dry landscapes.

flavum p. 208
Sulfur flower, yellow buckwheat
WM. Perennial. Zone 4
Height: 4–12 in. Spread: 12 in.
Clean, matted velvety foliage, dark green above, whitish below, makes a fine plant for the front of a border or the rock garden. Tight clusters of pale yellow or creamy white flowers last several weeks from late May to June. Good for drying.

How to Grow
Full sun. Prefers dry soil, tolerates poor soil and heat. Sold as seeds and in containers. Increase by seeds, not division. Plant seedlings in spring, 6–8 in. apart.

giganteum p. 156
Giant buckwheat
CA. Evergreen shrub. Zones 9–10
Height: 6–10 ft. Spread: 8 ft. or more
A bold accent plant, its rounded shape is superb with boulders. Large sprays of tiny white to pinkish flowers form a canopy over the thick, leathery, grayish foliage from April to October. Flowers turn russet-red as seeds mature. Combine with sages, encelias, romneyas, and zauschnerias. *E. arborescens* is smaller (3–4 ft. tall).

How to Grow
Full sun. Tolerates poor or dry soil and heat. Sold in containers. Allow for at least a 6-ft. spread. Deadhead in late fall or winter.

umbellatum p. 208   Pictured on p. 329
Sulfur buckwheat
WM CA. Perennial. Zones 7–9
Height: 1 ft. Spread: 2 ft.
A choice rock garden plant prized for its brilliant yellow flowers in summer and its neat mat of foliage. Leaves are green above, woolly beneath. Flowers, which may also be pale yellow, cream, or red, borne in umbels on 3–12-in. stems from June to September. They turn rusty red as they mature. A widespread and variable species; select plants carefully.

How to Grow
Sun or partial shade. Tolerates poor or dry soil and heat. Sold in containers. Plant in fall where winters are mild, in spring where they are colder. Increase by seed.

Eriophyllum
E-ri-oh-fil′um
Compositae. Daisy family

Description
A small group of western natives with woolly leaves and daisy-like flowers. They do best in gardens in arid and semiarid climates.

lanatum p. 229
Woolly sunflower (a.k.a. *E. caespitosum*)
WM. Perennial. Zone 5
Height: 4–16 in. Spread: 12 in.
The large (2-in.) yellow "sunflowers" are a striking contrast to the white, woolly leaves. Blooms late spring to midsummer. Good in groups or larger masses in a dryland border or rock garden. Attractive when combined with sage and junipers in naturalized plantings. The species is variable, with some plants upright, others sprawling. *E. l. integrifolium* has smaller flowers.

How to Grow
Full sun. Best in sandy soils. Tolerates poor or dry soil and heat. Sold as seeds or in containers. Plant 8–12 in. apart. Can be difficult to transplant. Prune dead branches. Don't over-water; susceptible to crown rot in wet soils.

Eschscholzia
Es-showlt′si-a
Papaveraceae. Poppy family

Description
A small group of bright, colorful western natives grown world-wide for their spectacular late winter to spring floral displays.

In the wild, these carpets of flowers attract appreciative audiences to the desert. In cultivation, plants can come up anywhere once they've obtained a toehold on the site. Pretty and graceful, they're seldom unwanted.

californica p. 209   Pictured on p. 331
California poppy
CA WM. Perennial (grown as annual in cold zones)
Height: 9–24 in. Spread: 9–24 in.
California's state flower, these easy-to-grow plants are perfect for naturalizing with other wildflowers in a drought-tolerant garden. Flowers, vivid orange with a satiny sheen, bloom most heavily March–May under natural conditions; they will bloom throughout the year in cultivation. 'Alba' has white flowers. *E. caespitosa* 'Sundew' is a miniature, with small, soft, yellow flowers.

How to Grow
Full sun. Tolerates poor or dry soil. Sold as seeds and in containers. Best plants obtained from sowing seed on site in fall or winter in mild-winter areas, spring in cold areas. Water during dry weather to encourage bloom. Self-sows.

mexicana p. 210
Mexican gold poppy, amapola del campo
WD. Annual
Height: 8 in. Spread: 8 in.
Most effective planted in broad sweeps, which ignite in a blaze of color from February to May when moisture and temperature are right. The cup-shaped flowers are golden orange and spicy. When not in bloom, the lacy, deeply dissected foliage is attractive.

How to Grow
Full sun. Tolerates poor or dry soil. Sold as seeds. Sow on site in fall or early winter. Rake in and keep moist in absence of winter rains. Self-sows.

Euonymus
You-on'i-mus
Celastraceae. Staff-tree family

Description
Many of the cultivated species in this large genus are medium-size shrubs or vines, with deep green foliage and brightly colored fruits.

americanus p. 157
Hearts-a-bustin, strawberry bush
EW. Deciduous shrub. Zones 6–9
Height: 4–6 ft. Spread: 6–10 ft.
These trouble-free, easy-to-grow plants are useful massed, as ground covers, screens, naturalized, or as specimens. The late spring flowers aren't as showy as the hot-pink seed capsules, which open to reveal bright orange pendant seeds. The foliage, dark green in summer, often provides a long-lasting splash of yellows, pinks, and reds in fall. Plants form clumps by suckering. Eastern wahoo (*E. atropurpurea*) is similar, with purple flowers and more subdued fruits. Running strawberry bush (*E. obovatus*) has trailing stems.

How to Grow
Full sun or shade. Tolerates heat. Sold in containers. Plant 5–8 ft. apart. Increase by separating suckers or by stem cuttings spring or summer. Susceptible to euonymus scale and crown gall.

Eupatorium
You-pa-toe'ri-um
Compositae. Daisy family

Description
Many of the cultivated species in this vast genus are perennials prized for their bold form and large, puffy fall flowers.

coelestinum p. 210
Mistflower, wild ageratum
EW CP. Perennial. Zones 6–10
Height: 2–2½ ft. Spread: 5 ft. or more
Crowded clusters of small powder-blue flowers enliven the

garden for 4–6 weeks in late summer and fall. The lush, light green foliage is attractive throughout the growing season. Ideal for moist, sunny meadows or creek banks. 'Alba' has white flowers.

How to Grow
Sun or partial shade. Tolerates constant moisture and heat. Can be invasive in rich, moist soils. Sold as seeds or in containers. Sow seeds in fall or stratify before sowing in spring. Space plants 1½–3 ft. apart. Increase by division in spring or by stem cuttings. Remove seed head to limit spread.

purpureum p. 211   Pictured on p. 333
Joe-Pye weed
EW CP. Perennial. Zones 4–9
Height: 5–9 ft. Spread: 2 ft.
Brings a bold form and, in fall, eye-catching color to the rear of a border: a single, mature plant is an effective focal point. Glossy purple stems and large whorled leaves. Large (12–18-in.) dome-shaped clusters of pinkish mauve flowers bloom for 3–4 weeks in late summer. *E. maculatum* and *E. fistulosum* are similar.

How to Grow
Full sun. Native to open woods and moist meadows, it prefers fertile, organic soil. Tolerates heat. Sold as seeds and in containers. Sow seed after last frost. Space plants 3–5 ft. apart. Increase by division in fall or early spring. Can cut back in late spring to reduce height.

Eustoma
You-stow′ma
Gentianaceae. Gentian family

Description
The species below is the only cultivated member of this small genus.

grandiflora p. 211
Tulip gentian, prairie gentian
WD GP. Annual or short-lived perennial. Zone 4
Height: 18–24 in. Spread: 12 in.
Large, showy, cup-shaped flowers, dark blue-purple, add color June–September to moist borders or naturalized plantings in swales or seep areas. Looks good combined with a low, mounded plant like dusty miller. Native stands are disap-

pearing (it's listed as rare and endangered in Colorado). Cultivars developed in Japan (sold as *Lisianthus russellianus*) make excellent cut flowers; colors fade in the native species.

How to Grow
Sun or partial shade. Prefers moist soil. Tolerates short dry spells. Can take heat if water is available. Sold as seeds or in containers. Slow growing from seed. Space plants 1 ft. apart in spring. Deadhead to prolong flowering.

Fallugia
Fa-loo'gee-a
Rosaceae. Rose family

Description
The single species in this genus is described below.

paradoxa p. 157   *Pictured above*
Apache plume
WD. Semi-evergreen shrub. Zones 5–10
Height: 4–6 ft. Spread: 4–6 ft.
An easy-to-grow, highly ornamental shrub. From May through September, the dark green leaves (silver beneath) contrast pleasingly with loose clusters of white, apple-blossom-like flowers and feathery, pink seed heads. Plant as specimen, massed, or naturalized. Fast growing and uniform, it makes a very tidy hedge without shearing.

How to Grow
Full or partial sun. Tolerates poor or dry soil and heat. Sold as seeds and in containers. Seed sown in spring and summer germinates easily. Transplant anytime the soil can be worked. Space 4–6 ft. for hedge, slightly wider for naturalized thicket.

Increase by rooting soft cuttings of new growth or by transplanting root sprouts in winter and early spring. Deep-water every 2–4 weeks. Cut oldest woody stems to ground to rejuvenate.

Forestiera
For-es-ti-air′a
Oleaceae. Olive family

Description
A small genus of primarily southwestern natives grown as multitrunked specimens, windbreaks, and wildlife habitat.

neomexicana p. 125
Desert olive, mountain ash, palo blanco
WD. Deciduous tree or large shrub. Zone 4
Height: 10–18 ft. Spread: 10–15 ft.
A versatile plant with fine-textured bright green foliage, smooth gray bark, and angular branching pattern. Early spring flowers are inconspicuous but fragrant. Clusters of tiny blue fruits attract songbirds to female plants from late summer into winter. Blends well with most other plants.

How to Grow
Sun or shade. Widely adaptable: tolerates poor or moist or dry soils and heat. Sold as seeds, in containers, bare root, and balled-and-burlapped. Plant from containers anytime. Space at least 20 ft. apart as specimens, 12–15 ft. apart for a grove, and 8 ft. apart for screen or windbreak. Thin interior branches in early summer to create tree form; tip-prune in spring to increase density of screen. Mites sometimes form galls on flowers; treat with dormant oil.

Fothergilla
Foth-er-gil′a
Hamamelidaceae. Witch hazel family

Description
Two species of eastern shrubs prized for their profuse spring flowers and wildly colorful fall foliage.

major p. 158 *Pictured on facing page*
Large fothergilla, witch alder (a.k.a. *F. monticola*)
EW. Deciduous shrub. Zones 4–8
Height: 5–10 ft. Spread: 5–10 ft.

At its best massed in a shrub border. As a specimen or in a small group it provides a focal point in a small setting. White "bottlebrush" flowers bloom for 2–3 weeks in early to mid spring and have a sweet, honey scent. Dwarf witch alder (*F. gardenii*) is about 3 ft. tall; *F. g.* 'Blue Mist' has glaucous blue leaves.

How to Grow
Sun or partial shade. (Light shade is best in the South.) Well-drained acid soil is essential. Tolerates dry soil. Sold in containers and balled-and-burlapped. Space 6–8 ft. apart. Increases easily by stem cuttings in summer or by separation of suckers. Grows slowly.

Fragaria
Fra-gay'ri-a. Strawberry
Rosaceae. Rose family

Description
Mostly grown for their well-known sweet, juicy fruit, some strawberries serve as ground covers or cascade over the rim of a container.

virginiana p. 212
Wild strawberry
WM CP EW. Perennial. Zone 5
Height: 4–16 in. Spread: 8–12 in.
An ideal ground cover, spreading by rooting runners; particularly suitable for naturalizing among trees and shrubs. Bluish green foliage blends well with other plants. Small white flowers are borne on upright stems for 2–3 weeks from midspring to early summer. Fruits are small and light red.

How to Grow
Sun or partial shade. Sold as seeds, in containers, and bare root. Space 8–12 in. apart; plant level with soil surface. Easily increased by division. Susceptible to spider mite if too hot and dry, to root rot if too wet.

Fremontodendron
Free-mon-toe-den'dron
Sterculiaceae. Sterculia family

Description
Two closely related species of evergreen shrubs (or small trees) native to the West. Several hybrid cultivars are grown for their spectacular display of large yellow flowers.

Fremontodendron 'California Glory' *p. 158   Pictured above*
Flannel bush, fremontia
CA. Evergreen shrub. Zone 9
Height: 15–20 ft. Spread: 20–30 ft.
Perfect for dry landscapes, especially spacious slopes, this is the showiest of California's spring-blooming shrubs. From March through June its branches are thickly covered with large (3-in.-wide), waxy, lemon-yellow flowers. Thick, leathery, dark green leaves are handsome but have irritating hairs, as do the branches. Ideal companion for blue-flowered ceanothus and orange California poppies. 'Pacific Sunset' and 'San Gabriel' are similar; 'Ken Taylor' has orange flowers and a low, mounding-spreading habit.

How to Grow
Full sun. Needs dry soil. Tolerates poor soil and heat. Sold in containers. Plant in fall, give plenty of room, stake securely

against wind. Grows quickly. Water weekly (if no rain) to establish. Once established, do not water in summer.

Gaillardia
Gay-lar'di-a
Compositae. Daisy family

Description
Members of this smallish genus are found in most regions of North America. Easy to grow, drought and heat tolerant; the showy flowers brighten gardens for months.

aristata p. 212
Blanket flower
WD WM GP CP. Perennial. Zones 5–10
Height: to 12 in. Spread: to 12 in.
From April to October, large (2–3-in.) daisies with red and yellow ray flowers and red disk flowers cover mounds of coarse, hairy foliage. Effective in borders or naturalized. The species is more drought tolerant and less gaudy than the many cultivars; notable are 'Goblin', with red and yellow bicolor flowers on compact plants, and 'Burgundy', with rich wine-red flowers on 18-in.-tall stems.

How to Grow
Sun or partial shade. Needs well-drained soil. Tolerates poor or dry soil and heat. Sold as seeds and in containers. Easy from seed; sow anytime soil can be worked. Add 1 oz. seed per 500 sq. ft. for meadow mixes. Space plants 12 in. apart. Deadhead to prolong flowering.

pulchella p. 213   *Pictured above*
Indian blanket, blanket flower, fire wheels
EW CP GP. Annual (perennial along Gulf Coast). Zones 5–9

Height: 1–2 ft. Spread: 1–2 ft.
Brownish red to yellow or purple ray flowers tipped with yellow provide color during hot, dry midsummer weather (blooms June–October). Tolerant of sea spray, it makes a striking accent in a coastal garden.

How to Grow
See *G. aristata*. Full sun. Space 24 in. apart.

Garrya
Gar'i-a. Silk tassel
Garryaceae. Silk tassel family

Description
A small group of evergreen shrubs or small trees with attractive dangling catkins in winter. Dense foliage makes them good hedge or screen plants.

elliptica 'James Roof' *p. 159*
Silk-tassel bush
CA. Evergreen shrub. Zone 8
Height: 10 ft. or more. Spread: 10 ft. or more
A splendid accent for the winter garden. From December through February, clusters of foot-long light green catkins with a silvery sheen contrast with the dense, dark green foliage. Female plants of the species bear small purple fruits from early summer into fall, attracting birds. *G. flavescens* and *G. fremontii* are similar, less showy in bloom, but more tolerant of heat and drought.

How to Grow
Sun or partial shade. Tolerates dry soil and heat if given afternoon shade. Hot winds will scorch the leaves. Sold in containers. Plant in fall, 6 ft. apart, for screen. Increase by cuttings in cool weather.

Gelsemium
Jel-see'mi-um
Loganiaceae. Logania family

Description
Three species of woody, climbing vines with evergreen foliage and yellow flowers.

sempervirens *p. 265   Pictured above*
Yellow jasmine, Carolina jasmine
CP EW WD. Evergreen vine. Zones 8–9
Height: 10–20 ft.
A versatile plant, it climbs well on fences, trellises, lamp posts, and mailboxes or can serve as a ground cover. Clusters of fragrant yellow blossoms in very early spring. 'Pride of August' has fragrant double flowers; *G. rankinii,* native to swamps and bogs, isn't fragrant. Plant is toxic if eaten.

How to Grow
Sun or partial shade. Tolerates heat. Sold in containers. Plant 3 ft. apart for ground cover. Increase by cuttings in midsummer. Prune to keep tidy.

Gordonia
Gor-doe′ni-a
Theaceae. Tea family

Description
Cultivated species of this smallish genus are magnificent evergreen shrubs and trees displaying showy, fragrant flowers for months.

lasianthus *p. 159*
Loblolly bay
CP. Evergreen tree or shrub. Zones 7–9
Height: 40 ft. Spread: 8 ft.
A native of Coastal Plain wetlands that grows well in the Piedmont and mid-Atlantic states. Most effective in groups of 3–5. Excellent glossy foliage, large fragrant flowers with white petals, and showy yellow to cream stamens bloom from June to frost.

How to Grow
Full sun. Prefers moist, fertile soil. Tolerates heat. Sold in containers. Space 10–12 ft. apart. Slow to establish; root rot can be a problem when young.

Halesia
Ha-lee′zhi-a
Styracaceae. Storax family

Description
A small genus of small trees or large shrubs whose abundant displays of showy white flowers in early spring make them excellent focal points in the landscape.

carolina p. 125   *Pictured above*
Carolina silverbell (a.k.a. *H. tetraptera, H. monticola*)
EW CP (rare). Deciduous tree/shrub. Zones 4–8
Height: 30–50 ft. or more. Spread: 30 ft.
Small clusters of pendulous, bell-shaped flowers cover the plant for 1–2 weeks in early spring. Clustered woody fruits are attractive after leaves fall. On young trees the bark has distinctive light stripes; with age, bark develops flakes of rich antique grays and browns. Single or multitrunked, they're good as specimens or in casual groups, especially in open woodland or on the woods' edge.

How to Grow
Sun or partial shade. Needs acid, well-drained organic soil (as for rhododendrons, azaleas). Sold in containers and balled-and-burlapped. Difficult to increase yourself. Often sprouts from base; retain some sprouts to replace damaged stems. Problems often result from improper soils or poor drainage.

Hamamelis
Ham-a-mee'lis. Witch hazel
Hamamelidaceae. Witch hazel family

Description
Multistemmed small trees or large shrubs with softly scalloped foliage and fragrant late fall to winter flowers.

virginiana p. 160
Witch hazel
EW CP. Deciduous shrub/tree. Zones 3–8
Height: 15–30 ft. Spread: 15–20 ft.
Best in informal screens or naturalized groups, witch hazel mixes easily into an established shrub border. Medium-green foliage turns clear yellow in fall. Fragrant yellow flowers appear for 2–4 weeks from fall to early spring. Woody seed capsules explode in spring, hurling seeds 20 ft. or more. *H. vernalis* is similar (some sources don't recognize it as a separate species) and flowers in spring.

How to Grow
Sun or partial shade. Prefers fertile, organic, acid soil and even moisture. Tolerates heat (best when shaded). Sold in containers and balled-and-burlapped. Choose plants with few stems for tree form, multiple stems for shrub. Prune only to shape.

Helenium
Hel-lee'ni-um. Sneezeweed
Compositae. Daisy family

Description
Well suited to a sunny border, the cultivated members of this medium-size genus are grown for their cheerful, long-blooming daisy flowers.

autumnale p. 213   *Pictured on p. 344*
Sneezeweed, Helen's flower
EW GP CP. Perennial. Zones 3–8
Height: 4–5 ft. Spread: 1½–3 ft.
Highly adaptable to various climates and conditions, sneezeweeds are easy to grow and blend well with most other late summer and fall flowers. Good in small groups at the middle to rear of a border or naturalized. (Can become leggy or weedy in the South.) Large (2–3-in.) blossoms with yellow ray flowers and raised dark or yellow disk flowers bloom for up to 10

weeks from mid to late summer. Numerous cultivars offer other flower colors (orange to bronze) and sizes.

How to Grow
Full sun. Prefers fertile, organic soil. Tolerates constant moisture. Sold as seeds and in containers. Sow seeds after last frost. Space 1½–2 ft. apart. Increase by division in fall or spring. May need support. Can prune in early summer to reduce floppiness later.

hoopesii p. 214
Sneezeweed
WM. Perennial. Zones 4–8
Height: 2–3 ft. Spread: 12–15 in.
A coarse plant with striking flowers, it is a great accent for perennial beds or among shrubs in an informal garden. Loose clusters of large orange-yellow flowers with darker centers are borne on long stems July–September. Excellent cut flowers.

How to Grow
See *H. autumnale.* Space 15 in. apart.

Helianthus
Hee-li-an′thus. Sunflower
Compositae. Daisy family

Description
A large genus, sunflowers have provided pleasure and sustenance to both man and beast for millennia.

angustifolius p. 214
Swamp sunflower (a.k.a. *H. simulans*)
EW CP. Perennial. Zones 6–9

Height: 5–10 ft. Spread: 2–3 ft.

Excellent plants for large borders or for naturalizing in damp meadows. Large, lustrous leaves are perfect foil for early-blooming plants. Flowers are large (2–3 in.), golden yellow, and abundant for 2–4 weeks in late summer and fall. Seed heads attract birds fall and winter. *H. salicifolius* has very narrow leaves; *H. giganticus* is larger in all parts (aggressive rhizomatous growth); *H. tomentosus,* the hairy sunflower, is great for birds; *H. rididus* is native to the Midwest and plains.

How to Grow

Full sun. Prefers fertile, organic soil. Tolerates constant moisture and heat (if kept moist). Sold as seeds and in containers. Sow seeds outdoors in fall or stratify for 6 weeks and sow in spring. Space 3–5 ft. apart. Divide in fall or spring. Avoid excess water until established. Prune in early summer to reduce height.

***maximiliani** p. 215   Pictured above*

Maximilian sunflower

WD GP EW. Perennial. Zones 5–10

Height: 6–8 ft. Spread: 4–6 ft.

A long-lived plant whose 3-in. yellow daisies make a spectacular display August–October. (Individual plants bloom for about 1 month.) Dark green leaves are lance-shaped. Highlight against a wall or fence or along a swale. Finches eat seeds in early winter.

How to Grow

Sun or partial shade. Tolerates poor or dry soil and heat. Sold as seeds and in containers. Sow seeds in fall or spring. Space plants 3–4 ft. apart to create solid mass in 1–2 years. Increase by division in late fall or spring; divide every 3–5 years to invigorate planting. Best results with deep watering every 2 weeks, though it can survive without irrigation for several years.

Hesperaloe
Hes-per-a′low
Agavaceae. Agave family

Description
The three southwestern natives in this genus are closely related to agaves and yuccas and provide the same kind of landscaping impact as specimens, in groups, or as ground covers. They adapt to a range of soils and exposures.

parviflora p. 160 *Pictured above*
Red yucca
WD. Evergreen shrub. Zones 6–10
Height: 2 ft. (flower stalks to 5 ft.). Spread: 4 ft.
From March through September, arching, wandlike stems bearing small, tubular, coral to salmon-pink waxy flowers rise above long (2–3-ft.), straplike leaves. Leaves are plum-colored in winter, blue-green other times. Effective near pools, paths, and patios, in borders, silhouetted singly or in groups against a backdrop, or massed as a coarse ground cover. Try it with ornamental grasses or threadleaf sage.

How to Grow
Sun or shade. (Flowering diminished in full shade.) Tolerates poor or dry soil and heat. Sold as seeds and in containers. Seeds germinate readily in warm soil. Transplant in spring or summer in zone 6, anytime in warmer zones. Remove flower stalks as they dry. Susceptible to aphids on flowers; deer love the stems.

Heteromeles
Het-er-oh-mee′leez
Rosaceae. Rose family

Description
The single species in this genus (the "holly" of Hollywood) is described below.

arbutifolia p. 161
Toyon, California holly, Christmasberry
CA. Evergreen shrub/tree. Zone 8
Height: 30 ft. Spread: 15 ft.
Adaptable, long-lived, drought-tolerant shrub or small tree. Leathery, dark green leaves make it effective as a screen, but profuse summer bloom and long-lasting display of bright red berries qualify it as a specimen. Clusters of small, fragrant white flowers are borne on second-year wood in June and July. Huge crop of tiny berries lasts from November to February, attracts birds.

How to Grow
Sun or partial shade. Tolerates poor or dry soil and heat. Sold in containers. Plant in fall, 6 ft. apart for screen. Subject to fire blight; sanitize shears with 10 percent bleach solution when cutting berries or pruning out infected wood.

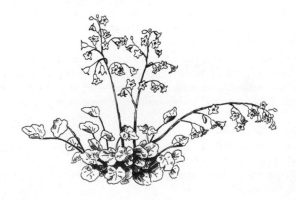

Heuchera
Hue′ker-a
Saxifragaceae. Saxifrage family

Description
A fairly large genus of North American natives, some grown primarily as evergreen or semi-evergreen ground covers, others for their airy spikes of flowers.

americana
Alumroot, rock geranium
EW GP CP. Evergreen or semi-evergreen perennial.
Zones 5–8
Height: 1½ ft. (flowers to 3 ft.). Spread: 1½ ft.
Large leaves, varying from all green to green marbled with whites and maroons, can be attractive year-round. (Foliage may freeze at about 10 degrees F, turning brown and unattractive.) Tall spikes of tiny, greenish white flowers bloom for about 4 weeks from late spring to early summer — best in groups. Good for woodland gardens or other shaded, well-drained sites. Good choice for southern gardens. *H. villosa* has larger leaves of solid green or maroon.

How to Grow
Partial sun or shade. Prefers fertile, organic soil. Tolerates poor or dry soil and heat (if kept moist). Sold as seeds and in containers. Space 1½–2 ft. apart, cover stems of crown to base of foliage when planting. Avoid overwatering. Divide to increase or every 3–4 years to rejuvenate. Susceptible to crown rot in poorly drained or overwatered soils.

maxima
Island alumroot
CA. Evergreen perennial. Zone 9
Height: 1½–2½ ft. Spread: 1–2 ft.
A versatile plant tolerant of many conditions. It is ideal for growing in the dry shade of native oaks or other woodland settings. Handsome leaves are large, scalloped, and dark green. Stout, leafy stalks bear dense panicles of small white flowers February–April (longer in irrigated gardens). A number of hybrids with *H. sanguinea* are available; one of the best is 'Santa Ana Cardinal', with rose-red flowers over a long season.

How to Grow
Partial sun or shade. Tolerates constant moisture or dry soil, poor soil, and heat. Sold in containers. Plant in fall. Increase division every third year. Deadhead for long bloom. Susceptible to mealybugs.

sanguinea p. 215   Pictured on p. 347
Coral bells, alumroot
CA. Evergreen perennial. Zone 5
Height: leaves 6 in., flower stalks 2 ft. Spread: 8 in.
An old favorite all over the U.S. for edging beds of roses and borders. Great for woodland gardens with summer rain. Panicles of tiny, nodding, dark red flowers rise above dark green

foliage April–August. Numerous selections and hybrids offer flowers in many shades of pink, red, and white.

How to Grow
Partial sun or shade. Tolerates constant moisture and heat (if well watered). Sold in containers. Space 6 in. apart for edging. Increase by division every third year in fall (mild-winter areas) or spring. Deadhead for long bloom. Susceptible to mealybugs.

Hibiscus
High-bis'kus
Malvaceae. Mallow family

Description
A large genus of tropical trees and shrubs and North American perennials grown in greenhouses and gardens for their showy flowers.

coccineus p. 216
Wild red mallow
CP EW. Perennial. Zones 6–9
Height: 6 ft. Spread: 5 ft.
A handsome plant for large borders or as a specimen. Slow to emerge in the spring, it offers large reddish green leaves and vivid red flowers, 5–6 in. wide, blooming from midsummer into September. *H. militaris* has pinkish flowers with purple centers; *H. lasiocarpus* has white or pink flowers with dark centers.

How to Grow
Full sun. Tolerates constant moisture. Sold in containers. Increase by cuttings in summer. Plant 6 ft. apart. Remove stems after frost.

moscheutos p. 216
Rose mallow
EW CP. Perennial. Zones 6–9
Height: 5–6 ft. Spread: 4 ft.
A vigorous plant with huge (6–7-in.) creamy white flowers with dark centers and large light green leaves. Blooms midsummer. Plant in large border or as specimen. Many hybrids include 'Disco Belle', a dwarf cultivar. *H. palustris,* common along the mid-Atlantic coast and wetlands, is similar, with pink flowers.

How to Grow
See *H. coccineus*. Sow seeds in late winter. Space 4–5 ft. apart.
Butterfly larvae may defoliate plants.

Hydrangea
High-dran'jee-a
Hydrangeaceae. Hydrangea family

Description
A small but widespread genus of mostly low shrubs that bring
attractive foliage and showy flowers to borders, mass plantings, or informal hedges.

quercifolia *p. 161   Pictured above*
Oakleaf hydrangea
EW CP. Deciduous shrub. Zones 5–9
Height: 5–6 ft. Spread: 8–10 ft.
An outstanding native of the hardwood forest, this large shrub
has something to offer year-round: large clusters of white flowers in spring; textured, greenish brown, oaklike leaves in summer; colorful peeling bark in winter. Flowers fade to brown
and remain into autumn. Numerous cultivars.

How to Grow
Partial sun or shade. Tolerates heat. Sold in containers. Space
6 ft. apart. Increase by cultivating suckers or layering. Prune
to maintain size and shape; in the north, remove winter-killed
branches.

Ilex
Eye'leks. Holly
Aquifoliaceae. Holly family

Description
Lush, often evergreen, foliage and bright berries are common
among the members of this large genus of trees and shrubs.
Popular as hedges, foundation plants, or specimen trees. Evergreens make excellent wildlife cover and food source. (Females bear berries if a male plant is nearby.)

cassine p. 162
Dahoon
CP. Evergreen shrub/tree. Zones 7–10
Height: 20–30 ft. Spread: 10–15 ft.
A good plant for southern gardens as a hedge or informal
barrier. Attractive leaves and often heavy crops of small red
berries fall and winter. Many crosses made with *I. opaca* are
grouped as *I. × attenuata* and are hardier.

How to Grow
Sun or partial shade. Prefers fertile, organic, moist, well-
drained soil. Tolerates heat. Sold in containers and balled-and-
burlapped. Plant in fall or early spring, 8–12 ft. apart.

glabra p. 162
Inkberry, gallberry
CP. Evergreen shrub. Zones 5–9
Height: 6 ft. Spread: 8 ft.
A relatively compact plant with fine-textured light green leaves
and black fruit in the fall. Good hedge or foundation plant.
'Compacta' is particularly compact; 'Ivory Queen' and 'Leu-
cocarpa' have white berries; 'Shamrock' resembles boxwood.

How to Grow

Sun or partial shade. Tolerates heat. Sold in containers. Space 6 ft. apart. Mites can be problematic on dry sites.

opaca p. 126   *Pictured on p. 351*
American holly
EW CP. Evergreen tree. Zones 6–9
Height: 40 ft. Spread: 18 ft.
A slow-growing tree with interesting spiny leaves and bright red berries. Many cultivars selected for superior foliage and berries. Ask local nurseries to recommend those adapted to your region and climate.

How to Grow

Sun or shade. (Best fruiting and compact growth in full sun.) Tolerates heat. Sold in containers. Space 12–18 ft. apart. Susceptible to leaf miner and leaf spots.

verticillata p. 163   *Pictured above*
Common winterberry, black alder
EW CP. Deciduous shrub/tree. Zones 3–9
Height: 5–10 ft. Spread: 10–15 ft.
Superb for winter color; after the leaves drop, the tiny, bright red fruits are sensational against a light-colored wall. Commonly grown as multitrunked shrub, sometimes as small, single-trunk tree. Numerous cultivars include 'Chrysocarpa', with yellow berries, 'Autumn Glow', with good fall leaf color, and 'Nana', a dwarf form.

How to Grow

See *I. cassine.* Native to wet woods, it tolerates wet soils well; does fine with ordinary moisture, too. Susceptible to leaf spots and powdery mildew.

vomitoria *p. 163*
Yaupon
CP. Evergreen shrub/tree. Zones 8–9 as tree; 7–9 as shrub
Height: 20 ft. Spread: 12 ft.
An easy plant to grow, with many cultivars available. Some
have compact form, good for hedges or foundation plantings;
others useful as screens. Some can be pruned as graceful, free-
standing specimens. Lustrous gray-green leaves are arranged
sparsely on stems, revealing gray bark. Bright red berries fall
and winter.

How to Grow
See *I. glabra*. Space according to form selected. Relatively pest
and disease free.

Ipomopsis
Ip-o-mop′sis
Polemoniaceae. Phlox family

Description
A group of herbaceous plants primarily of western North
America, they are best suited to natural landscapes, enhancing
grassy meadows or open woodlands with a flash of colorful
bloom.

aggregata *p. 217*   *Pictured above*
Skyrocket gilia, scarlet gilia (a.k.a. *Gilia aggregata*)
WM. Biennial. Zone 4
Height: 1–3 ft. Spread: 4–6 in.
Among grasses or shrubs, this plant has wands of trumpet-
shaped bright red to coral-pink flowers that are eye-catching
(to hummingbirds as well as people) from June to August. A
biennial, the first year produces a rosette of finely divided

leaves, the second a flowering stalk. *I. a. attenuata* has pink flowers tinged with white or yellow.

How to Grow
Sun or partial shade. Well-drained soil; tolerates dry soil and some heat. Sold as seeds. Sow spring, summer, or fall (every year if plants don't self-sow). Transplant 6 in. apart in mass plantings.

Iris
Eye′ris
Iridaceae. Iris family

Description
A large and extremely diverse genus, irises have long been cultivated for the beautiful form and colors of their flowers. Ranging in the wild from swamps to alpine meadows to semi-arid areas, there is an iris for almost any condition or garden, from formal borders to water gardens to naturalized plantings in sun or shade.

Irises have sword-shaped or grassy foliage, flowers composed of 3 inner segments (petals or standards) and 3 outer segments (sepals or falls). Some increase by rhizomes, others by bulbs. Most form clumps that spread with age, so no figures for spread are given below. To increase or rejuvenate an old clump, divide the rhizomes or bulbs in late summer or fall. Irises have been bred intensely, and cultivars offer a range of characteristics (usually flower color and form) for most species.

cristata p. 217
Dwarf crested iris
EW. Perennial. Zones 3–9
Height: 4–7 in.

Delightful, spring-blooming miniatures, these irises spread easily given the right conditions, creating a long-lived ground cover. A must for mixing with other woodland wildflowers or tucking into a rock garden. Flowers, usually light to dark bluish lavender or white, bloom for 1–2 weeks in early spring. Light green foliage.

How to Grow
Partial or light shade. Well-drained soil. Heat tolerance increases with shade. Sold in containers. Plant 1 ft. apart, covering rhizomes lightly (if at all) with soil.

douglasiana p. 218
Douglas iris
CA. Evergreen perennial. Zone 9
Height: to 3 ft.
A vigorous, shade- and drought-tolerant iris, it is ideal for dry woodlands but also thrives in irrigated gardens. From March through May, a 30-in.-tall stalk with up to 4 branches rises through dark green foliage, each branch bearing 3 large (3-in.) flowers in pale cream, lavender, or deep red-purple. Crosses with *I. innominata* and other West Coast species are collectively called Pacific coast hybrids. They offer more and larger flowers, longer bloom, and more colors.

How to Grow
Partial or light shade. Tolerates constant moisture, dry soil, and heat. Sold as seeds and in containers. Space rhizomes 1 ft. apart.

missouriensis p. 218
Western blue flag, Rocky Mountain iris
WM GP. Perennial. Zones 3–6
Height: 1–2 ft.
A native of marshes, wet prairies, and sedge meadows, it needs adequate spring and early summer moisture but is otherwise extremely drought tolerant. Flowers in June, pale to dark blue, with a yellow stripe on the falls.

How to Grow
Full sun. Tolerates poor soil and heat. Sold as seeds, in containers, and bare root. Spreads to form colonies; if space is constricted, needs to be divided regularly.

versicolor p. 219   Pictured on facing page
Blue flag, wild flag
CP EW. Perennial. Zones 3–7
Height: 3 ft.

A vigorous aquatic iris for a water or bog garden. Its lavender or blue flowers last only 3 weeks in spring, but the waxy, arching leaves contrast with other plantings all season. Southern blue flag, *I. virginica,* is similar; *I. fulva,* with bronze-red flowers, is also good in wetlands.

How to Grow
Full sun. Needs fertile, organic soil and constant moisture. Grows best with rhizome barely covered with water; does well when just kept moist. Sold in containers and bare root. Plant 3 ft. apart.

Itea
It′ee-a
Saxifragaceae. Saxifrage.

Description
A small genus including easy-to-grow trees and shrubs with showy, fragrant flowers and attractive foliage.

virginica p. 164
Virginia sweetspire, Virginia willow
EW CP. Shrub. Zones 5–9
Height: 3–6 ft. or more. Spread: forms spreading colonies
Mixes easily in a shrub border and naturalizes well. Good for damp or wet sites. Dense, pendulous racemes of bell-shaped, white, very fragrant flowers bloom for 2–3 weeks in early spring. Medium-green foliage turns to bright yellows and reds in fall and may persist until spring in warmer climates. 'Henry's Garnet' has rich maroon fall color.

How to Grow
Sun or partial shade. Prefers moist, fertile, organic soil. Tolerates heat if kept moist. Sold in containers and balled-and-burlapped. Plant 6–10 ft. or more apart. Increase by division in fall or spring.

Juniperus
Joo-ni′per-us
Cupressaceae. Cypress family

Description
The variety of junipers available for landscaping is staggering, from tall, columnar trees to creeping shrub ground covers. They are most effective in groups, where their dark foliage

provides a perfect background. All have small, evergreen leaves, needlelike on young plants, scalelike on adults. Many change color from green to reddish brown during winter and spring. Mature trees have distinctive shredding bark. Female plants form small, waxy blue berrylike cones.

Native across the U.S. in one form or another, junipers are highly adaptable. Often found in the wild on the very worst soils, they thrive in ordinary garden soil as well as in dry, scorched, urban landscapes. Requiring minimal care, they are relatively pest and disease free.

communis p. 164 *Pictured above*
Common juniper
WM. Evergreen shrub. Zone 2
Height: 2–15 ft. Spread: 5–15 ft.
Widely distributed throughout the northern and mountain states, it is the hardiest of all junipers. Numerous varieties and cultivars offer a wide range of habits. The low-growing forms are excellent in groups or as specimens for foundations, informal natural plantings, or rock gardens.

How to Grow
Sun or partial shade. Prefers well-drained soil. Tolerates poor or dry soil and heat. Sold in containers. Space according to form. After watering to establish, an occasional deep watering is appreciated.

horizontalis p. 165 *Pictured on p. 358*
Creeping juniper
EW GP WM. Evergreen shrub. Zones 3–9
Height: 1–1½ ft. Spread: 1 ft. per year
One of the most popular junipers for low ground cover, especially in poor soils and all-day sun. Its many cultivars include 'Wiltonii', very low growing, and 'Bar Harbor', an old favorite from Maine.

How to Grow

See *J. communis*. Full sun. Space 3–5 ft. apart. Susceptible to juniper blight and bagworms.

monosperma
One-seed juniper
WD. Evergreen shrub/tree. Zones 5–8
Height: 6–20 ft. Spread: 8–20 ft.
A tough native of hillside grasslands, mesas, rimrock, and escarpments, it withstands abrupt shifts in temperature and drying summer and winter winds, providing shelter for more tender plants, people, and wildlife.

How to Grow

See *J. communis*. Susceptible to mistletoe (prune it out) and, on stressed plants, spider mites and scale.

scopulorum *p. 126*
Rocky Mountain juniper
WM GP. Evergreen tree. Zone 4
Height: to 30 ft. Spread: 10–15 ft.
A reliable plant for dry, exposed areas. In general, it has a loose pyramidal form with graceful branches. Many selections, including *J. s. pendula,* a weeping form, and *J. s.* 'Medora', a columnar form (2–3 ft. wide).

How to Grow

See *J. communis*. Full sun.

virginiana *p. 127*
Red cedar
EW CP. Evergreen tree/shrub. Zones 3–9
Height: to 60 ft. Spread: to 30 ft.
As with other junipers, this species exhibits a wide variety of

forms, from shrubby ground covers to large trees. Especially common on abandoned farmland all over the eastern U.S. Excellent source of food and shelter for wildlife. Among the choices are 'Cupressifolia', tightly branched, broad-based, and upright; 'Silver Spreader', an excellent ground cover for poor soil; 'Skyrocket', narrow and columnar.

How to Grow
See *J. communis*. It is alternate host to apple-rust fungus.

Kalmia
Kal'mi-a
Ericaceae. Heath family

Description
A near relative of rhododendrons, this small genus of largely North American evergreen shrubs make ideal "backbone" plants in a landscape or handsome specimens.

latifolia p. 165
Mountain laurel, calico-bush, ivybush
EW CP. Evergreen shrub. Zones 4–9
Height: 8–20 ft. Spread: 8–20 ft.
These long-lived plants are tough and adaptable — found in the wild clinging to harsh, rocky slopes in bright sun or nestled comfortably in deep soils at the bottom of a shady ravine. Medium-size, glossy, dark green leaves cover the open framework of gnarled branches year-round. Clusters of small but distinctive flowers, white to pink with lacy highlights of dark pink, bloom for 1–3 weeks in late spring. Cultivars offer a variety of colors, including 'Alba', with white flowers, 'Nipmuck', with red buds, pink flowers. 'Myrtifolia' reaches 6 ft. at maturity. *K. angustifolia,* a rounded shrub that spreads by stolons, is only 1–3 ft. tall.

How to Grow
Partial sun or shade. Needs well-drained, acid soil. Prefers fertile, organic soil; tolerates poor or dry soil and heat. Sold in containers and balled-and-burlapped. When planting, add plenty of medium-grade pine bark to help drain and acidify soil; in poorly drained sites, leave half of root ball above ground when planting and mulch heavily with pine bark. Susceptible to leaf spots; root rots in poorly drained or overwatered sites. Avoid regular overhead watering.

Kosteletzkya
Kos-tel-etz′kee-a
Malvaceae. Mallow family

Description
Only a few members of this smallish genus (about 30 species) of perennials and subshrubs are cultivated, grown primarily for their numerous hibiscus-like flowers.

virginica p. 219   *Pictured above*
Seashore mallow
CP. Perennial. Zone 5
Height: 5 ft. Spread: 4 ft.
Native to the edges of salt marshes near the coast, seashore mallow also grows well inland with ordinary moisture. It is useful in wild seascapes or as background in a perennial border. A full-grown plant can display 50 or more large (3-in.) pink blossoms every day for 6–8 weeks in August and September.

How to Grow
Full sun. Tolerates constant moisture. Sold in containers. Plant 5 ft. apart. Increase by seed or summer cuttings. Cut back to ground after frost.

Larrea
Lar′ree-a
Zygophyllaceae. Caltrop family

Description
A small genus of shrubs with resinous, aromatic evergreen leaves, small flowers, and fuzzy seeds. A specimen in the Mohave Desert is currently thought to be the oldest living plant on earth.

tridentata *p. 166   Pictured above*
Creosotebush, greasewood
WD. Evergreen shrub. Zones 6–10
Height: 3–10 ft. Spread: 3–10 ft.
Grows in the hottest, driest conditions the Western Deserts
can offer. Tiny, rich green leaflets contrast nicely with the gray-
green foliage of many desert shrubs. The layered, open form
has an "oriental" feel, making it a good specimen. Also attractive when mass planted or naturalized or as an informal
hedge. Small yellow flowers, with silky petals and many stamens, bloom intermittently from spring into fall.

How to Grow
Sun or partial shade. Tolerates poor or dry soil and heat. Sold
as seeds and in containers. Sow seeds or transplant in warm,
well-drained soil. Once established, can be left completely untended. Tip-pruning or deep watering increases foliage density.
Thin branches to enhance layered structure.

Layia
Lay'i-a
Compositae. Daisy family

Description
Members of this small genus of annual wildflowers are native
almost exclusively to California. Attractive naturalized or in
more formal gardens.

platyglossa *p. 220*
Tidy-tips
CA. Annual
Height: 12–18 in. Spread: 18 in.

Dependable and easy-to-grow plants ideal for naturalizing in summer-dry areas with California poppies (which bloom at the same time) and lupines or with native shrubs, particularly blue-flowered ceanothus. Numerous 2-in.-wide flowers rise above fuzzy, light green leaves March–June. Yellow ray flowers are neatly tipped with creamy white. Prolific bloomers.

How to Grow
Full sun. Tolerates dry or poor soil and heat. Sold as seeds. In mild-winter areas, broadcast seed in fall; elsewhere sow in spring.

Leucophyllum
Loo-koh-fil'um
Scrophulariaceae. Figwort family

Description
A small group of evergreen shrubs native to the Western Deserts, planted for their compact, mounded form, attractive flowers and leaves, and adaptability to heat and drought.

frutescens p. 166   *Pictured above*
Texas sage, Texas ranger, purple sage, barometer bush, cenizo
WD. Evergreen shrub. Zones 7–10
Height: 4–8 ft. Spread: 3–6 ft.
One of the best shrubs for warm-desert gardens. Handsome alone, in groups, in beds and borders, and as a dense screen or unclipped hedge. Small, woolly, oval leaves are silver to green. Tubular flowers, 1 in. long, white, pink-lavender to purple, appear intermittently from spring to fall in response to rain. 'Green Cloud' has dark green leaves and purple flowers; 'White Cloud', silver leaves, white flowers. *L. candidum*

is smaller (to 4 ft.) and very dense; *L. minus* 'Silver Cloud' is 3 ft. tall with deep purple flowers.

How to Grow

Full sun. Tolerates dry or poor soil and heat. Best in gravelly soils with no fertilizer — do not amend soil with compost. Sold as seeds and in containers. Space according to use. Deep-water periodically; overwatering produces floppy plants. Tip-prune to increase density.

Liatris
Lie-a′tris
Compositae. Daisy family

Description

A group of versatile North American wildflowers whose strik-ing flower spikes rise above clumps of grassy foliage. Scattered through a prairie or meadow, they are spectacular in bloom, inconspicuous otherwise. Equally effective grouped in a sunny perennial border. Butterflies love them. They have become a popular cut flower.

punctata p. 220
Gayfeather
WD GP WM. Perennial. Zones 4–8
Height: 18–24 in. Spread: 18–24 in.
Easy to grow and very long lived. A 5-year-old plant may produce 25 tall spikes of reddish purple flowers for 2–3 weeks in September. The species does better than cultivars in the Western Deserts.

How to Grow

Full sun. Well-drained soil. Tolerates dry or poor soil and heat. Sold as seeds and in containers. Plant container-grown plants anytime spring—autumn, bare-root seedlings in spring. Space 2 ft. apart. Established plants do not transplant well. To establish, water deeply every 2 weeks late spring—autumn, monthly in winter.

pycnostachya p. 221
Gayfeather
GP EW. Perennial. Zones 3–8
Height: 2–4½ ft. Spread: 2 ft.
A native of moist prairies. Long (to 2 ft.) spikes of lilac to purple flowers bloom for several weeks in midsummer — a striking sight when visited by monarch butterflies. Best naturalized; the spikes tend to tumble.

How to Grow
Full sun. Needs uniformly moist (not wet) soil. Tolerates poor soil and heat. Sold as seeds, in containers, and bare root. Moist-stratify seeds for 2 months.

spicata p. 221   *Pictured on p. 363*
Blazing star
CP EW. Perennial. Zones 4–9
Height: 3–4 ft. Spread: 2 ft.
A good choice for beds and borders, where its foliage and erect spikes of rosy lavender flowers provide interesting texture. (Larger plants may require support.) One of the best cultivars is 'Kobold', whose form and flower spike are compact.

How to Grow
Full sun. Grows best in ordinary, well-drained soil. Tolerates heat. Sold in containers and bare root. Increase by division in spring. Do not overwater or overfertilize.

Lilium
Lil′i-um
Liliaceae. Lily family

Description
A large genus much loved for their distinctive, trumpet-shaped flowers. Commonly grown in beds and borders, where small or large groups provide drama, lilies can also be naturalized. Extensively bred, they come in many sizes and colors.

Lilies can be propagated by a variety of means — seeds, bulbils, bulb scales, and, on older plants, division of more

fully formed bulbs. Depending on the species and the method, it can take up to 4 years to produce a flowering plant.

canadense p. 222   *Pictured above*
Canada lily, wild yellow lily
EW. Perennial bulb. Zones 4–9
Height: 4–7 ft. Spread: 2 ft.
A good plant for moist beds and borders, Canada lily is a real treat in a naturalized setting, where the perfection of its flowers contrast with the "untamed" surroundings. Stems bear whorls of straplike leaves and 5–20 large (3-in. by 3-in.) orange to yellow, sweet-smelling flowers, splashed with many purplish red spots. Blooms for 1–3 weeks in mid to late summer.

How to Grow
Partial sun. Needs fertile, moist, well-drained, slightly acid soil, fortified with plenty of organic matter. Sold in containers and as bulbs. Plant 4–6 in. deep and 9–24 in. apart. Susceptible to leaf fungus and bulb rot. Provide good air circulation and avoid overhead watering. Voles and mice eat bulbs; trap or discourage them by adding sharp gravel to the planting area.

superbum p. 222
Turk's cap lily
EW. Perennial bulb. Zones 4–9
Height: 4–7 ft. Spread: 2 ft.
Similar to *L. canadense*. Mature plants bear up to 50 flowers in a candelabra pattern for 1–3 weeks in mid to late summer. Nodding flowers have strongly recurved orange or reddish petals with rust-colored spots.

How to Grow
See *L. canadense*.

Linum
Lie'num
Linaceae. Flax family

Description
This large genus includes the plants from which linen and linseed oil are made. Several species are grown in beds and borders or naturalized for their wispy foliage and clouds of delicate flowers.

perenne lewisii p. 223
Lewis flax
WM GP. Perennial. Zones 5–8
Height: 1–2 ft. Spread: 1–1½ ft.
These airy plants are excellent in meadows or grouped in informal beds. The bluish green leaves are fine textured. From midspring to early summer the plant is covered with small (¾-in.) sky-blue flowers. The petals open in the early morning and fade in the afternoon sun; ample replacements appear the following morning. 'Sapphire' has sapphire-blue flowers.

How to Grow
Sun or partial shade. Well-drained soil; tolerates dry or clay soil and heat. Sold as seeds and in containers. Sow seeds anytime; space plants 6–8 in. apart. Increase by division in spring or cultivate self-sown seedlings.

Lobelia
Low-bee'li-a
Campanulaceae. Bellflower family

Description
The North American members of this huge genus are largely annuals and perennials. Their stately, erect stems provide ver-

tical interest throughout the growing season. Spikes of tubular flowers rising above the foliage are a colorful addition to beds, borders, and meadows for a few weeks in summer.

cardinalis p. 223   Pictured on facing page
Cardinal flower
EW GP CA CP. Perennial. Zones 2–9
Height: 4–6 ft. Spread: 2 ft.
Spikes of brilliant crimson-red flowers are like candy to hummingbirds. As many as 50 flowers, about 1½ in. long, blaze on the upper portions of the stems for 4–8 weeks in midsummer. Effective with rudbeckias, helianthus, and aster. 'Alba' has white flowers; 'Rosea', pink flowers.

How to Grow
Sun or partial shade. Native to wet sites, will do well in drier spots if watered regularly. Needs fertile soil. Tolerates heat if kept moist. Sold as seeds and in containers. Space 1½–2½ ft. apart. Raise the crown slightly on a mound of soil and keep mulch away from basal leaves to avoid rot. Plants are short-lived, especially when crowded — divide every 2–3 years. Also increase by cultivating self-sown seedlings. Overhead watering may cause leaf and stem spot.

siphilitica p. 224
Great blue lobelia
EW GP. Perennial. Zones 4–9
Height: 2–3 ft. Spread: 1–2 ft.
More tolerant of dry conditions than *L. cardinalis,* this lobelia looks best in small, closely spaced groups in the middle or front of a border or naturalized at the edge of a woodland. Popular with hummingbirds, moths, and bumblebees. The light blue flowers, sometimes with white throats, bloom for 4–8 weeks in midsummer. 'Alba' has white flowers.

How to Grow
See *L. cardinalis.*

Lonicera
Lah-nis′er-a
Caprifoliaceae. Honeysuckle family

Description
A varied group of woody shrubs and vines, honeysuckles are prized for their showy, often fragrant, flowers and by bees for their abundant nectar.

sempervirens p. 266
Coral honeysuckle, trumpet honeysuckle
EW CP. Perennial vine. Zones 3–9
Height: 10–20 ft.
One of the easiest and most rewarding vines, effective draped over a mailbox or small tree or twining along a fence or up a trellis. Not aggressive, like its popular Japanese relative, it blooms heavily for 3–5 weeks in early summer, then intermittently through the fall. The 2-in.-long tubular flowers are scarlet, often with yellow to orange throats. The paired, glossy, oval leaves are evergreen to semi-evergreen in the South. Yellow-flowered cultivars are sometimes available.

How to Grow
Sun or partial shade (best bloom in full sun). Average to rich soil. Tolerates heat. Sold in containers. Space 5 ft. or more apart. Increase by layering stems or sowing seed outdoors in fall. Susceptible to mildew, leaf curl, and, on young growth, aphids.

Lupinus
Loo-pie′nus. Lupins
Leguminosae. Pea family

Description
This large group of annuals, perennials, and shrubs ranges

from the tropics to the tundra; California alone counts some 80 native species. Gardeners enjoy their striking spires of colorful flowers and handsome leaves.

argenteus *p. 224* *Pictured on facing page*
Silvery lupine
GP WM. Perennial. Zones 3–6
Height: 1½–3 ft. Spread: 2 ft.
A meadow of silvery lupines in bloom is a spectacular sight, but they are equally effective grouped in more formal plantings. Spikes of light to deep blue flowers rise above silvery-green palmately compound leaves in June and July. An important food plant for butterflies. Similar but with different natural ranges are sundial lupine (*L. perennis,* Maine to Florida), lady lupine (*L. villosus,* North Carolina to Florida and Mississippi), and Texas bluebonnet (*L. texensis,* Texas).

How to Grow
Full sun. Tolerates poor or dry soil and heat. Sold as seeds. Sow in the fall; scarify seed coats. Established plants are difficult to transplant.

latifolius *p. 225*
Canyon lupine
CA WM. Perennial. Zone 9
Height: 3–6 ft. Spread: 3–6 ft.
This spectacular, easy-to-grow perennial produces quantities of wonderfully fragrant flowers, excellent for cutting, April–August. Ideal for massing in openings among trees. Small blue, rose, and lavender flowers densely cover robust spikes above smooth, green foliage.

How to Grow
Full or partial sun. Tolerates constant moisture, poor soil, and heat (goes dormant). Sold as seeds and in containers. Sow seeds in fall where they are to bloom. Plant requires water during active growth, but can dry out after it goes dormant in mid to late summer. Genista moth caterpillars can defoliate plants in late spring; spray with *Bacillus thuringiensis.*

polyphyllus *p. 225*
Washington lupine, streamside lupine
WM. Perennial. Zone 5
Height: 3–5 ft. Spread: 1½ ft.
This native of mountain streams and meadows is one of the parents of the well-known Russell Hybrid lupines. It is a robust

plant with bold, rich green leaves and stately spires of deep blue, purple, or reddish flowers that bloom for 2–3 weeks in May. Good for cutting.

How to Grow
Sun or partial shade. Tolerates poor soil. Does best in cooler areas but tolerates some heat; mulch to keep soil cool. Sold as seeds and in containers. Sow seeds in fall. Space plants 15–18 in. apart. Divide in spring or late summer. Susceptible to mildew if air circulation is poor.

succulentus
Arroyo lupine
CA. Annual
Height: 3 ft. Spread: 2 ft.
Spikes covered with whorls of small purplish blue, sweetly fragrant flowers contrast nicely with the dark green foliage. Blooms February–May. Other annual California lupines include dwarf lupine (*L. nanus*), with blue flowers; spider lupine (*L. benthamii*), with fine leaf segments and purplish blue flowers; and *L. densiflorus* 'Ed Gedling', whose golden yellow flowers bloom May–June.

How to Grow
Full sun. Tolerates dry or poor soil. Sold as seeds. Broadcast seeds in fall in warm-winter areas, spring elsewhere. Seeds germinate easily in any season in California. Sprouted in early autumn, they can be blooming in December and January with the first of the season's California poppies.

Magnolia
Mag-no'li-a
Magnoliaceae. Magnolia family

Description
The cultivated species in this large genus of trees and shrubs are grown for their showy flowers and handsome, often evergreen, foliage.

grandiflora p. 127   *Pictured on facing page*
Southern magnolia, bull bay
CP. Evergreen tree. Zones 7–9
Height: 60 ft. Spread: 45 ft.
One of the grandest broadleaf evergreen trees, it makes a splendid specimen. The large (8–10-in.-long) leaves are lus-

trous, dark green, and leathery, with gray-green to rust undersides. The fragrant white flowers are huge (8 in. across) and bloom from late spring to early summer. Reddish brown to greenish fruits, 3–4 in. long, expose red seeds as they ripen. Cultivars include 'Little Gem', a heavy-blooming dwarf; 'Saint Mary', with a compact form and early flowers; and 'Majestic Beauty', with immense leaves and a magnificent pyramidal form.

How to Grow
Sun or partial shade. Best in fertile, moderately moist soil. Tolerates heat. Sold in containers and balled-and-burlapped. Space 50 ft. apart. Leaf litter can be messy.

virginiana p. 128
Sweet bay (a.k.a. *M. glauca*)
CP. Deciduous to evergreen tree/shrub. Zones 5–9
Height: to 60 ft. Spread: to 20 ft.
A light, airy, slow-growing plant, often grown as a multi-trunked shrub or small tree. Effective against a wall, singly, or in groups. The silvery undersides of the large (5–6-in.) lustrous leaves shimmer in the breeze. The fragrant flowers and showy fruits are smaller versions of those of southern magnolia. *M. v.* var. *australis* is evergreen; 'Henry Hicks' is unusually cold-hardy.

How to Grow
Sun or partial shade. Tolerates constant moisture and heat. Sold in containers and balled-and-burlapped. Space 12 ft. apart in shrub border. Prune to train as shrub or tree.

Mahonia
Ma-hoe'ni-a
Berberidaceae. Barberry family

Description
These rugged, adaptable broadleaf evergreen shrubs are versatile, effective as specimens, in borders and hedges, and as ground covers. They naturalize well in rock gardens or woodland landscapes. Good wildlife habitat.

aquifolium p. 167
Oregon grape (a.k.a. *Berberis aquifolium*)
WM. Evergreen shrub. Zone 4
Height: 6–8 ft. Spread: 3–4 ft.
A four-season plant. The stiff, thick, spine-tipped leaflets are glossy green, turning reddish in fall. Racemes of bright yellow, fragrant flowers bloom for 1½–2 weeks in midspring. Clusters of tiny blue, grapelike fruit attract wildlife in late summer. 'Compacta' reaches 4 ft., has denser foliage; the new leaflets of 'Orange Flame' are bronze.

How to Grow
Full sun or shade. Tolerates some heat if soil is kept moist. Sold as seeds and in containers. Protect from drying winter winds. Pinch new growth to keep compact and dense.

repens p. 167   *Pictured above*
Creeping holly grape (a.k.a. *Berberis repens*)
WM. Evergreen shrub. Zone 4
Height: 2–3 ft. Spread: 2–3 ft.
An excellent ground cover for sun or shade, clay or loam soils. It withstands cold, dry weather. Leaflets are dull green above, paler green beneath, bronze in winter. Dense racemes of fragrant yellow flowers bloom for 2–3 weeks April–June. Blue, grapelike fruit in late summer.

How to Grow
See *M. aquifolium*. Tolerates dry soil and heat.

Melampodium
Mel-am-poh'di-um
Compositae. Daisy family

Description
A group of annuals and perennials of the Western Deserts, Central and South America. Their perky daisies brighten meadows, beds, and borders for long periods during the growing season.

leucanthum p. 226
Blackfoot daisy, rock daisy
WD GP. Perennial. Zones 5–10
Height: 12–18 in. Spread: 12–18 in.
Mounds of small, narrow, gray-green leaves are covered with small (¾-in.) white daisies with yellow centers March–November in warm deserts, April–October in colder areas. Crisp, tidy plants, they can be used in many garden settings, from formal to naturalized. Particularly attractive in massed plantings with penstemons and evening primroses. *M. paludosum* is a yellow-flowered, large-leaved annual recently available for bedding or pot culture. Requires more consistent watering than *M. leucanthum*.

How to Grow
Sun or partial shade. Well-drained soil. Tolerates poor or dry soil and heat. Sold as seeds and in containers. Plant when soil is warm, space 12–24 in. apart for mass planting. Sensitive to overwatering, it can be difficult to establish, especially in heavier soils. Once established, however, it seems to prosper when ignored.

Mertensia
Mer-ten'si-a
Boraginaceae. Borage family

Description
Members of this medium-size genus are grown in woodland or rock gardens for their spring flowers. One plant can be effective in a small garden; small to large groups are especially pleasing.

virginica p. 226   *Pictured above*
Virginia bluebells
EW. Perennial. Zones 3–9
Height: 1–2 ft. Spread: 1–2 ft.
An old favorite for spring gardens. The lush foliage seems to appear overnight; delicate, nodding, bell-shaped flowers, pastel blue fading to pink, follow quickly (1–4 weeks in early to mid spring). Combines perfectly with foamflowers, bleeding hearts, celandine poppy, phlox, and bloodroot. Plant goes dormant by late spring, allowing overplanting. 'Alba' has white flowers; 'Rubra', pink flowers.

How to Grow
Partial sun or shade. Prefers moist, organic soil, fertile and adequately drained. Sold in containers. (Bare-root plants have often been collected in the wild.) Space 1½–3 ft. apart. Increase by sowing fresh seeds or by division: take a generous section of crown with at least one bud. Susceptible to crown rot in boggy soils.

Mimulus
Mim'you-lus
Scrophulariaceae. Figwort family

Description
A large, widespread genus with numerous species native to western North America. They vary from streambank perennials to drought-tolerant shrublets of chaparral hillsides.

guttatus p. 227
Common monkey flower
WM CA. Perennial. Zones 9–10
Height: 3 ft. Spread: creeping rootstocks

Found in moist places up to 10,000 feet, from Alaska to Mexico, it grows well in beds and borders or naturalized. Racemes of cheerful, snapdragon-like flowers, yellow, usually spotted with red, bloom March–August. Soft, light green leaves are ½–3 in. long. Perennial in warm zones, it blooms in the first year from seed and is grown as a half-hardy annual in colder places. Cultivars of *M. hybridus* (a cross of *M. guttatus* and *M. luteus*) bear large flowers in many colors.

How to Grow
Full sun. Needs moist soil. Tolerates poor soil and heat if it has plenty of water. Sold as seeds and in containers. Broadcast seeds in fall or spring. One plant spreads widely. Divide dormant rootstocks in fall or winter or when growth begins in spring.

Mirabilis
Mi-rab'i-lis. Four-o'clocks
Nyctaginaceae. Four-o'clock family

Description
Many members of this genus are native to the Southwest. The flowers are often large and showy; the forms range from tall and skeletal to low, sprawling, and dense.

multiflora p. 227
Giant four-o'clock, desert four-o'clock
WD GP. Perennial. Zones 5–10
Height: to 18 in. Spread: to 6 ft.
This long-lived, undemanding plant makes a colorful ground cover. The smallish, tubular, rose-pink to magenta flowers open in the late afternoon and close in late morning — perfect near a patio used in the cooler times of day. Also handsome draping a retaining wall. Deep-watered every few weeks, it will bloom April–September; otherwise for a few weeks at a time in response to rainfall. Hummingbirds and hawk moths visit the flowers; quail love the seeds. No cultivars, but it's worth seeking out forms native to your area.

How to Grow
Sun or partial shade. Needs well-drained soil. Tolerates poor or dry soil and heat. Sold as seeds and in containers. Space 2–4 ft. depending on use and available moisture. Too much water in poorly drained or highly organic soil will kill plant. Don't give up too soon on "dead" plants; they can regenerate from deep and extensive root systems.

Monarda
Moh-nar′da
Labiatae. Mint family

Description
Members of this small group of North American natives are old favorites for their highly aromatic foliage, bright flowers, and medicinal properties. Effective as specimens, in massed plantings, in beds and borders, and naturalized.

didyma p. 228   *Pictured above*
Bee balm, Oswego tea
EW. Perennial. Zones 4–9
Height: 2–4 ft. Spread: 3–5 ft.
A flamboyant plant for the wild or tame garden. A favorite of hummingbirds and bees. Narrow, tubular scarlet flowers are tightly packed to form a head like a pompom, 2–3 in. across. They bloom for 3–5 weeks in early to mid summer. Ripe seed heads are used in dried arrangements. Cultivars include 'Adam', a compact plant with clear red flowers, more drought tolerant. 'Cambridge Scarlet' has bright red flowers; 'Croftway Pink', rosy, pastel pink flowers; 'Violet Queen', deep lavender to violet flowers. Spotted horse mint, *M. punctata*, with interesting pink and cream flowers, and *M. citriodora*, with pink flowers and lemon-scented leaves, are annuals except in the South.

How to Grow
Sun or partial shade (best in full sun). Native to moist lowlands and creek banks, it prefers fertile, moist soil. Tolerates some heat with afternoon shade and ample water. Sold as seeds and in containers. Sow seeds in early spring. Space 3–5 ft. apart. Increase by divisions in spring or stem cuttings spring and early summer. Crowded plants are susceptible to mildew. Japanese beetles will defoliate, though usually not kill, plant.

fistulosa p. 228
Bergamot
EW GP CP WM. Perennial. Zones 3–9
Height: 2–4 ft. Spread: 2–4 ft.
A native of prairies, open woodlands, and savannas, bergamot tolerates drier conditions and poorer soil than *M. didyma*. Good for prairie plantings or more formal uses. Lavender flowers bloom in midsummer.

How to Grow
Sun or partial shade. Tolerates poor or dry soil and heat. Sold as seeds, in containers, and bare root. Easy to grow from seed. Spreads rapidly in fertile soil. Susceptible to mildew.

Muhlenbergia
Mew-len-berg′i-a
Gramineae. Grass family

Description
This large genus of grasses varies greatly in appearance from vertical clumps to open, spreading forms. Their fine texture lends a soft, flowing quality to the landscape.

dumosa p. 259
Bamboo muhly, bush muhly
WD. Perennial bunchgrass. Zones 8–10
Height: to 5 ft. Spread: to 5 ft.
Grown for its fine foliage and fountainlike form rather than for flowers or seed heads, this desert grass is most effective in mass plantings or as individual clumps. Narrow basal leaves rise about 1 ft.; shorter (4–6-in.) leaves grow from the tall, bamboolike flower canes. Native to elevations of 3,000 to 5,500 ft., Lindheimer muhly (*M. lindheimeri*, 2–5 ft.) and deergrass (*M. rigens*) are similar.

How to Grow
Sun or partial shade. Tolerates poor or dry soil and heat. Sold as seeds and in containers. Space 4 ft. apart for massing, 6 ft. as specimens. Increase by making large divisions in March and April. (You may need a saw or an ax.) To clean up a messy, mature clump, thin oldest canes in April, cutting as close to crown as possible.

Myrica
Mi-rye′ka
Myricaceae. Bayberry (or wax myrtle) family

Description
A widespread genus of shrubs and small trees, a few of which are cultivated for their attractive, aromatic foliage and ornamental fruits. They attract birds but not deer.

cerifera p. 168   *Pictured above*
Wax myrtle, southern wax myrtle
CP EW. Evergreen shrub. Zones 6–9
Height: to 30 ft. Spread: to 20 ft.
A good low-maintenance shrub for much of the South, especially along the coast (it tolerates salt spray and wind). Ideal for screening. The fine-textured leaves are linear, light green, and fragrant when crushed; used in Christmas arrangements. In fall and winter, numerous tiny gray fruits attract the eye and birds. 'Evergreen' is an unusually hardy, fast-growing cultivar.

How to Grow
Sun or partial shade. Tolerates poor soil and heat. Sold in containers. Space 8–10 ft. apart. Can be pruned to shape if desired.

pensylvanica p. 168
Bayberry
CP EW. Deciduous or semi-evergreen shrub. Zones 4–9
Height: 8–10 ft. Spread: 8–10 ft.
Hardier than *M. cerifera,* bayberry is useful as a border or screening plant. It also tolerates salt spray and wind. With clean, bright to dull green aromatic foliage, and copious waxy, gray fruit on female plants in fall and winter. Wax coating on

fruit is used to make bayberry candles. *M. heterophylla* is the evergreen, southern form of bayberry. *M. inodora* is an attractive native of the Gulf Coastal Plain — not aromatic.

How to Grow
Full sun. Tolerates heat. Sold in containers. Space according to use. Shearing destroys character of plant.

Nelumbo
Nee-lum'bow
Nelumbonaceae. Water lotus family

Description
One of the two species in this genus of striking aquatic plants is native to eastern North America, the other to Asia and Australia.

lutea p. 229   *Pictured above*
American lotus, yellow lotus, water chinquapin (a.k.a. *N. pentapetala*)
CP EW. Aquatic perennial. Zones 4–9
Height: 1–4 ft. Spread: 6–20 ft.
A bold plant, suitable for naturalizing in a pond or growing singly in a tub. The dull bluish green leaves are huge (9–18 in. across); some float, some rise above the water. For 6–8 weeks in midsummer large stalks rise out of the water, bearing very large (10-in.-wide) creamy yellow flowers. The fruiting receptacle lasts well into winter and is excellent for dried arrangements.

How to Grow
Full sun. Plant the bare rootstock about 4 in. deep in fertile soil (in pond or in container 1–1½ ft. deep) under 8–12 in.

of still water. Takes 1 year to establish. Hardy as long as rootstock does not freeze. Increase by dividing the rootstock.

Nemophila
Nee-mof′i-la
Hydrophyllaceae. Waterleaf family

Description
A small genus of North American annuals cultivated for their charming early spring blooms.

menziesii p. 229
Baby blue eyes
CA WM. Annual.
Height: 6 in. Spread: 1 ft.
A western native great for naturalizing in woodland gardens or on cool, moist northern exposures. Perfect underplanting in beds and borders for early spring bulbs. Its small, bowl-shaped flowers, bright blue with white centers, bloom February–June. Several seed strains have been derived from natural variations, including 'Pennie Black', with blackish purple flowers with a white edge. Fivespot (*N. maculata*) has white flowers veined with blue-violet.

How to Grow
Sun or shade. Prefers fertile soil. Tolerates constant moisture. Sold as seeds, occasionally in containers. Broadcast seeds in fall in warm-winter areas, spring in cold-winter areas.

Nymphaea
Nim-fay′a
Nymphaeaceae. Water lily family

Description
A widespread genus of aquatic plants admired for their gorgeous flowers.

odorata p. 230
Water lily, pond lily, fragrant white water lily (a.k.a. *Castalia odorata*)
CP EW. Aquatic perennial. All zones
Height: 6 in. Spread: 2 ft. or more
The large floating leaves and fragrant white flowers impart

tranquillity to a pond or barrel planting all summer. Numerous cultivars are available.

How to Grow
Full sun. Place rhizome, bud end up, horizontally on the surface of soil at bottom of pond or on surface of 8 in. of soil in a container. Soil surface should be 8–12 in. below water surface. Fertilize soil with a complete fertilizer (1 lb./plant). Plant February–October in mild-winter areas, April–July in cold-winter areas. Do not allow rhizomes to freeze.

Nyssa
Nis′a
Nyssaceae. Tupelo (or sour gum) family

Description
Long used as specimen shade trees, the native North American tupelos (3 of the 5 species in this genus) have an attractive, pyramidal form and handsome foliage, which begins to color as early as midsummer and continues through the fall.

sylvatica p. 128   Pictured above
Black gum, black tupelo, sour gum
EW CP. Deciduous tree. Zones 3–9
Height: 30–60 ft. or more. Spread: 20–30 ft.
Able to withstand harsh conditions, black gum makes a handsome specimen tree or can be naturalized, especially in moist, wet soils near a pond or creek. Flowers are insignificant; fruit is appreciated by wildlife. The medium-size leaves are dark green and glossy; color begins early and lasts long. Other noteworthy species include water tupelo (*N. aquatica,* hardy to zone 6), Ogeechee-lime (*N. ogeche,* with large, edible fruits), and swamp tupelo (*N. biflora,* possibly a variety of *N. sylvatica*).

How to Grow

Sun or partial shade. Prefers fertile, organic soil. Tolerates constant moisture, dry or poor soil, and heat. Sold in containers and balled-and-burlapped. (Taproot is least disturbed when container-grown.) Space 20 ft. or more apart.

Oenothera
Ee-noth'er-a
Onagraceae. Evening primrose family

Description
A largish, variable group of annual, perennial, and biennial plants native to North and South America. Cultivated for their showy flowers, which bloom over a long season, often opening at dusk for night pollination. A variety of forms allow use as specimens, ground covers, massed plantings, naturalized in meadows, or placed in beds and borders.

berlandiera p. 230   *Pictured above*
Mexican evening primrose
WD. Perennial. Zones 5–10
Height: 12–18 in. Spread: to 24 in. or more
A good ground cover in sun or part shade, it can be invasive in beds and borders. Saucer-shaped, 2-in.-wide flowers, pale to bright pink, provide a vibrant carpet of color in the spring. Open in daylight hours. Effective on hot sites mixed with prostrate dalea (*Dalea greggii*). Species varies greatly in height and flower color; 'Siskiyou' is supposed to be reliably compact.

How to Grow
Sun or shade. Tolerates poor or dry soil and heat. (Goes dormant in extreme heat.) Sold in containers. Plant in spring in

cooler areas. Space 18 in. apart for fast cover. Increase by division in spring. Can mow to 4 in. high when dormant. Mexican flea beetles can defoliate the plants; control with *Bacillus thuringiensis* 'San Diego' strain and beneficial nematodes.

fruticosa p. 231
Sundrops
EW CP. Perennial. Zones 4–9
Height: 2–3 ft. Spread: 1–2 ft.
Bright lemon-yellow flowers, 1–2 in. wide, cheer up an open border or meadow for 2–4 weeks or more from midspring to early summer. Daylight bloom. Medium-green leaves are spotted deep maroon-red. *O. tetragona*, slightly taller, usually without red spots on leaves, is often interchanged with *O. fruticosa*.

How to Grow
Full sun. Tolerates poor or dry soil and heat. Sold as seeds and in containers. Sow seed after last frost. Space container-grown plants 1–2 ft. apart; raise crown slightly to avoid crown rot. Increase by division in spring or fall or cultivate self-sown seedlings. Avoid too much watering. Susceptible to slugs and Japanese beetles; crown rot in poorly drained soils.

missouriensis p. 231
Missouri evening primrose
EW GP. Perennial. Zones 4–8
Height: 8–10 in. Spread: 15 in. or more
A low-growing plant with exceptional drought tolerance, it is a top candidate for smallish, dry properties. Large (3–6-in.-wide) flowers of clear canary-yellow open in the evening from late spring to early fall. White-tufted evening primrose (*O. caespitosa*), another low-growing plant, has large, fragrant white flowers April–October. Tooth-leaved evening primrose (*O. serrulata*) has smaller flowers that are open most of the day. The biennial species *O. biennis* and *O. rhombipetala* are valuable for providing quick cover and food for birds and butterflies.

How to Grow
Full sun. Tolerates poor or dry soil and heat. Sold as seeds. Sow seeds in spring. Increase by division in spring.

speciosa p. 232
Showy primrose
EW GP CP. Perennial. Zones 5–9
Height: 1½ ft. Spread: 3 ft. or more
Large (to 2½ in. wide) pink or white, slightly scented flowers

bloom prolifically in midsummer for 4–8 weeks. Foliage is blue-green, sometimes tinged with red. An ideal plant for dry, infertile conditions, it can be extremely invasive in richer, moister soils.

How to Grow
Full sun. Tolerates poor or dry soil and heat. Sold as seeds and in containers. Sow seeds after last frost. Space plants 1–2 ft. apart. Increase by division anytime. Edging at least 8 in. deep needed to contain spread where invasive. Same pests as *O. fruticosa.*

Opuntia
Oh-pun′shi-a
Cactaceae. Cactus family

Description
A large and tremendously variable genus of cacti whose many cultivated members are grown as accent specimens, ground covers, even living fences. Many have strikingly colorful flowers. The species below bear spines on leafless jointed stems that are cylindrical or flattened and padlike.

bigelovii p. 169
Teddy bear cholla
WD. Cactus. Zones 7–10
Height: 2–5 ft. Spread: 3 ft.
Adds regional flavor to the garden as accents or massed in a hedge or barrier. They are particularly effective when backlit. Spines are 1 in. long, soft and hazy looking from a distance, prickly up close on cylindrical joints 2–10 in. long and up to 2 in. thick. Small, inconspicuous flowers bloom in spring. Other noteworthy species include Christmas cactus (*O. lep-*

tocaulis), smaller with pencil-like stems, gold spines, small yellow flowers, and bright red fruits in winter. *O. kleiniae,* 4 ft. tall, 6 ft. wide, has narrow stems, dusty rose flowers.

How to Grow
Full sun. Tolerates poor or dry soils and heat. Sold in containers and bare root. Plant in warm weather, 2 ft. apart for barrier. Increase by cuttings: sever cleanly, allow to callous, then insert in well-drained, warm soil. Avoid sites with blowing litter (leaves, paper), as cleanup is difficult. Susceptible to cochineal, a scale/mealy bug relative; control by hosing them off a few times a year.

humifusa p. 169 Pictured on facing page
Prickly pear (a.k.a. *O. compressa*)
EW CP. Cactus. Zones 4–9
Height: 1 ft. Spread: 5 ft.
This low-growing cactus can help define space or express "natural character" in a dry, sandy habitat, or it can form an effective barrier on a beachfront property. The showy yellow flowers are large (3 in. wide) and bloom May–June, followed in late summer by a smallish, soft, purple to reddish brown fruit. The flattened joints are round or oval, 2–6 in. long.

How to Grow
See *O. bigelovii.* No pest or disease problems.

polycantha p. 170
Plains prickly pear
GP. Cactus. Zones 3–6
Height: 4 in. Spread: 4–5 ft.
The large, waxy flowers (yellow, occasionally pink or carmine) are spectacular in late June. Small cream- to beige-colored fruit ripen in August. Flattened joints are round, 2–4 in. wide. Native to the driest sites of non-windblown sandy or rocky hills, this is a tough ground cover where all else fails.

How to Grow
See *O. bigelovii.* Grows in any well-drained soil, but must be kept weeded. No pest or disease problems.

Orthocarpus
Or-tho-kar′pus
Scrophulariaceae. Figwort family

Description
A group of annuals characteristic of the western grasslands, they are conspicuous in the landscape for their richly colorful flower spikes.

purpurascens p. 232
Owl's clover
WD CA. Annual
Height: 4–14 in. Spread: 4 in.
A mass of owl's clover covering a hillside is one of the West's highlights. Beautiful when naturalized alone or with other native annuals in any sunny, open area. The plant's impact comes from the velvety rose-purple flower bracts overlapping densely on erect spikes. Blooms March–May.

How to Grow
Full sun. Tolerates poor or dry soil. Sold as seeds. Broadcast in fall in warm-winter areas, spring in cold-winter areas.

Oryzopsis
Oh-rye-zop′sis
Gramineae. Grass family

Description
A genus of some 20–50 species of mostly perennial grasses, only a few of which are cultivated.

hymenoides p. 259   *Pictured on facing page*
Indian ricegrass
WD. Perennial bunchgrass. Zones 5–10
Height: 18 in. Spread: 18 in.
A tough plant with a light, airy appearance, it is one of the most heat- and drought-tolerant cool-season grasses. Its sage-green, wiry foliage and ethereal seed heads are a wonderful textural accent in beds and borders or naturalized plantings and also provide excellent forage for wildlife. Foliage cures blond in summer. Grown commercially as a filler for dried arrangements and wreaths.

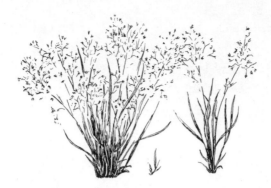

How to Grow
Full sun. Needs dry soil. Tolerates poor soil and heat. Sold as seeds and in containers. Sow seeds 1–2 in. deep in late fall or winter, 1 lb./1,000 sq. ft. (May take a year or more to sprout.) Space plants 1½–2 ft. apart. Increase by division in early spring. Can be mowed 8 in. high in early fall. Normally lives 6 years; remove old clumps to allow self-sown seedlings room to develop.

Osmanthus
Os-man'thus
Oleaceae. Olive family

Description
A small group of evergreen shrubs and small trees, some grown for their handsome foliage and fragrant white flowers.

americanus p. 170
Devilwood, wild olive
CP. Evergreen shrub/tree. Zones 6–8
Height: to 30 ft. Spread: to 30 ft.
Grown outdoors in the South as specimens, in hedges and screens, or naturalized landscapes. An irregularly rounded and open plant, its long leaves are light green and leathery; blue-black fruit resembles small cherries. The small, creamy white flowers will perfume the air within 100 ft. of a 6-ft. plant. (In colder areas, it is grown in conservatories for the fragrance.)

How to Grow
Partial sun or light shade. Best in good soil with light shade and adequate moisture. Tolerates heat. Sold in containers. Space 6–8 ft. apart. Can be liberally pruned to maintain shape.

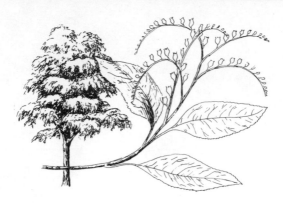

Oxydendrum
Ok-si-den'drum
Ericaceae. Heath family

Description
The single species in this genus, a native of the eastern U.S.,
is described below.

arboreum p. 129   *Pictured above*
Sourwood
EW CP. Deciduous tree. Zones 4–9
Height: 30–50 ft. Spread: 20 ft.
An extraordinary specimen tree with year-round interest. In
early summer, lacy clusters of white, beadlike flowers drape
gracefully over the large, glossy, dark green leaves. In summer,
clusters of fruit ripen into dry, tawny lace. As early as midsummer the leaves begin mottling with burgundy, turning later
to glorious yellows, oranges, reds, and purples. In winter, sourwood's bark and distinctive branching pattern give it a wizened, oriental appearance. Plant in the open or in a woodland
understory.

How to Grow
Sun or partial shade. Prefers fertile, organic soil, if possible
acidic and well drained. Tolerates poor or dry soil and heat.
Sold in containers and balled-and-burlapped.

Parthenocissus
Par-then-oh-sis'us
Vitaceae. Grape family

Description
A small group of fast-growing, leafy, climbing vines with colorful fall foliage. Effective for covering masonry walls or trellises or as creeping ground covers.

quinquefolia p. 266   *Pictured above*
Virginia creeper, woodbine (a.k.a. *Ampelopsis quinquefolia*)
EW GP CP. Deciduous vine. Zones 3–9
Height: grows up to 10 ft. per year
An easy, well-behaved vine for almost any situation needing leafy cover. Numerous large, palmately compound leaves, deep green and slightly glossy, obscure the midsummer flowers and fall berries. Rich red fall color. 'Engelmanii' and 'Saint Paulii' have smaller leaflets.

How to Grow
Sun or partial shade. Tolerates poor or dry soil, heat, and salty coastal conditions. Sold in containers. Stems root along the ground; increase by transplanting these in fall or spring. Prune to keep in bounds.

Passiflora
Pass-i-flo'ra
Passifloraceae. Passionflower family

Description
This huge genus of perennial vines includes many tropical members. Flowers are unusual and beautiful.

incarnata p. 267
Passionflower, maypops
EW CP. Perennial vine. Zones 5–10
Height: 20 ft. or more. Spread: 20 ft. or more
Grow on a trellis or allow to ramble over a fence or hedgerow where you can get close enough to appreciate the intricate structure of the flowers. The light green leaves may be evergreen in the Deep South. Flowers, 2½–3½ in. across, bloom from late spring through summer: numerous narrow filaments of purple and white are displayed above wider sepals and petals, with pistils and stamens uniquely arranged above the filaments. Attracts butterflies. Large, green, podlike edible fruits ripen in late summer and fall. 'Alba' has white flowers; yellow passionflower (*P. lutea*) has "miniature" yellowish green flowers.

How to Grow
Sun or partial shade. Prefers fertile, well-drained, organic soil. Tolerates dry or poor soil and heat. Sold as seeds and in containers. Space 1–3 ft. apart in fall or spring. Increase by planting sections of suckering stem in spring or fall. In the north, can be grown in containers or in the ground as annuals. Insects may defoliate plant late in the season, without lasting harm to mature plants.

Paxistima
Pax-is'ti-ma
Celastraceae. Staff-tree family

Description
The only two species in this genus of low-growing evergreen shrubs are described here. (The genus is sometimes misspelled *Pachystima*.)

canbyi p. 171   *Pictured on facing page*
Mountain lover
EW. Evergreen shrub. Zones 3–8
Height: 1 ft. Spread: 3–5 ft. or more
A good ground cover or low hedge, border edging, rock garden
specimen, or underplanting in a naturalized garden. The small,
shiny, deep green leaves are of more interest than the spring
clusters of small greenish flowers. Very cold-hardy, it doesn't
stand up well to the heat of the Deep South. Although mountain lover roots where its branches touch soil, it spreads very
slowly, taking several years to fill in between plants.

How to Grow
Sun or partial shade. Needs well-drained soil; prefers fertile,
organic soil. Tolerates dry soil. Sold in containers. Space 2–3
ft. apart, closer for quicker coverage. Increase by layering
branches.

myrsinites p. 171
Oregon boxwood, mountain lover
WM. Evergreen shrub. Zone 4
Height: 1–3 ft. Spread: 8–10 in.
Often more upright, Oregon boxwood can be used in the same
ways as its eastern relative. Small, lush green leaves; small,
fragrant, but inconspicuous flowers.

How to Grow
Sun or shade. Needs well-drained soil; prefers fertile, organic
soil. Sold as seeds and in containers. Plant in spring in area
protected from winter winds. Space 8–12 in. apart for hedge
or ground cover. Increase by tip cuttings in summer. Can be
sheared (spring and fall) for formal hedge.

Penstemon
Pen-stee'mon (commonly pen'ste-mon)
Scrophulariaceae. Figwort family

Description
All but one species in this vast genus (250 species) of wildflowers and subshrubs is native to North America. They range
from tufted alpines to tough, robust plants of the deserts and
dry prairies. Some large, lush penstemons are stars of the
perennial border. Other low-growing, diminutive species provide ground cover or accents in a rock garden. Most penstemons have attractive foliage and showy snapdragon-like
flowers in a wide variety of colors. A great many species are

cultivated. The descriptions below provide a sampling from across the country.

As a rule, penstemons require very well drained soil, and they do best in full sun. (Wet soil rots roots and invites other problems.) They tolerate poor or dry soils and heat. They are usually sold as seeds or in containers. Most are considered short lived (less than 6 years), but they often self-sow readily.

ambiguus p. 233 *Pictured above*
Sand, bush, or gilia penstemon
WD. Perennial. Zones 5–10
Height: 1–2 ft. Spread: 1½–2½ ft.
This long-lived plant (25 years or more) produces billows of flowers in extremely hot and dry conditions. It gets better with age, as the woody base produces more stems and flowers. Some of the threadlike medium-green leaves persist year-round. Smallish flowers have pale pink or white pansylike faces and a deep, narrow, darker pink tube. Blooms most heavily in May, then continues until October, depending on availability of water. A wonderful complement in desert gardens to thread-leaf sage and apache plume.

How to Grow
See description of genus. Also partial sun. Best in dry soils. Sow seeds in cool soil, spring or early autumn. Space plants at least 2 ft. apart to emphasize mounded form.

digitalis p. 233
White beardtongue, foxglove beardtongue
EW. Perennial. Zones 3–9
Height: 3–5 ft. Spread: 2½ ft.
One of the larger, more robust penstemons, it is the best for white flowers, which resemble those of foxglove and bloom

for 2–5 weeks in early summer. Foliage can be semi-evergreen in the South. Attracts hummingbirds. Another eastern species, *P. australis,* is about the same size and has lavender flowers.

How to Grow
See description of genus. Also partial sun. Prefers fertile, well-drained, organic soil. More tolerant of less than perfect drainage than many penstemons. Sow seeds in late winter. Space plants 2½–3 ft. apart. Plant nursery stock in fall or spring.

gracilis
Slender beardtongue
GP. Perennial. Zones 3–4
Height: 1–1½ ft. Spread: 6–8 in.
Delicate, purplish violet late spring flowers, fine dark green foliage, and small stature make this native of sandy prairies and open woodlands ideal for small plantings. Attracts hummingbirds.

How to Grow
See description of genus. Also benefits from afternoon shade. Space 1 ft. apart for mass planting.

grandiflorus p. 234
Large-flowered beardtongue
GP. Perennial. Zones 3–5
Height: 12–40 in. Spread: 6–8 in.
Large showy lavender flowers bloom in late spring and attract hummingbirds. Foliage is gray-green. Ideal for naturalizing on a sandy site, it adapts to well-drained garden soil. This species is listed as threatened or endangered over part of its range; buy seeds or plants only from nurseries that propagate their own plants.

How to Grow
See description of genus. Also benefits from afternoon shade.

heterophyllus p. 234
Foothill penstemon
CA. Evergreen perennial. Zones 7–8
Height: 1–1½ ft. Spread: 1½–2½ ft.
Brings cool blue or violet flowers to the border April–July. Neat low plants with dark green foliage are good companions for sulfur buckwheat and other small perennials. More adaptable to garden conditions than most dryland penstemons. *P. h.* subsp. *purdyi* has rich blue flowers and is sometimes sold as 'Blue Bedder' penstemon.

How to Grow
See description of genus. Also benefits from afternoon shade on hot, dry sites. Plant seeds or nursery stock in fall in warm-winter areas, in spring in cold-winter areas. Space 2 ft. apart for mass planting. Deadhead to prolong bloom.

pinifolius p. 235
Pineleaf penstemon
WD. Evergreen perennial. Zones 5–10
Height: 1 ft. Spread: 8–12 in.
Orange-red flowers have long yellow hairs in the throat; blooms most heavily May–June, recurring through September. The evergreen cushion of very fine, bright green leaves contributes nicely to a mixed ground cover with fringed sage or cerastium. Also effective as rock garden accent, in perennial border, or as edging for beds and pathways. Attracts hummingbirds. *P. crandallii* is similar, with blue-purple flowers. Both species tolerate clay soils better than many penstemons.

How to Grow
See description of genus. Also, partial sun or shade. Don't add organic matter to the soil. Plant nursery stock anytime the soil can be worked. Deep-water every 2 weeks in summer. Remove old flower stems. New growth is susceptible to aphids.

smallii p. 235 *Pictured above*
Small's beardtongue
EW. Perennial. Zones 6–8
Height: 1–2½ ft. Spread: 1½ ft.
Particularly effective when allowed to seed itself down a dry bank; also works well in dry meadows (with sundrops) or in dry soils around tree roots. Dark green foliage is usually evergreen. Lavender flowers bloom for 3–6 weeks from late

spring through early summer. *P. canescens* is similar, with light lavender to near white flowers.

How to Grow
See description of genus. Also tolerates heat best in partial shade.

strictus *p. 236*
Rocky Mountain penstemon
WD WM. Evergreen perennial. Zones 5–10
Height: to 3 ft. Spread: 12–18 in.
An adaptable plant, it forms a low (3-in.) mat of foliage, from which arise tall stems capped with clusters of blue-purple flowers in May and June. Tolerates heavy soils and too much water better than most penstemons. Canyon beardtongue (*P. pseudospectabilis*) has large, crisp, evergreen leaves and rose-pink flowers April–June; a hummingbird magnet. Blue-mist penstemon (*P. virens*), a Western Mountain native, is smaller (6–10 in. high), with numerous spikes of bright blue, sometimes white or pink, flowers in late May and June.

How to Grow
See description of genus and *P. pinifolius*.

Phlox
Floks
Polemoniaceae. Phlox family

Description
Garden favorites for many years, all but 1 of the 60 or so species of phlox are North American natives. They range from low, creeping ground covers ideal for rock gardens to stately, 5-ft.-tall standards of the perennial border. Beloved for their clusters of simple, 5-lobed flowers (½–1½ in. wide) in a variety

of colors, phlox are in bloom for much of the season, beginning with the woodland species in early spring, continuing with long-blooming annual species and ending with the late summer displays of the tall border plants. Often seen in cottage gardens and other traditional settings, phlox also enhance natural landscapes, particularly woodlands.

There are many selections and hybrids to choose from, but all phlox are simple to grow. Their main problem is powdery mildew brought on by the heat and humidity of summer. Control by avoiding overhead watering, reducing crowding and increasing air circulation, avoiding drought stress, or applying preventive sprays. Many gardeners ignore all but the worst cases of mildew; although unsightly, it doesn't seriously harm the plant. Phlox interbreed easily; deadhead to prevent growth of seedlings that may be significantly different from the parent plants.

carolina p. 236   *Pictured on p. 395*
Thick-leaf phlox, Carolina phlox (a.k.a. *P. suffruticosa*)
EW. Perennial. Zones 3–9
Height: 1–4 ft. Spread: 1–2 ft.
Widespread in the East along moist shady roadbanks, thick-leaf phlox is a good plant for a sunny border or naturalizing in open woodlands or moist meadows. Flowers are lavender, pink, sometimes white, and lightly scented, blooming most heavily in late spring or early summer and continuing sporadically through late summer. Leaves are deep green and glossy. Resists mildew better than many phlox. 'Miss Lingard' has large heads of white flowers; spotted phlox (*P. maculata*) is similar to but usually taller than *P. carolina*.

How to Grow
Sun or partial shade. Prefers fertile, organic soil. Tolerates constant soil moisture and heat (better in shade). Sold in containers. Plant 1½–2 ft. apart. Increase by division in fall or spring.

divaricata p. 237
Wild sweet William, woodland phlox (a.k.a. *P. canadensis*)
EW. Perennial. Zones 3–9
Height: 8–12 in. Spread: 2 ft. or more
An ideal ground cover or fill-in plant for a shade garden, where the slightly fragrant pastel blue flowers wandering among foamflowers and bleeding hearts is the essence of spring. Foliage is medium to dark green. 'Alba' has fragrant white flowers; 'Dirgo Ice', light blue flowers. 'Fuller's White' is a smaller plant with profuse white flowers; *P. d.* var. *laphamii* has deep

blue to purple flowers; *P.* × *chattahoochee* has deep blue flowers with a red eye.

How to Grow
See *P. carolina.* Also partial sun or shade, not full sun; blooms well with morning sun. Spreads by rhizomes easily in moist, organic soils.

drummondi p. 237
Drummond's phlox
GP. Annual
Height: 4–20 in. Spread: 8 in.
A native of east-central Texas, this phlox is a good garden plant and quick cover for poor, bare soils. Clusters of small red, pink, or white flowers bloom from spring to frost if faded flowers are removed. (Plant dies after going to seed.) Cultivars offer many colors and heights. Another Plains species, alyssum-leaved phlox (*P. alyssifolia*) is a perennial mat-forming northern native adapted to harsh conditions.

How to Grow
Full sun. Tolerates poor or dry soils and heat. Sold as seeds and in containers. Sow seeds around last frost date; space container plants 6 in. apart. May persist by self-seeding, though not on fertile soils.

glaberrima p. 238
Smooth phlox
EW GP CP. Perennial. Zones 3–8
Height: 2½–5 ft. Spread: 2 ft.
Similar to *P. carolina* and *P. maculata,* equally useful for sunny borders or naturalizing at the edge of a woodland. Slightly fragrant flowers are reddish purple, pink, and sometimes white; blooms for 2–4 weeks in mid to late spring. Native to low meadows, woodland borders, and swamps.

How to Grow
See *P. carolina.*

paniculata p. 238
Summer phlox (a.k.a. *P. decussata*)
EW CP. Perennial. Zones 4–8
Height: 4–6 ft. Spread: 2–3 ft. or more
One of the best of the tall phlox, it is an essential member of a sunny or lightly shaded border and a welcome addition to a naturalized area. Large clusters of highly fragrant flowers vary in color; usually pink, lavender, or white, sometimes blue, red, or salmon. Blooms for 2–5 weeks in mid to late summer.

Attracts butterflies and hummingbirds. Plants spread to form large patches. Many cultivars, including 'Mt. Fuji', with large heads of pure white flowers; 'Bright Eyes', whose pale pink flowers have red eyes; 'Star Fire', with flowers of cherry-red; and 'Blue Boy', with pastel blue flowers.

How to Grow
See *P. carolina*. Also sold as seeds. Only moderately heat tolerant. Particularly susceptible to powdery mildew.

pilosa *p. 239* *Pictured above*
Prairie phlox, downy phlox
GP EW CP. Perennial. Zones 3–9
Height: 1–2 ft. Spread: 2 ft. or more
A cheerful addition to a sunny bank, border, or woodland edge. Clusters of bright pink flowers bloom for 3–6 weeks from midspring into midsummer and contrast nicely with the glossy, dark green foliage. Spreads by underground runners into loose clumps that combine well with sundrops or eared coreopsis. 'Eco Happy Traveler' has very bright flowers and is semi-evergreen in the South. Hairy phlox (*P. amoena*) is a low-growing plant similar to prairie phlox; moss phlox (*P. subulata*), with bright pink, purple, blue, or white flowers, provides a thick ground cover for dry sites.

How to Grow
See *P. carolina*. Also prefers fertile, organic soil with good drainage. Tolerates poor or dry soil and heat.

stolonifera *p. 239*
Creeping phlox
EW. Perennial. Zones 2–9
Height: 6–10 in. Spread: 1–2 ft. or more
Loose mats of medium-green foliage and clusters of large flow-

ers add a soft texture to a shade garden. Flowers, lavender, blue, or white with yellow centers, bloom in midspring for 2–4 weeks. Plants spread where space allows. 'Bruce's White', one of the very best cultivars, has bright white flowers; 'Blue Ridge', soft blue flowers; 'Pink Ridge', clear pink flowers. 'Millstream' has pink petals with red and white rings in the center.

How to Grow
Partial sun or shade. Tolerates heat if shaded. Sold as seeds and in containers. Increase by division in spring. Slugs can be troublesome in very moist soil.

Physostegia
Fi-so-stee'ji-a
Labiatae. Mint family

Description
A small group of North American perennials, only one of which (described below) is widely cultivated.

virginiana p. 240   *Pictured above*
Obedient plant, false dragonhead
EW CP. Perennial. Zones 2–9
Height: 3–4 ft. Spread: 3 ft.
If you're willing to tolerate or control its aggressively invasive growth, this is a fine addition to sunny beds or naturalized plantings in moist or wet soils. Spikes of pink to lavender snapdragon-like flowers rise above dense, glossy foliage for 3–6 weeks in late summer and fall. Flower spikes are floppy. 'Alba' has white flowers; 'Summer Snow' has white flowers and is less aggressive than the species; 'Variegata' has leaves edged in creamy white; 'Vivid' is a more compact plant.

How to Grow
Full sun. Prefers fertile, organic, acid soil. Tolerates constantly moist soil and heat. Sold as seeds and in containers. Sow seeds after last frost; space nursery stock 2–3 ft. apart. Increase by divisions anytime. Prune in early summer to reduce height and floppiness. Restrain spread by limiting water and nutrients and by pulling new plants that sprout from running underground stems.

Pinus
Py′nus
Pinaceae. Pine family

Description
Nearly all of the 90 or so species in this genus of outstanding evergreen trees are native to North America. All pines have long, needlelike leaves in bundles of 2–5; their habit and rate of growth vary considerably. Some provide high, open shade when mature. Others have sinuous, gnarled branches that give the landscape a "Japanese" look. Inexpensive nursery stock can be planted in quantity for erosion control, windbreaks, and screens.

   In general, pines prosper in poor soil, but they adapt to a wide variety of conditions as long as the site is well drained. Drying summer winds may turn the needles brown. Most pines develop deep roots, making them very drought tolerant but difficult to transplant once established. In addition to pruning, you can shape young pines by thinning and breaking off part of the expanding buds, called candles, in the spring. Selective pruning and candle pinching can create the look of a gnarled, wind-blown mountain specimen in a much younger tree.

aristata p. 129
Bristlecone pine
WM. Evergreen tree. Zone 4
Height: 20–25 ft. Spread: 12–15 ft.
An excellent tree for western landscapes, it is adaptable to high and low elevations and urban conditions. Slow growing, it becomes more picturesque with age. A native of exposed mountain sites and dry rocky soils, it survives where other plants fail. Bundles of 5 short, stout, dark green needles; cones 2–4 in. long.

How to Grow
Sun or partial shade. Tolerates dry soil and heat. Sold in containers and balled-and-burlapped. Plant in spring before bud break. Do not overwater.

edulis p. 130 Pictured on facing page
Pinyon pine
WM. Evergreen tree. Zone 5
Height: 12–15 ft. Spread: 10–12 ft.
A slow-growing, single- or multitrunk tree with a compact pyramidal to spreading form, rounded top, and, with age, twisted branches. Makes an excellent dense screen or picturesque specimen. Native to the rocky soils of foothills, mesas, and slopes, it needs very little water. Bundles of 2 short, stout, light green needles; short, oval cones. The seeds, well known as pinyon nuts, provide food for wildlife.

How to Grow
Full sun. Prefers dry soil; tolerates poor soil and heat. Sold in containers and balled-and-burlapped. Plant in spring before bud break. Pinch candles to maintain compact form. Susceptible to pitch mass borer if watered too much.

flexilis p. 130
Limber pine
WM. Evergreen tree. Zone 4
Height: 25–50 ft. Spread: 15–25 ft.
A slow-growing tree, its broad, pyramidal form becomes more open with maturity. Native to summits and rocky, exposed ridges, it withstands strong winds, hot sun, and dry, alkaline soil, making it an ideal substitute for eastern white pine in harsher areas. Excellent as a specimen, screen, or windbreak. Bundles of 5 rigid, bluish to dark green needles; resinous yellow-brown cone, 3–5 in. long. 'Pendula' is a weeping form.

How to Grow
Full sun. Well-drained or dry soil. Tolerates heat. Sold in containers and balled-and-burlapped. Plant in spring before bud break.

palustris p. 131
Longleaf pine (a.k.a. *P. australis*)
CP EW. Evergreen tree. Zones 7–9
Height: 80–100 ft. Spread: 30 ft.
The most distinctive of southern pines, longleaf pine is the characteristic tree of the Coastal Plain from southeastern Virginia to east Texas. The high, airy, fragrant canopy of a mature stand makes fine shade; individuals make striking specimens. Easily grown, they tolerate almost any conditions except the most swampy. They start slowly but grow rapidly after a few years. Bundles of 3 long (10–18-in.), dark green needles; cones, 6–10 in. long. Slash pine (*P. elliottii*) and spruce pine (*P. glabra*) are also noteworthy.

How to Grow
Full sun. Tolerates dry or poor soil and heat. Sold in containers and as bare-root seedlings. Space 10–12 ft. apart. Susceptible to pine beetles.

ponderosa p. 131
Ponderosa pine (a.k.a. *P. scopulorum*)
WM GP. Evergreen tree. Zone 4
Height: 60 ft. or more. Spread: 15–30 ft.
A large tree suitable for specimen or group planting. Pyramidal when young, it opens with age, revealing colorful, deeply furrowed bark. Native to sunny mountain slopes, high plateaus, and valleys. Bundles of 3 long, coarse yellow-green to dark green needles; cones, 2–3 in. long, are reddish to yellow-brown.

How to Grow
See *P. flexilis*.

pungens p. 132
Prickly pine, Table Mountain pine
EW. Evergreen tree. Zones 5–8
Height: 40–60 ft. Spread: 25–30 ft.
The bold branching pattern in mature specimens has the look of a huge bonsai, making this a distinctive specimen tree. Short (1–3-in.), dark green needles in bundles of 2–3. Large cones remain on the limbs for several years. Extremely drought tolerant once established. Pitch pine (*P. rigida*) is similar and striking.

How to Grow
See *P. palustris*. Sold in containers and balled-and-burlapped.
Space 25 ft. or more apart.

strobus p. 132   *Pictured above*
Eastern white pine
EW. Evergreen tree. Zones 3–8
Height: 80 ft. or more. Spread: 20–40 ft.
The pine used most widely for ornamental purposes. Its soft
texture, attractive form, and fast rate of growth make it ideal
as a specimen, screen, in groups, or naturalized. The dense,
low foliage is a superb winter habitat for birds. Can be sheared
to form tall hedges. The branches form conspicuous whorls
around the trunk, one whorl per year. Bundles of 5 soft, bluish
green needles; pendant cones, 6–8 in. long. The many cultivars
include 'Compacta', a smaller, compact form; 'Fastigata', a
pyramidal form; 'Pendula', a weeping form. Western white
pine (*P. monticola*) is similar.

How to Grow
Sun or partial shade. Prefers fertile, organic soil. Tolerates
moist soil if well drained. Sold in containers and as seedlings. Provide even moisture until well established; water during
dry spells to maintain. Doesn't tolerate polluted environments. Susceptible to white pine blister rust and white pine
weevil.

taeda p. 133
Loblolly pine
CP EW. Evergreen tree. Zones 7–9
Height: 90–100 ft. Spread: 30–40 ft.
Conical when young, this is a fast-growing tree, useful for
shade or screening. Its top rounds and its lower branches drop
off with age. Reddish brown bark fissures handsomely into

heavy, scaly plates. With great endurance of poor soils and exposed sites, it is valuable for planting around homes on badly eroded sites. Bundles of 3 long (6–9-in.), bright green needles; cones, 4–5 in. long, prickly. Shortleaf pine (*P. echinata*) is a large tree with a more northerly range, to zone 6. Virginia pine (*P. virginiana*) maintains its lower branches, making it an excellent long-term screening tree.

How to Grow
Full sun. Tolerates moist or dry soil and heat. Sold in containers or as bare-root seedlings. Susceptible to borers and pine beetles.

Pityopsis
Pit-i-op′sis
Compositae. Daisy family

Description
A small genus of perennials grown in borders, rock gardens, or naturalized in meadows for their bright autumn flowers. (Species are sometimes included in the genera *Chrysopsis* or *Heterotheca*.)

graminifolia
Golden aster
CP EW. Perennial. Zones 6–9
Height: 2 ft. Spread: 6 in.
A drought-tolerant plant valuable for naturalizing on poor, dry sites. Its linear gray leaves are covered with silky hairs. Bright golden yellow daisies, about 1 in. across, bloom from August to October. They spread by stolons to form a patch.

How to Grow
Sun or partial shade. Tolerates poor or dry soils. Sold in containers. Space plants 18 in. apart. Remove dead stems for winter cleanup.

Populus
Pop′you-lus
Salicaceae. Willow family

Description
Widely distributed in the Northern Hemisphere, these deciduous trees are adaptable and fast growing.

tremuloides p. 133 *Pictured above*
Quaking aspen
WM. Deciduous tree. Zone 2
Height: 20–30 ft. Spread: 8 ft.
A lively, striking, small tree, quaking aspen takes its name from the shimmery flutter of its two-tone leaves (bright green above, lighter beneath) in the breeze. It makes a beautiful specimen for small properties. In groups, it captures the feel of its mountain habitat. Pendulous reddish catkins appear in early spring before the leaves. In fall the leaves turn golden yellow, sometimes red. (In warmer climates at lower elevations, fall color is often disappointing.)

How to Grow
Sun or partial shade. Needs moist soil. Sold in containers and bare root. Doesn't do well in heat; plant in cool spots — the shady side of a building or beneath larger trees. Susceptible to cankers, galls, leaf spot, and scale.

Prosopis
Proh-soh′pis
Leguminosae. Pea family

Description
A group of tough desert natives, these trees and shrubs have picturesque gnarled branches and fine-textured leaves, deciduous or evergreen. Deep roots make them very drought tolerant, allow planting near walls and paved areas without structural damage.

glandulosa p. 134 *Pictured on p. 406*
Honey mesquite
WD. Deciduous tree or shrub. Zones 6–10
Height: to 30 ft. Spread: to 20 ft.

Its long, very fine, bright green compound leaves and asymmetrical, spreading form, single or multitrunked, make it a handsome specimen. Groups form thickets, making good barriers and wildlife habitat. In spring and early summer, small, narrow, frilly clusters of yellow, sweet-smelling flowers appear, followed in late summer by long (8-in.) straw-colored pods, sometimes flecked with red. Species varies greatly from area to area. Found in wild to 4,500-ft. elevation.

How to Grow
Full sun. Does well in poor, dry soil and heat. Sold in containers and balled-and-burlapped. Plant during warm weather; space 10 ft. apart for grove or barrier. Deep roots make transplanting established plants difficult. Thin and shape to create tree form. Water deeply and infrequently. Susceptible to borers and tip-girdler beetles.

pubescens p. 134
Screwbean mesquite, tornillo
WD. Deciduous tree or shrub. Zones 6–10
Height: to 20 ft. Spread: 15 ft.
Stiff, vaselike, multitrunked plant has very fine, dull, gray-green foliage. Narrow clusters of pale yellow flowers bloom in spring and summer. Tightly coiled tan seedpods, bunched in clusters, serve as accents in dried arrangements. Good as barrier, screen, or wildlife habitat. Natural habitat is along streams and bottomlands, where it benefits from periodic flooding.

How to Grow
Sun or partial shade. Tolerates dry or poor soil and heat. Plant during warm weather; space 6 ft. apart for barrier or grove. Deep-water monthly during rainless periods. Thin and shape for tree form; tip-prune to increase density.

Pseudotsuga
Sue-do-sue′ga
Pinaceae. Pine family

Description
A small group of pyramidal evergreen trees. Given room to grow, they make stately specimens. Their dense foliage and branching make them excellent windbreaks and wildlife habitat when planted in groups. Leaves are soft, flat, and needle-like.

menziesii p. 135
Douglas fir
WM. Evergreen tree. Zone 4
Height: 50–80 ft. Spread: 30 ft.
The most prominent tree in the Pacific Northwest, it makes a magnificent specimen in a large, formal landscape. Young plants are well known as Christmas trees. Topped and trimmed when young, Douglas fir can make an effective tall hedge. It adapts to a wide range of conditions and survives drought. *P. m. glauca* has blue foliage and is hardier to winter cold; *P. m. fastigiata* is slower growing, with ascending branches; *P. m. pendula* has pendulous branches.

How to Grow
Sun (survives in shade, but growth is straggly). Tolerates most soils except those that are swampy or poorly drained. Easy to transplant or start from seed. Sow in fall; protect from wildlife. To establish, keep soil moist and cool.

Quercus
Kwer′kus
Fagaceae. Beech family

Description
Evergreen or deciduous, solemn tree or gnarled shrub, oaks help define the character of practically every North American region. For gardeners, oaks are supreme specimen and shade trees, revered for their handsome leaves and stately habit. They are also effective in mass plantings, screens and hedges, and naturalized landscapes. Oak flowers and fruit (acorns) are ornamentally insignificant but provide fodder for wildlife. Deciduous leaves may be colorful in autumn; they often cling to branches through the winter.

The great many oaks in the residential landscape attest to their adaptability to cultivation. But they are often slow growing, and they can be difficult to transplant and sensitive to soil pH. Construction damage and lawn fertilizers high in soluble salts pose problems in urban areas. Choose species suitable for your conditions.

agrifolia p. 135   *Pictured above*
Coast live oak
CA. Evergreen tree. Zone 9
Height: 20–50 ft. Spread: 20–50 ft.
The emblematic tree of coastal southern and central California, it provides welcome shade in hot valleys, and its broad canopy shelters plantings of low-water-use perennials and shrubs. Can be sheared to make a tall hedge. Thick, slightly glossy, gray-green leaves are rounded, 1–3 in. long. Old trees can reach 100 ft. high and wide and are to be treasured. Plant new trees where summer irrigation can be restricted; the deadly oak root fungus (*Armillaria*) is encouraged by a wet trunk and root crown. Engelmann oak (*Q. engelmannii*) is similar, with blackish, sinuous branches.

How to Grow
Sun or partial shade. Needs dry soil. Tolerates poor soil and heat. Sold in containers. Plant in fall. Prune in summer to remove deadwood and to shape.

alba p. 136   *Pictured on facing page*
White oak
EW GP CP. Deciduous tree. Zones 3–9
Height: 50–100 ft. Spread: 1½ times height
Native to moist woodlands throughout the East, this is one of the most beautiful oaks. Its broad, open-domed canopy

provides shade for plants and people, food and shelter for many forms of wildlife. Leaves are large, medium green, with rounded, deep lobes. Male catkins are noticeable in spring. Swamp white oak, *Q. bicolor,* has shallowly scalloped leaves and is native to moist and wet soils (zones 3–8).

How to Grow
Sun or partial shade. Adaptable, but best in deep, moist soils with adequate drainage. Does not transplant well once established. Avoid compacting the soil and mulch generously with organic matter over root zone.

gambelli
Gambel oak, scrub oak
WM. Deciduous tree or shrub. Zone 4
Height: 30 ft. Spread: 8–15 ft.
A hardy tree or shrub with low water needs, it is an excellent specimen for a small property or, when grouped, a good screen. The deeply lobed leaves are bright green above, paler below, turning brown or sometimes red in fall. Native to dry hills, slopes, and canyons in Colorado, Arizona, and New Mexico.

How to Grow
Full sun. Tolerates dry soil and heat. Sold in containers and balled-and-burlapped. Space 6–8 ft. apart for screen. Train as tree by pruning off suckers when young.

lobata p. 136
Valley oak
CA. Deciduous tree. Zone 9
Height: to 70 ft. or more. Spread: to 70 ft. or more
A highly picturesque native of California's Central Valley, it

has a massive trunk, broad crown, and weeping branches. Leaves, with 7–11 rounded lobes, are deep green above, paler below. Grows fastest where roots can tap groundwater; less drought tolerant than *Q. agrifolia*.

How to Grow
Full sun. Tolerates dry soil and heat. Sold in containers. Plant in fall or spring.

macrocarpa p. 137
Bur oak
GP EW. Deciduous tree. Zones 3–8
Height: 70–80 ft. Spread: 60 ft. or more
Plant this slow-growing tree as a gift to the future. Even when small, the deeply furrowed bark and irregular form add to the landscape. Large leaves, 6 in. long, turn beige to dark brown in fall; small, light green flowers in spring, large acorns in autumn. Provides food and shelter for wildlife. Native to prairie, savanna, and dry forests.

How to Grow
Full sun. Tolerates poor or dry soil and heat. Sold in containers, bare root, balled-and-burlapped. Drip irrigation during first growing season is beneficial. Highly resistant to oak wilt. Partial defoliation by insects is rare but fatal.

palustris p. 137
Pin oak
EW. Deciduous tree. Zones 4–9
Height: 50–100 ft. Spread: 25–40 ft.
A popular, fairly fast growing selection, pin oaks have an erect, pyramidal shape with gracefully drooping lower branches. Medium to large leaves with deep, pointed lobes are medium green, turning copper to deep red in fall.

How to Grow
Full sun. Prefers acid soil. Very tolerant of wet, clayey soils and heat. Sold in containers and balled-and-burlapped. Space 25–35 ft. apart. Susceptible to chlorosis; acidify soil or provide iron supplement.

rubra p. 138
Northern red oak (a.k.a. *Q. borealis*)
EW CP. Deciduous tree. Zones 4–8
Height: 50–90 ft. Spread: 40–50 ft.
Faster growing than most oaks, red oaks are widely used as shade and street trees. Large leaves with deep, pointed lobes are glossy green in summer and bright red in fall. Black oak,

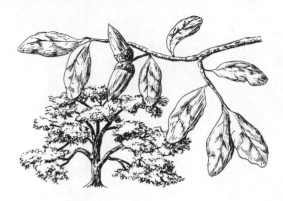

Q. velutina, is common on upland dry soils and clay slopes, has little color in fall.

How to Grow
Full sun. An adaptable tree, native to soils ranging from rich and moist to gravelly or clay. Prefers adequate drainage and acid conditions. Tolerates heat. Sold in containers and balled-and-burlapped.

virginiana *p. 138   Pictured above*
Live oak
CP. Evergreen tree. Zones 8–9
Height: to 60 ft. or more. Spread: to 120 ft. or more
One of the most picturesque trees, it dominates the maritime forests from North Carolina south. Typically, a short, massive trunk supports large, twisted branches that spread to form a low, rounded crown. Small leaves, dark green and shiny above, paler below, are not lobed.

How to Grow
Full sun. Tolerates poor soil and heat. Sold in containers. Very slow growing, it won't outgrow a 25-ft. spacing for decades.

Ratibida
Ra-tib′i-da
Compositae. Daisy family

Description
Members of this small group (5 or 6 species) of prairie wild-flowers enliven meadow plantings and borders with showy, long-blooming daisylike flowers with prominent central cones.

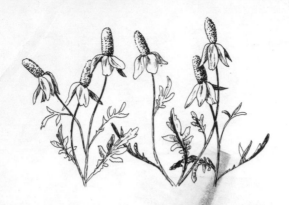

columnifera p. 240   *Pictured above*
Coneflower, Mexican hat (a.k.a. *R. columnaris*)
WD GP CP. Perennial. Zones 4–10
Height: 12–18 in. Spread: 12–18 in.
A good meadow plant, it has fine medium-green leaves that blend inconspicuously with neighboring grasses. When in bloom, May–September, it's an eye-catcher. The blossoms are elongated, the ray flowers (yellow, mahogany-red, and yellow-red bicolor) drooping from the base of a columnar cluster (¾–1 in. long) of rust-colored disk flowers (the cone).

How to Grow
Full sun. Tolerates poor or dry soil and heat. (It is relatively short lived in amended garden soil but reseeds well.) Sold as seeds and in containers. Sow seeds in April; plant nursery stock 12–18 in. apart anytime soil is workable. Can be mowed 4–6 in. high for fall cleanup. Roots will rot if soil stays too wet.

pinnata p. 241
Prairie coneflower
EW CP GP. Perennial. Zones 6–8
Height: 3–5 ft. Spread: 2–2½ ft.
One of the most striking wildflowers, it has a purple central disk shorter than that of *R. columnifera*, drooping ray flowers longer (to 2 in.). Blooms profusely in midsummer.

How to Grow
Full sun. Does well in medium to dry soils, especially well in clays. Tolerates alkaline soil and heat. Sold as seeds and in containers. Space plants 4 ft. apart.

Rhododendron
Roh-doh-den'dron
Ericaceae. Heath family

Description
Rhododendrons are among the most beautiful shrubs, offering attractive deciduous or evergreen foliage and spectacular spring or summer flowers. Produced in a wide range of colors, the flowers are often gathered in rounded clusters, called trusses, containing as many as 15 trumpet-shaped blossoms, each 1–6 in. wide.

The genus is vast (some estimate 1,200 species) and the number of cultivars overwhelming: there are 10,000 registered named varieties, many of which are currently available. The genus includes shrublets a few inches high and 100-ft. trees, but many cultivated rhododendrons are between 3 and 15 ft. tall. They are equally effective as specimen plants or grouped in shrub borders, screens, or around foundations. The plants described below introduce you to the many fine North American natives.

Although gardeners often consider azaleas a separate group of plants, botanists include them with rhododendrons. As a rough rule of thumb, azaleas are usually deciduous, with funnel-shaped flowers; rhododendrons are usually evergreen, with bell-shaped flowers.

Rhododendrons need acid soil that drains well but doesn't dry out. Richly organic soil, mulched to conserve water, fills this seemingly contradictory requirement. If your soil is alkaline or poorly drained, grow rhododendrons in mounds or raised beds, 1–2 ft. deep, adding about half peat moss and a quarter sand to the soil. Place the top of the root ball slightly above the soil line when you plant.

In general, rhododendrons do best when lightly shaded. In full sun, they risk bleached or burned leaves; in heavy shade, plants can be lanky and bloom poorly. Wind may burn leaves, particularly winter winds on evergreen leaves; plant in sheltered locations or wrap the plants with burlap over the winter.

If necessary, feed with acid fertilizers (following the manufacturer's directions). Tip-prune evergreen species or young plants after bloom to produce bushy growth or maintain compact form. Remove faded flowers, taking care not to damage the new buds that form just beneath the old. Rhododendrons are generally free of serious pests and diseases; check with a reputable nursery about the ones you choose.

austrinum p. 172   *Pictured on p. 414*
Yellow wild azalea, Florida azalea
CP. Deciduous shrub. Zones 7–9
Height: 12 ft. Spread: 5–6 ft.

Native to woodlands of the Deep South, it has small, light green leaves and abundant clusters of fragrant flowers that appear in spring before the leaves or as the leaves develop. Flowers are clear yellow to golden, sometimes with pink to strawberry tubes. One of the easiest native azaleas to grow.

How to Grow
See description of genus. Also tolerates heat. Space 8–10 ft. apart.

canescens p. 172
Wild azalea, wild honeysuckle, Piedmont azalea
CP EW. Deciduous shrub. Zones 7–8
Height: 10–15 ft. Spread: 4–5 ft.
Native from North Carolina to Florida and Texas, it is found in diverse habitats that include streamsides, moist woods, and dry ridges. Small, light green leaves. Abundant flowers from March to early April are fragrant and pure white to light or deep pink. Hybridizes naturally with a number of species, producing numerous color variations.

How to Grow
See description of genus. Also tolerates heat. Space 8–10 ft. apart.

maximum p. 173   Pictured on p. 415
Rosebay rhododendron
EW. Evergreen shrub. Zones 4–8
Height: 8–15 ft. or more. Spread: 10–20 ft.
One of the largest and hardiest of the evergreen species, it creates a cool mood in a shady garden and brings color to the winter landscape. Medium to deep green leaves are oblong (4–8 in. long) and whitish green underneath. Clusters may contain as many as 30 flowers, each 1–2 in. across and rose-

pink (can vary from white to pinkish lavender), the throat spotted with green or orange. Blooms from late spring to early summer for 1–3 weeks. *R. m.* forma *album* has white flowers; *R. m.* forma *purpureum* has dark pink to purple flowers.

How to Grow
See description of genus. Space 10 ft. or more apart.

periclymenoides p. 173
Pinxterbloom azalea (a.k.a. *R. nudiflorum*)
EW CP. Deciduous shrub. Zones 3–9
Height: 4–10 ft. Spread: 10 ft. or more
A hardy, luxuriously fragrant azalea, it spreads by stolons to gradually colonize an area, making it well suited for naturalized plantings. Adapted to drier sites than many azaleas, it is quite drought tolerant once established. Clusters of up to a dozen flowers, each 1½ in. across. The fragrant blossoms, off-white to pink or violet, bloom in midspring for 1–3 weeks.

How to Grow
See description of genus. Also tolerates drier soil and heat.

prunifolium p. 174
Plumleaf azalea
EW CP. Deciduous shrub. Zones 7–9
Height: 15–20 ft. Spread: 15–20 ft.
The most distinctive of the southern deciduous azaleas, plumleaf azalea adds color to a shade garden in July and August. The orange to deep red flowers contrast vividly with the dark green foliage. They require more shade than do some azaleas, particularly during the hottest part of the day. *R. calendulaceum,* with red, orange, and bright gold flowers, was once called "the most gay and brilliant shrub yet known."

How to Grow
See description of genus.

viscosum p. 174
Swamp azalea
EW CP. Deciduous shrub. Zones 3–9
Height: 3–15 ft. Spread: 5–8 ft.
One of the hardiest deciduous natives, its rich fragrance, later
bloom time, and low stature add diversity to a mixed planting
of azaleas. Fragrant white, sometimes pink, flowers, in clusters
of 4–9, bloom for 1–3 weeks from late spring to midsummer.
Spreads by stolons. *R. v.* var. *rhodanthum* has bright pink
flowers.

How to Grow
See description of genus.

Rhus
Rus. Sumac
Anacardiaceae. Cashew family

Description
A large genus of shrubs, trees, and vines with members found
throughout North America, sumacs are both sought after and
assiduously avoided by gardeners. Cultivated varieties offer
year-round interest: the foliage is rich green in summer and
very colorful in fall. Some species offer large, brightly colored
seed heads that last many months and attract wildlife. In winter, the distinctive, leafless stems of the taller species catch the
eye. Sumacs can be used as specimens, in massed plantings,
as ground covers, screens, in large borders, and in naturalized
settings.
   Very easy to grow, sumacs often thrive in poor, dry soils.

But they can be highly invasive and some — poison oak (*Rhus diversiloba*), poison ivy (*R. radicans*), and poison sumac (*R. vernix*) — are highly irritating to the skin.

aromatica p. 175
Aromatic sumac
GP CP EW. Deciduous shrub. Zones 3–7
Height: 4–6 ft. Spread: 6–10 ft.
A good candidate for a screen or windbreak, especially in poor, dry soils where few other shrubs prosper. Yellowish flowers are insignificant. Leaflets, 1½–3 in. long, are aromatic when crushed, turn red in fall. Spreads rapidly in fertile soils. 'Low Grow' reaches 2½ ft. high, has glossy leaves.

How to Grow
Sun or partial shade. Tolerates dry or poor soil and heat. Sold as seeds, in containers, bare root, and balled-and-burlapped. Plant 6–8 ft. apart.

copallina p. 175   *Pictured on facing page*
Dwarf, shining, or winged sumac
EW CP. Deciduous shrub. Zones 4–9
Height: 10–30 ft. Spread: 20–30 ft.
Given room, winged sumac spreads to form beautiful dome-shaped colonies. But it can be easily pruned to suit a smaller area. Leaves are bright red, yellow, or orange in fall. In fall and winter, the dense clusters of tiny bright red seeds stand out; steeped in boiling water, they make a tart, pink "lemonade." Similar but taller species are smooth sumac (*R. glabra*) and staghorn sumac (*R. typhina*). Several attractive forms are available.

How to Grow
Full sun. Easily established in all but wet or poorly drained soils. Tolerates heat. Sold as seeds, in containers, and balled-and-burlapped. Space 10 ft. or more apart to allow for spread. Contain by mowing or cutting new suckers to the ground. Established plants can be cut to the ground in winter for attractive spring growth.

microphylla p. 176
Littleleaf sumac, lemita
WD. Deciduous shrub. Zones 6–10
Height: 6–12 ft. Spread: 8–14 ft.
Dense, mounded network of branches makes an excellent screen or informal hedge. In summer, the tiny compound leaves are green with a plum cast, turning deep burgundy-red in fall.

In August and September, plants carry a profuse crop of tiny orange-red berries, used to make a lemony, tart drink.

How to Grow
Full sun. Prefers poor, dry soil; tolerates heat. Sold as seeds and in containers. Space 6–8 ft. apart for screen; 15–20 ft. apart to show off mounding form. Water deeply and infrequently. Large specimens can be pruned to multitrunked tree form.

trilobata *Pictured above*
Threeleaf sumac, squawbush, skunkbush
WD WM GP. Deciduous shrub. Zones 4–10
Height: 4–12 ft. Spread: 4–12 ft.
Excellent for hedges, backdrops, wildlife thickets. Naturalized, it gives a pleasing, soft, mounding roll to the landscape. Small, crisp, clean, dark green compound leaves turn red, yellow, and orange in fall. Clusters of tiny red berries June–July. Bare winter stems are clean and smooth, with a reddish cast. Whole plant is aromatic — unpleasantly so to some people. Combines well in mass plantings with chamisa and/or Apache plume. 'Autumn Amber', to 18 in. high, spreading to 8 ft., is a good ground cover.

How to Grow
Sun or partial shade. Tolerates constantly moist or dry conditions; tolerates poor soil and heat. Space 4–6 ft. for dense thicket. Withstands severe pruning, but selecting uniform plants for a hedge can eliminate the need to do so.

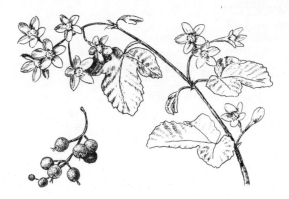

Ribes
Rye'bees
Grossulariaceae. Gooseberry family

Description
Some members of this largish genus (150 species) of shrubs are grown for their edible fruit (currants and gooseberries). Others are valued in the landscape for their flowers and foliage. They are especially valuable in woodland gardens as specimens, in groups, or as ground covers. Several are handsome enough to include in more formal gardens. Many species are early to leaf out, and their delicate new leaves add welcome color to the remnants of the winter. Butterflies and birds are also attracted to the flowers and fruit. Some species are hosts for white pine blister rust, a destructive fungus affecting certain pines, and in some areas their cultivation is discouraged. Check with your nursery before purchasing.

cereum
Wax currant, squaw currant
WM. Deciduous shrub. Zone 4
Height: 3–5 ft. Spread: 3–5 ft.
A compact, mounded shrub with smooth, cherrylike bark and tidy foliage, it makes a good transition from larger background plants to a meadow or grassy area. Clusters of light pink flowers bloom from spring to early summer. Leaves are light green, turning yellow in fall. The bright red, fuzzy currants, borne in summer, are not tasty.

How to Grow
Sun or partial shade. Native to dry slopes and ridges, it tolerates dry soil and some heat. Sold as seeds and in containers. Plant in spring or summer, space 3–5 ft. apart. Thin too-vigorous shoots if necessary.

odoratum p. 176
Buffalo currant
GP. Deciduous shrub. Zones 4–6
Height: 3–6 ft. Spread: 4 ft.
A low-growing, thicket-forming shrub, it is valuable in windbreak plantings. Lovely racemes of golden yellow, clove-scented flowers appear in May, followed in July by edible gooseberry-like fruit. Smallish leaves are deeply lobed and pale green. Golden currant (*R. aureum*), a related Western Mountain species, is similar but taller.

How to Grow
Full sun. Tolerates dry or poor soil and heat. Sold in containers and bare root. Plant spring or fall, 3–4 ft. apart. Increase by division in spring.

sanguineum p. 177   *Pictured on p. 419*
Flowering currant
CA WM. Deciduous shrub. Zone 6
Height: to 12 ft. Spread: to 15 ft.
Long a popular shrub in England, flowering currant is especially desirable for its very early bloom (January–March). Short, erect racemes contain 10–20 small tubular flowers in deep pink to deep red. Small blue-black berries with a whitish bloom appear in summer. 'Elk River Red' and 'King Edward VII' are well suited to cool, wet climates. 'Mesa Red' does well in southern California. *R. s.* var. *glutinosum* is more drought tolerant and has longer, drooping clusters of pink flowers; its cultivar 'Spring Showers' flowers profusely.

How to Grow
Sun or shade. Native to moist shady spots in a coniferous forest, it tolerates constant moisture and some heat (check specific cultivars). Sold in containers. Plant in fall. Increase by layering branches. Prune when dormant to shape or control size.

speciosum p. 177
Fuchsia-flowered gooseberry
CA. Deciduous shrub. Zone 7
Height: to 10 ft. Spread: to 15 ft.
A lively ornament for a winter garden, when its bristly branches are thickly hung with small crimson flowers. Excellent for planting in the dry shade of native oaks. The flowers (December–May) are an important nectar source for Anna's hummingbirds. Small bristly berries in spring are more or less inedible. Canyon gooseberry (*R. californicum*) has white petals, reddish brown sepals, and very attractive arching branches.

How to Grow

Partial sun or shade. Tolerates dry or poor soil and heat. Sold in containers. Plant in fall. Increase by layering branches. Remove old, straggly canes during dormancy in late summer to fall to encourage new growth.

Romneya
Rom'ni-a
Papaveraceae. Poppy family

Description

The single species in this genus is described below.

coulteri p. 241   *Pictured above*
Matilija poppy
CA. Perennial. Zones 8–10
Height: 8 ft. Spread: to 8 ft. (wider over time)
One of California's most famous wildflowers. From May through July, the tall stems are tipped with 5–8 poppylike flowers, each up to 9 in. wide, with crinkled or pleated petals surrounding a large ball of golden stamens. (Good for cutting; flowers cut in bud will open.) The huge, slightly fragrant flowers are welcome in formal gardens, but the plant's habit of spreading widely by deep, lateral roots makes it more suitable for naturalizing on dry flats and slopes. *R. c.* var. *trichocalyx* is similar to the species; 'White Cloud' has petals that are pleated lengthwise.

How to Grow

Full sun. Tolerates dry or poor soil and heat. Sold in containers. Plant in fall; one plant spreads widely. Increase by cuttings of root stocks in fall or winter; seedlings take several years to flower. Cut back to within a few inches of the ground in fall.

Rosa
Roh'za
Rosaceae. Rose family

Description
Few plants are more popular than the rose. Intensively bred, roses are best known in their hybrid forms — lush, many-petaled flowers in a rainbow of colors (save, as yet, blue) and a wide range of sizes.

Given the overwhelming choice among hybrid roses (there are at least 20,000 cultivars), it isn't surprising that wild or species roses, whose flowers appear plain by comparison, have been frequently overlooked. But the charm and grace of their simple, five-petaled flowers and their much less demanding cultural requirements have recently brought them into favor. Like their showy offspring, species roses can be used in traditional plantings, but they also make excellent hedges, screens, living fences, and wildlife habitat in naturalized settings.

To grow species roses, it's helpful to think of them as native shrubs rather than roses; they have far fewer cultural requirements and problems than temperamental hybrids. Choose species from or adapted to your area, give them the same sort of conditions and care you provide your other native shrubs, and they'll most likely thrive.

arkansana p. 178
Prairie rose
GP EW. Deciduous shrub. Zone 3
Height: 12–18 in. Spread: spreads freely

The clear pink, aromatic flowers of this diminutive native of the dry prairies are pretty running through a natural planting, shrubby border, or mixed windbreak. Leaves are compound with small, dark green leaflets. Flowers, 1–2 in. across, bloom in late spring. The crimson rose hips provide food for many species of birds. *R. blanda* is similar and almost thornless.

How to Grow
Full sun. Does well in poor or dry soil and heat. Sold in containers and bare root. Space 4–6 ft. apart. Increase by dividing suckers in spring. Blooms on new growth.

palustris p. 178
Swamp rose
CP EW. Deciduous shrub. Zones 5–9
Height: 5–8 ft. Spread: 3 ft.
Native to swamps and low ground, often in standing water, swamp rose is a great plant for the edge of a pond or a garden with drainage problems. Compound leaves are dull green and smooth above, pale and downy beneath. Fragrant pink flowers, 2 in. across, bloom in May and June, followed from July through October by red hips.

How to Grow
Sun or very light shade. Needs constantly moist soil. Sold in containers. Space 4–5 ft. apart for mass plantings. Prune occasionally to maintain shape.

woodsii p. 179 *Pictured above*
Wood's rose
WM. Deciduous shrub. Zone 4
Height: 3–5 ft. Spread: 2–3 ft.
A versatile rose, it is effective in a formal border, a shrub border, as a screen, hedge, or barrier, or as a ground cover for a bank or hillside. Compound leaves are dull to bright green, turning red to maroon in fall. Groups of 3–4 fragrant pink to deep rose flowers, about 2 in. across, bloom in spring, then sporadically through the summer. Large red hips used for tea, jelly, and candy. Another western native, *R. pisocarpa*, has smaller pink flowers.

How to Grow
Sun or partial shade. Native to streamside and damp mountain sites, it grows in ordinary soil and moisture and tolerates heat. Sold in containers and bare root. Space 3–5 ft. apart. Increase by transplanting suckers. Remove weak, damaged, or diseased canes in midspring. Susceptible to spider mites in arid climates.

setigera
Prairie rose, climbing rose
GP EW. Deciduous shrub. Zones 5–8
Height: 6–18 ft. (individual canes). Spread: 8–10 ft.
An ideal plant for the forest edge, where its long canes can clamber freely over trees and shrubs. Also good for fence rows. Clusters of 2-in., clear pink flowers are not fragrant; blooms from May (in the South) to July (in the North). Compound leaves are medium green.

How to Grow
Sun or partial shade. Tolerates heat. Sold bare root and balled-and-burlapped. Space 6 ft. or more apart. Increases easily by tip rooting or layering in spring. Prune to contain growth. Blooms on second year's growth.

Rudbeckia
Rud-bek′i-a
Compositae. Daisy family

Description
This small genus of North American annuals, perennials, and biennials is familiar to many as black-eyed Susans. Grown as specimens, in beds and borders, massed, and naturalized in meadows, rudbeckias provide cheerful yellow flowers in summer and autumn. They can be grown easily on almost any site.

fulgida p. 242   *Pictured above*
Black-eyed Susan, orange coneflower
EW CP. Perennial. Zones 6–9
Height: 24–30 in. Spread: 24 in.
The species is highly variable. The most widely grown cultivar is 'Goldsturm', which produces bushy, compact plants, large

dark green leaves, and large, dark yellow blossoms with a blackish central cone.

How to Grow
Full sun. Sold in containers. Plant in spring or fall, 24–30 in. apart. Increase by division or by seeds. (*R. fulgida* is apomictic — it produces asexual seed — and its cultivars, including 'Goldsturm', will come true from seed.)

hirta p. 242
Black-eyed Susan
EW WM GP CP. Annual, biennial, or short-lived perennial. Zones 3–9
Height: 12–20 in. Spread: 6 in.
A plant for those who like spontaneity, it self-sows readily and seems to skip merrily about a planting. (Mostly behaves as a biennial.) Rosettes of bristly green leaves carry the characteristic yellow daisies from June until hard frost. *R. laciniata* is a perennial of moist, shaded habitats. Sweet black-eyed Susan, *R. subtomentosa,* is a perennial of moist areas of the tallgrass prairie.

How to Grow
Full sun. Tolerates poor or dry soil and heat. Sold as seeds, in containers, and bare root. Extremely easy to grow from seed.

Salvia
Sal'vi-a
Labiatae. Mint family

Description
This huge (900 species) and varied group of fragrant herbs and shrubs has long been grown for medicinal, culinary, and ornamental purposes. Offering brightly colored flowers and

attractive, sometimes evergreen, foliage, salvias include one of the most familiar bedding plants (the Brazilian native *S. splendens*). North American natives match imported plants and hybrids for attractiveness; they are also drought tolerant and are often better adapted to harsh conditions. They're suited to a broad range of landscape uses: all work well in beds and borders; some are colorful ground covers; others enhance meadow plantings. Most produce abundant nectar, attracting insects and hummingbirds.

azurea p. 243
Pitcher sage
WD GP CP EW. Perennial. Zones 5–10
Height: 3–5 ft. Spread: 1–3 ft.
Produces wonderful arching fountains of clear blue flowers in August and September (into October in the Great Plains). Bees and butterflies love it. A native of open grasslands and woodlands, it is a good meadow plant; it competes well with grasses, and its coarse, grayish green foliage is inconspicuous and can be mowed periodically.

How to Grow
Sun or partial shade. Prefers poor, dry soil; tolerates heavy, moist soils better than most salvias. Tolerates heat. Sold as seeds and in containers. Sow seeds in March and April (1 oz./500 sq. ft.) for meadows. Space plants 2–4 ft. apart; plant anytime soil is workable. Pinch growing tips once or twice before August for a shorter, more floriferous plant.

chamaedryoides
Mexican blue sage, germander sage
WD. Perennial subshrub. Zones 8–10
Height: 8–18 in. Spread: 8–18 in.
A welcome addition to borders or as accents in dry-desert gardens, along streambeds, in rock gardens. Short spikes of blue-violet, sweetly aromatic flowers stand above mounds of tiny, delicate, silver leaves in summer and fall.

How to Grow
Full sun or shade. Prefers poor or dry soil. Tolerates heat. Sold as seeds and in containers. Sow seeds on warm soil in spring. Space plants 1–2 ft. apart. Shear off spent flowers periodically. Susceptible to root rot when too wet, especially in heavy soils.

clevelandii p. 179 *Pictured on p. 425*
Cleveland sage
CA. Evergreen shrub. Zone 10
Height: 4 ft. Spread: 6 ft.

The heavy bloom of violet-blue flowers in late spring and early summer complements pink rockroses and white Matilija poppies on dry, sunny hillsides. Bloom continues through August. Very fragrant wrinkled gray leaves can be used in cooking in place of the European garden sage (*S. officinalis*).

How to Grow

Full sun. Tolerates poor or dry soil and heat. Sold in containers. Plant in fall, 4 ft. apart for mass plantings. Prune off old flower stalks. Avoid overwatering in summer.

coccinea p. 243
Scarlet sage
EW CP. Annual/perennial. Zones 8–10
Height: 3 ft. Spread: 2–3 ft.
Most often grown as an annual, scarlet sage will overwinter in mild climates. It offers an open, bushy form and profuse spikes of tubular scarlet flowers from early summer (from seeds started indoors) through the first hard frost. A native of sandy woodlands, it is drought tolerant and a favorite of hummingbirds and butterflies. 'Bicolor' has white and pink flowers; 'Lactea', white flowers.

How to Grow

Full sun. Tolerates poor or dry soil and heat. (Grows larger in better soils.) Sold as seeds and in containers. Sow seeds outdoors after last frost. Space plants 3–5 ft. apart. Mulch lightly in summer heat. Fertilize lightly in poor soils.

farinacea p. 244   *Pictured above*
Mealy blue sage
GP. Perennial. Zones 6–8
Height: 2–3 ft. Spread: 2–3 ft.

Grown as an annual in colder climates, mealy blue sage provides an attractive mass of color in beds and borders, as a foundation planting, or naturalized. Gray-green, lance-shaped leaves in mounds. Blue flowers bloom April–November.

How to Grow
Sun or partial shade. Tolerates dry or poor soil and heat. Sold as seeds, in containers, and bare root. Space 1 ft. apart for mass plantings.

greggii p. 180
Cherry sage, autumn sage
WD. Deciduous or evergreen shrub. Zones 6–10
Height: 1–2 ft. Spread: 2–3 ft.
Trim and tailored, this long-blooming (May–November) shrub with a soft, mounding form is a colorful unifying element when threaded through the garden. Small green leaves, crisp and fine, are evergreen in warm climates (zone 8). Minty-aromatic flowers are most often rose-pink (on the most cold-tolerant plants), can be deep red, salmon, purple, or white. 'Cardinal' has deep red flowers.

How to Grow
Sun or shade. Prefers poor, dry soil and heat. Very adaptable to a range of sun, shade, and moisture as long as soil is well drained. Sold in containers. In colder areas, plant in May and June. Space 3–4 ft. apart. Increase by transplanting self-sown seedlings in spring. Trim off spent flowers periodically to stimulate further bloom.

Schizachyrium
Sky-zak'ri-um
Gramineae. Grass family

Description
Little bluestem, one of 60 species in this genus of largely tropical grasses, is an important constituent of almost all of the Great Plains prairies.

scoparium p. 260   *Pictured on facing page*
Little bluestem. (a.k.a. *Andropogon scoparius*)
EW CP GP EW WD. Perennial grass. Zones 3–8
Height: 1½–2½ ft. Spread: 1–2 ft.
One of the most widespread and most beautiful of native grasses. During the growing season its fine, blue-green foliage is part of the prairie carpet. When dormant, its beige to bril-

liant bronze-red color and fluffy seed heads provide autumn excitement. In the wild it forms discrete bunches on dry sites; on moister sites it forms part of the continuous prairie sod. Plant clumps as specimens or grow as ground cover.

How to Grow
Full sun. Tolerates poor, dry soil and heat. Sold as seeds, in containers, and bare root. Sow seeds in spring on site or in flats for transplanting.

Sedum
See'dum
Crassulaceae. Orpine family

Description
This very large group of succulent plants provides excellent specimens and ground covers for beds, borders, rock gardens, and container plantings. The colorful, thick, fleshy foliage usually spirals and overlaps on the stems. Long-lasting flowers are star-shaped, often profuse.

lanceolatum p. 244 Pictured on p. 430
Lance-leaved stonecrop
WM. Perennial. Zone 5
Height: 3–7 in. Spread: 4–6 in.
A small plant ideal for containers or tucking among rocks. The linear leaves are very small (¼–¾ in. long), green in summer, bronze in fall. Clusters of small flowers hover about 4 in. above the foliage for several weeks from midspring to midsummer. Does not tolerate foot traffic. *S. oreganum* has light yellow flowers; *S. spathulifolium,* broad, bluish leaves and yellow flowers.

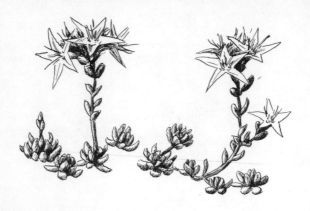

How to Grow

Full sun. Native to exposed rocky sites, it does best in shallow, gravelly soil. Tolerates dry soil and heat. Sold as seeds and in containers. Space plants 4–6 in. apart. Increase by division or stem cuttings.

ternatum p. 245
Stonecrop
EW. Perennial. Zones 4–8
Height: 2–6 in. Spread: 1–2 ft. per year
Able to find a toehold in the worst conditions (rocky slopes and walls), stonecrop doesn't compete well against more aggressive neighbors. Does best in shady locations, where it can creep lazily across bare spots or stones. Good container plant, too. Numerous delicate white flowers rise on drooping stems above rosettes of small, roundish, light green leaves for 2–3 weeks in spring. 'Minus' is smaller in all its parts.

How to Grow

Partial sun or shade. Tolerates heat. Sold in containers. Space 2 ft. or more apart (fills in quickly). Increase by division anytime; broken stems covered with soil easily root. Susceptible to botrytis rot in overly wet conditions.

Silphium
Sil'fi-um
Compositae. Daisy family

Description

A smallish genus of large North American perennials offering spectacular displays of sunflower-like flowers.

laciniatum p. 245
Compass plant
CP GP EW. Perennial. Zones 3–8
Height: 3–12 ft. Spread: 1–3 ft.
Compass plant rivals big bluestem as the symbol of the tall-grass prairie. Best in meadow or prairie plantings, it can be used in medium-size landscapes if it is introduced into an established stand of grass; competition will keep it smaller. Flowers, 3–4 in. across with yellow rays, bloom in early summer. The coarse, deeply divided leaves orient themselves along a north-south axis, hence the common name. An important source of food and shelter for birds and butterflies. Prairie dock (*S. terebinthinaceum*) is native to the moist prairies of the Eastern Woodlands. Rosinweed (*S. asperrimum*) and white-flowered rosinweed (*S. albiflorum*) are Texas natives.

How to Grow
Full sun. Tolerates dry or poor soil and heat. Sold as seeds, in containers, and bare root. Easy from seed. Space plants 3 ft. or more apart. (In the wild they're 15–30 ft. apart.) Mow or burn in fall to remove foliage if desired.

Sisyrinchium
Sis-i-ring'ki-um
Iridaceae. Iris family

Description
Closely related to irises, with similar clump-forming habit and grasslike foliage, members of this genus are pretty enough for beds, borders, and containers but tough enough to naturalize, some even on unirrigated sites. The simple flowers are ephemeral but abundant. Plants are easy to grow in average garden soils.

angustifolium *p. 246   Pictured on p. 431*
Blue-eyed grass
EW WM GP CP. Perennial. Zone 5
Height: 1–1½ ft. Spread: 6–8 in.
Effective in meadows or around ponds and pools. Many light blue, star-shaped flowers cling to flattened, leaflike stems for 4–5 weeks May–July. Foliage is deep green. 'Album' has white flowers; *S. montanum* is similar, with blue to violet flowers.

How to Grow
Sun or partial shade. A native of wet mountain meadows, it prefers moist soil. Sold as seeds and in containers. Space plants 6 in. apart. Increase by division in early spring. Divide every 2–3 years to rejuvenate clumps.

bellum *p. 246*
Blue-eyed grass
CA WM. Perennial. Zone 8
Height: 3–18 in. Spread: 6 in.
A native of mostly open, grassy places, it naturalizes easily on dry-summer sites. Umbels of small blue, violet, or lilac flowers (rarely white) bloom March–May. Individual flowers last only a day but are produced in great quantity. Foliage may be evergreen, depending on moisture and temperature. Dwarf forms of *S. bellum* are available from rock garden specialists. Grass widow (*S. douglasii*) has nodding pink to purple flowers in early spring.

How to Grow
Sun or partial shade. Tolerates dry or poor soils and heat. Sold as seeds and in containers. Easily grown from seeds sown in fall.

Smilacina
Smy-la-si'na
Liliaceae. Lily family

Description
Several of the 30 or so members of this genus are grown for their lush, arching foliage, plumes of flowers, and abundant showy clusters of berries. Ideal for moist, shady spots, they spread slowly to form thick patches, in time making an attractive foundation to the shade garden.

racemosa *p. 247   Pictured above*
False Solomon's seal (a.k.a. *Vagnera racemosa*)
EW CP WM. Perennial. Zones 3–7
Height: 2–3 ft. Spread: ½–1 ft. per year
Provides a year-round focal point to the woodland garden.
Long, narrow, medium-green leaves on arching stems are a
perfect background for many spring ephemerals. For 2–3
weeks in early to mid spring, the end of each stem bears a
dense panicle of tiny, fragrant white flowers. Clusters of green
berries turn red in fall, attract wildlife. *S. r.* var. *cylindrica* has
a slightly more southern range; starflower (*S. stellata*) is
smaller and more subtle.

How to Grow
Shade. Best in deep, loose, organic soil, moist but well drained.
Sold as seeds and in containers. Sow seeds outdoors in fall.
Space plants 2–5 in. apart. Increase by division of established
plants (3 years old) into generous clumps with at least one
bud each.

Solidago
Sol-i-day′go. Goldenrod
Compositae. Daisy family

Description
The vivid golden flowers of the goldenrods herald the end of
summer in many parts of North America. This large and varied
genus provides plants for beds and borders, ground covers,
massed and naturalized plantings. Popular with butterflies,
they do not cause allergic reactions. (Giant ragweed, which
blooms at the same time, is the culprit.) In general, goldenrods

are easy to grow; some become weedy in soil that is too rich. Some spreading species can be invasive. Plants bloom in the second year when grown from seed.

canadensis p. 247 *Pictured above*
Goldenrod, Canada goldenrod
WM CP EW. Perennial. Zone 4
Height: 1½–4 ft. Spread: forms spreading colonies
An embellishment to a manicured flower garden or a natural planting, it combines well with asters, grasses, and gayfeather. Dense clusters of small yellow flowers bloom in August and September. Lance-shaped leaves are dark green. Spreads by underground stems. A number of hybrids offer tidier form and flowers in different shades and intensities of yellow.

How to Grow
Full sun. Tolerates dry soil and heat. Sold as seeds and in containers. Sow seeds in fall. Space plants 12–24 in. apart. Increase by division. Susceptible to rust if air circulation is poor.

missouriensis
Prairie goldenrod, Missouri goldenrod
GP EW WM. Perennial. Zones 3–6
Height: 4–24 in. Spread: forms spreading colonies
A low-growing plant, it forms loose colonies in dry soils. Golden yellow flowers are borne in compact panicles June–August. Fluffy seed heads produce silvery glow when backlit by the low sun in fall. Narrow leaves are green, occasionally red. Related prairie species include gray goldenrod (*S. nemoralis*), with graceful, wandlike inflorescences, and showy goldenrod (*S. speciosa*), with cylinders of densely clustered flowers.

How to Grow

Full sun. Tolerates dry or poor soil and heat. Sold as seeds and in containers. Sow seeds after last frost. Space plants 4 ft. apart or closer. Increase by division of rhizomes in spring.

mollis

Soft goldenrod
GP. Perennial. Zones 3–6
Height: 4–18 in. Spread: forms spreading colonies
Downy, gray-green velvety foliage is an ideal backdrop for the dense, pyramidal clusters of bright yellow flowers July–September. Ideal as a loose ground cover in thin soils. Combines well with other gray-green plants, such as prairie sage. Stiff goldenrod (*S. rigida*) is a robust, tallgrass native with striking, large, dense flower clusters. It holds its own in a dense stand of grass and can tolerate dry conditions.

How to Grow

See *S. missouriensis*. Sold only as seeds.

odora

Sweet goldenrod
CP EW. Perennial. Zones 6–9
Height: 2–4 ft. Spread: 12–18 in.
The 10-in. clusters of blazing yellow flowers stand out in any planting. Blooming July–October, it provides a welcome splash of color when many other flowers have come and gone. Leaves are smooth, bright green, and strongly anise scented. Plant as individual specimen or in groups of 3–5. *S. bicolor* has creamy flowers; *S. ulmifolia,* deep yellow flowers against dark green elmlike leaves. Rapidly spreading species good for meadows include *S. altissima, S. gigantea,* and *S. fistulosa.*

How to Grow

Full sun. Tolerates heat. Sold in containers. Space 2 ft. apart. Increase by division of the short rhizomes.

rugosa pictured on p. 436

Rough-leaved goldenrod
EW CP. Perennial. Zones 4–9
Height: 4–5 ft. Spread: 2–4 ft.
This well-behaved, clump-forming plant adds a distinctive texture to formal borders as well as to meadows and roadsides. Long, dark green leaves are crinkled and glossy. Many fine branches bear sprays of bright yellow flowers in midfall for 2–3 weeks. False goldenrod (*S. spathulata*) has similar arching sprays on a plant 1–3 ft. tall with broad, rich green foliage.

How to Grow

See *S. missouriensis*. Also grows in partial sun. Space 2½–4 ft. apart. Can be cut back in early summer to reduce mature height.

sempervirens *p. 248*
Seaside goldenrod (a.k.a. *S. mexicana*)
EW CP. Perennial. Zones 3–10
Height: 4–6 ft. Spread: 1–2 ft.
A good choice for the fall border, where its thick, bright yellow panicles of flowers arch toward the sun. (Excellent cut flowers.) Glossy leaves, deep green, are often mistaken for daylily foliage; basal leaves are evergreen. A native of coastal marshes and dunes, it tolerates salty conditions and can hold eroding soils.

How to Grow

See *S. missouriensis*. Will grow in sand. Space 2–3 ft. apart. Can be cut back in early summer to reduce mature height.

Sorghastrum
Sor-gas′trum
Gramineae. Grass family

Description

The only cultivated species in this small genus of African and American grasses is described below.

nutans *p. 260   Pictured on facing page*
Indian grass (a.k.a. *S. avenaceum*)
GP EW CP. Perennial grass. Zones 3–9
Height: 3–6 ft. Spread: 1 ft.

One of the premier elements of the tallgrass prairie, Indian grass forms graceful foot-wide clumps, green in summer, bronze in fall. Long, narrow panicles of light bronze flowers with bright yellow anthers are borne in summer, followed by bronze seed heads in fall. Can be grown as a specimen in a bed or border, ground cover, screen, or naturalized.

How to Grow
Full sun. Tolerates dry or poor soil and heat. Sold as seeds, in containers, and bare root. Forms a dense cover smothering other plants; use sparingly in prairie seed mixes. Mow or burn heavy stands in spring to remove old growth.

Sporobolus
Spore-ob′o-lis
Gramineae. Grass family

Description
Largely unused in traditional gardens, members of this genus of grasses are finding a place in natural plantings and in habitat recovery programs. They are tough, drought tolerant, relatively fine textured, and graceful.

heterolepis p. 261
Northern dropseed, prairie dropseed
GP EW. Perennial grass. Zone 4
Height: 1–2 ft. Spread: 1½ ft.
A low-growing, fine-textured grass of medium-moist prairies, it is ideal for making a transition from a traditional planting to a more natural one. Blades are light green in summer, turning yellow in fall. Midsummer flowers are inconspicuous but give off a sweet aniselike aroma, especially evident when humidity is high.

How to Grow
Full sun. Tolerates dry or poor soil and heat. Sold as seeds and in containers. Sow seeds in fall. Space plants 1 ft. apart. Benefits from prescribed burning.

wrightii p. 438
Giant sacaton
WD. Perennial bunchgrass. Zones 6–10
Height: 4–6 ft. Spread: 3–4 ft.
Well adapted to desert heat, giant sacaton is impressive as an accent planting; may be used to best advantage as a naturalized ground cover in runoff catchments. Narrow gray-green leaves cure blond. Minute flowers cluster on 10-in.-long spikes at the ends of 2–4-ft. stems for a month or so in late summer, followed by fine chaffy seeds in early autumn. Alkali sacaton (*S. airiodes*) is shorter and tolerates very alkaline soils.

How to Grow
Full sun. Prefers sites that are periodically flooded but tolerates dry soil, also poor soil and heat. Sold as seeds and in containers. For mass planting, sow seeds ½ in. deep in warm soils, 1 lb./2,000 sq. ft.; or space plants 3–6 ft. apart. Mow to 1 ft. in late winter or spring. If possible, burn every 2–3 years in early spring to remove old growth and stimulate new.

Stokesia
Stoh-key'zhi-a
Compositae. Daisy family

Description
The only member of this genus is described here.

laevis p. 248 *Pictured on facing page*
Stoke's aster (*S. cyanea*)
EW CP. Evergreen perennial. Zones 5–10
Height: 1–2 ft. Spread: 1½ ft.
An old favorite in perennial borders. Leaves are long, lance-shaped, and dark green; basal leaves are evergreen. Leafy stems bear 1–7 flowers, each up to 3 in. across with powdery blue lacy petals, for 3–5 weeks in the summer. Spiny bracts supporting the flowers dry and remain attractive through the summer. One of the few composites for use in light shade, where it is striking among ferns or along a path. Cultivars offer different flower colors, including white ('Alba'), lavender blue ('Blue Danube'), pink ('Rosea'), pale yellow ('Lutea'), and rich blue ('Wyoming').

How to Grow
Sun or partial shade. Tolerates dry or poor soil and heat. Avoid wet spots. Sold as seeds and in containers. Sow seeds in fall or late winter. Space plants 1–2 ft. apart. Increase by division spring or fall.

Stylomecon
Sty-low-mee'con
Papaveraceae. Poppy family

Description
The single species in this genus is described below.

heterophylla p. 249
Wind poppy (a.k.a. *Meconopsis heterophylla*)
CA. Annual
Height: 6–18 in. Spread: 6 in.
This exquisitely delicate annual is seldom seen in the wild, for it appears after wildfires. In cultivation, it is grown in beds and borders and naturalized under the light shade of high-branched trees. It is a good companion for *Nemophila menziesii* in cool north or east exposures. Orange or orange-red flowers, to 2 in. across, with maroon spots at the base of each petal, are borne on elongated stalks in April and May (when sown in fall).

How to Grow
Sun or partial shade. Tolerates poor or dry soils. Sold as seeds and occasionally in small containers ("six-packs"). Broadcast seeds in fall in mild-winter areas, in spring elsewhere.

Stylophorum
Sty-lof'o-rum
Papaveraceae. Poppy family

Description
The single North American member of this small genus (3 species) is described below.

diphyllum p. 249
Celandine poppy
EW. Perennial. Zones 4–9
Height: 1–2½ ft. Spread: 1–2½ ft.
One of the most useful plants for the shade garden. Large, deeply cut light green to blue-green leaves are a focal point all season and make a good foundation for the middle or rear of a spring bed. It self-sows readily and easily naturalizes in a moist woodland. Large, bright yellow poppies bloom for much of the spring and sporadically through summer if it's not too dry. Seedpods are pendulous, plump, and bristly. Combines well with Virginia bluebells, columbine, foamflower, and creeping phlox. Do not confuse this plant with *Chelidonium majus,* also called celandine, which is similar but extremely invasive.

How to Grow
Partial sun or shade. Prefers deep, organic soils. Tolerates constantly moist soils if well drained. Sold as seeds and in containers. Increase in fall or early spring by division or by transplanting self-sown seedlings.

Taxodium
Taks-oh'di-um
Taxodiaceae. Taxodium family

Description
Two of the three species in this genus are North American natives grown for their interesting form and soft, graceful foliage. Desirable as specimens, for naturalizing, or for massed plantings. They are deciduous, the needlelike leaves occurring on slender twigs, which drop with the leaves in autumn.

distichum p. 139   *Pictured on facing page*
Bald cypress
CP. Deciduous tree. Zones 6–9
Height: 70–100 ft. Spread: 20–30 ft.

A long-lived native of riverbanks and flood plains, it forms a narrow conical crown, even on open sites. Good for residential use. Branches are soft and featherlike, turning bronze-red in fall. Stately shape and handsome bark are interesting after leaf drop. Pond cypress (*T. ascendens*) is a smaller native of wet depressions in acid pinelands, with interesting form and twisted trunk.

How to Grow
Full sun. Grows rapidly on fertile, moist, well-drained soil. Tolerates heat. Sold in containers. Space 20 ft. apart.

Tecoma
Te-ko′ma
Bignoniaceae. Bignonia family

Description
A small group of shrubs or small trees native to the southern U.S. and south to Argentina. Foliage looks crisp and fresh; bright yellow flowers are profuse and very showy.

stans p. 180
Yellow bells
WD. Deciduous or evergreen shrub. Zones 7–10
Height: see below. Spread: see below
These fast-growing, long-flowering plants are useful as specimens, in massed plantings, as hedges, or in beds and borders. The long, lance-shaped leaflets are olive-green above, paler below. Clusters of large, bell-shaped flowers are borne in sprays at the ends of new growth intermittently from April to November. Long, thin pods are conspicuous in autumn. Plants vary considerably in form and cold-hardiness. The smallest shrub form and most northern representative, *T. s.* subsp.

angustata, is 3–6 ft. high, spreading 3–4 ft. The largest tree form, *T. s.* subsp. *stans,* grows to 24 ft. high and to 12 ft. wide. Ask at a nursery for the subspecies best suited to your area.

How to Grow
Sun or partial shade. Prefers dry, well-drained soil. Tolerates poor soil and heat. Sold as seeds and in containers. Space 3–4 ft. apart in zone 7, 12 ft. apart in zone 10. Water deeply every few weeks in warmer weather. In colder areas, withhold water in late summer and fall to prevent new frost-tender growth. May freeze back to ground in cold areas, but regrows fast enough to use as seasonal hedge. New growth is most attractive and bears the flowers, so you may elect to prune back to the ground even in warm areas. Thin to enhance tree form.

Thermopsis
Ther-mop′sis
Leguminosae. Pea family

Description
Members of this small genus are grown for their spires of lupinelike yellow flowers, which are excellent for cutting. If you can't grow lupines, try these as a substitute.

montana *p. 250   Pictured above*
Golden banner
WM. Perennial. Zone 4
Height: 3–4 ft. Spread: 2 ft. or more
Good candidates for the middle or back of a sunny border or in a naturalized planting along a stream or open woodland, they spread by rhizomes to form loose colonies. Small lemon-yellow flowers rise above the bright green, somewhat stiff compound leaves on 5–10-in. spikes in mid to late spring, sometimes through the summer.

How to Grow

Sun or partial shade. Needs well-drained soil. Sold as seeds and in containers. Sow seeds in fall or cold-stratify. Space plants 15 in. apart for dense group. Difficult to divide and does not transplant well.

villosa p. 250
Carolina bush pea
EW. Perennial. Zones 4–8
Height: 4–7 ft. Spread: 5–6 ft.
Single plants are dramatic in the middle or rear of a large border; groups of 3–5 plants are equally striking in a large naturalized planting. Leaves have 3 oblong, light green leaflets. Racemes 6–12 in. long of lemon-yellow pea flowers, each 1 in. or more across, bloom for 1–3 weeks in late spring. Numerous flattened pods ripen in midsummer.

How to Grow

Full sun. Prefers fertile, organic soil. Tolerates heat. Sold as seeds and in containers. Pour boiling water over seeds and allow to cool overnight before sowing. Space plants 5 ft. or more apart. Division is difficult. Foliage fades after plant blooms; cut it to the ground.

Tsuga
Soo'ga. Hemlock
Pinaceae. Pine family

Description

A small group of evergreen trees, hemlocks reach a great size in old-growth forests. They are versatile in cultivation, where they are handsome as specimens and useful in groups as windbreaks or visual screens or sheared to make dense hedges. With a soft, relaxed form, they bring a more natural feel to the landscape than many of the overused, stiff, exotic conifers. The short (¼–⅔-in.), fine needles are usually flattened.

canadensis p. 139   *Pictured on p. 443*
Hemlock
EW. Evergreen tree. Zones 3–7
Height: 50–100 ft. Spread: 25–35 ft.
One of the most graceful conifers, it has soft, relaxed branches and a full pyramidal form. Delicate cones are also attractive. *T. c.* var. *sargentii* is a weeping form. Carolina hemlock, *T. caroliniana,* with a slightly stiffer form and fuller branches, is best for hedges and better for urban conditions.

How to Grow
Sun or shade. Prefers fertile, acidic, organic soil. Tolerates constantly moist soil if well drained. Sold in containers and balled-and-burlapped. Space 25 ft. apart. A cooling mulch is helpful. Scales, worms, cankers, and rusts are occasionally serious.

Vaccinium
Vak-sin′i-um
Ericaceae. Heath family

Description
Members of this large genus are grown for their edible fruit, but their noteworthy flowers, foliage, and form make them effective ornamental shrubs.

arboreum p. 181
Sparkleberry, tree huckleberry
CP EW. Semi-evergreen shrub/tree. Zones 7–9
Height: 20–26 ft. Spread: 4–5 ft.

Ideal for naturalizing as a multitrunked shrub or small tree, sparkleberry also has value in screens or shrub borders. The picturesquely twisted, gnarled stems bear fine-textured, glossy, semi-evergreen leaves. Clusters of small white flowers bloom in late spring; glistening black berries persist into winter.

How to Grow
Sun or partial shade. Grows well in dry, acid soil. (Sensitive to lime and alkaline conditions.) Tolerates heat. Spreads and grows slowly. Sold in containers. Prune to train as shrub or tree.

corymbosum *p. 181*   *Pictured on p. 444*
Highbush blueberry
EW CP. Deciduous shrub. Zones 4–9
Height: 6–15 ft. Spread: to 8 ft.
An excellent shrub for naturalizing in moist, acid soil, it has small cylindrical white flowers in early spring, fine-textured foliage with good fall color, and an interesting informal growth habit. The dull black to blue berries are prized by birds, and pie makers will probably have to protect the crop with netting. Numerous cultivars have been selected for fruit production and fall color. *V. crassifolium* 'Wells Delight' is a choice evergreen ground cover. (*V. corymbosum* now includes plants previously assigned to the species *V. ashei*, *V. fuscatum*, *V. anoenum*, *V. myrtilloides*, *V. elliottii*, and *V. constablei*.)

How to Grow
Sun or partial shade. (The more shade, the fewer berries.) Best in fertile, moist, acid soil. Sold in containers. (Consult with nursery staff to select a cultivar hardy in your region.) Space 6–8 ft. apart. Increase by layering. Prune to maintain shape and to keep clean.

Viburnum
Vie-bur'num
Caprifoliaceae. Honeysuckle family

Description
Many species in this large group of shrubs have long been popular landscape plants. Upright and compact, they have attractive flowers and fruit and often bold autumn foliage. Effective as specimens or in borders, the native species are also at home in naturalized landscapes.

acerifolium *p. 182*   *Pictured on p. 446*
Maple-leaved viburnum

EW. Deciduous shrub. Zones 3–8
Height: 4–6 ft. Spread: 5 ft. or more
Ideal for naturalizing, these plants spread slowly to form a multistemmed colony. Flat-topped clusters of white flowers are attractive in late spring or early summer, but the fall foliage — vibrant salmon-pink or purple — is truly spectacular. Loose clusters of small, dark blue fruits last into fall. Hobblebush (*V. lantianoides*) has great form, foliage, and berries and terrific fall color. Arrowwood (*V. dentatum*) is extremely durable.

How to Grow

Sun or partial shade. Prefers adequately drained, slightly acid, moist soil. Tolerates heat if given a cooling mulch. Sold in containers and balled-and-burlapped. Space 5 ft. or more apart. Increase by dividing colonies in early spring. Pests and diseases are rarely serious; avoid sulfur sprays.

lentago p. 182
Nannyberry
EW. Deciduous shrub. Zones 2–8
Height: 15–20 ft. or more. Spread: to 10 ft. or more
A hardy, durable shrub for informal shrub borders and natural plantings. Oval leaves are glossy and medium green. Clusters of white flowers up to 8 in. across bloom for 1–3 weeks in spring. Dark blue fruit and good form are interesting in fall and winter.

How to Grow
See *V. acerifolium*.

nudum p. 183
Possum haw, withe-rod (a.k.a. *V. cassinoides*)
CP EW. Deciduous shrub. Zones 5–9
Height: 5–9 ft. Spread: to 5 ft.
Grown for its numerous clusters of lovely, small white flowers

in late spring and its red to purple fall foliage. In summer the oval to lance-shaped leaves, 2–5 in. long, are dark green. Pink fruit turns a light waxy blue from August to October. Black haw (*V. prunifolium*) has smaller leaves and tolerates drier soils.

How to Grow
Full sun. Sold in containers. (Consult with nursery staff to select a cultivar hardy in your region.) Space 6–8 ft. apart. Prune to remove deadwood and suckers. Susceptible to scale insects and borers, but fairly trouble free.

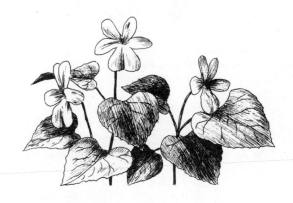

Viola
Vie′oh-la
Violaceae. Violet family

Description
Members of this very large genus are familiar to many as pansies and Johnny-jump-ups, with their gay, 5-petaled flowers and heart-shaped or divided leaves. In the wild, violas are found in a wide variety of flower colors and habitats — shaded and sunlit, dry and wet. Native species, like their highly bred relatives, are excellent for borders and containers; they also look good in rock gardens, as ground covers, or naturalized in drifts among other small plants. Most violas are very easy to grow; some spread widely by self-sowing.

canadensis *p. 251   Pictured above*
Canada violet
EW. Perennial. Zones 3–8
Height: 6–12 in. Spread: 6–10 in.
Its tall (for a violet), loose habit is best when massed on a woodland bank or border. Broad white flowers with purple on the backs of the petals bloom for 2–3 weeks in spring.

Once the flowers fade, the light green foliage begins to decline, making way for other plants. Round-leaved violet (*V. rotundifolia*) has bright yellow flowers and thick-leaved foliage held close to the soil.

How to Grow
Shade. Prefers fertile, moist, well-drained soil. Sold in containers. Increase by transplanting plentiful self-sown seedlings when dormant.

nuttallii
Nuttall's violet
WM GP. Perennial. Zone 4
Height: 2–10 in. Spread: 6 in.
Native to meadows and foothills in sandy or gravelly soil, this species provides outstanding spring color in arid areas. Effective in many traditional garden situations, it's good for naturalizing in shortgrass meadows or on sunny slopes. Yellow flowers with purplish to brown lines bloom May–early July. Leaves have downy undersides.

How to Grow
Sun or partial shade. Tolerates dry or poor soil and heat. Sold as seeds and in containers. Sow seeds in fall (they need a cold period). Space plants 6 in. apart. Increase by division. Susceptible to crown rot in wet, heavy soils.

pedata p. 251   *Pictured above*
Birdfoot violet
EW GP CP. Perennial. Zones 4–9
Height: 2–6 in. Spread: 12 in.
One of the showiest native violets. It has palmately lobed leaves and large (¾–1½-in.) multicolored flowers, most often in

shades of blue and violet, sometimes white, with yellow stamens. Blooms in spring for 1–3 weeks. *V. p.* var. *alba* has white flowers.

How to Grow
See *V. nuttallii*. Sun. Very well drained soil. Don't overfertilize. Keep it weeded; doesn't tolerate much competition.

pubescens p. 252
Downy yellow violet (a.k.a. *V. pensylvanica*)
EW GP. Perennial. Zones 3–7
Height: 6–8 in. Spread: 6 in.
An outstanding ground cover, its heart-shaped leaves (2–3 in. long) are covered with soft hairs, hence the common name. Small (½ in. across), clear yellow flowers bloom in early spring. It is one of the few woodland plants that tolerates the climatic extremes of the Great Plains if shaded and protected from wind. White wood violet (*V. rugulosa*) is a handsome, white-flowered native of the northern Great Plains.

How to Grow
Shade. Needs fertile, uniformly moist but not wet soil and a windless site. Sold as seeds, in containers, and bare root. Space 1 ft. apart. Increase by division.

sororia complex p. 252
Blue woods violet, confederate violet
GP CP EW. Perennial. Zones 3–8
Height: 6–8 in. Spread: 6 in. (forms colonies)
The most widespread violet in the eastern U.S., this group includes many forms that don't quite qualify as species, subspecies, or varieties in their own right, hence the designation "complex." All have lovely small flowers, pale to deep blue, often white with purple centers, that bloom in early spring. Good ground cover. Among the many species related to *V. sororia* are *V. adunca*, *V. papilionacea*, and *V. missouriensis*.

How to Grow
See *V. pubescens*.

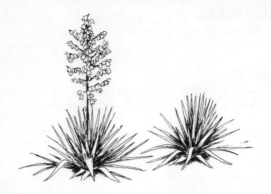

Yucca
Yuk'a
Agavaceae. Agave family

Description
Popularly associated with deserts, these North American natives are surprisingly widespread in the wild and hardy and adaptable in cultivation. The tall spikes of creamy flowers are spectacular, making yuccas a dramatic accent specimen. But the striking clumps of sword-shaped evergreen foliage also provide superb year-round architectural effects in borders, small groups, large masses, or natural settings. The 40 or so species range from small, coarse, grasslike plants to large, many-headed, treelike plants. In some species, the leaf rosettes rest on the ground; in others they are held aloft on thick stems.

Yuccas are easy to grow in most well-drained soils. They bloom several years after starting from seed or small transplants. Depending on the species, individual rosettes of leaves will send up a flowering stalk every year or every few years. Most yuccas form offsets — new rosettes at the base of the plant — which can be removed and transplanted to increase your stock.

brevifolia p. 183
Joshua tree
WD. Evergreen shrub/tree. Zones 6–10
Height: to 25 ft. or more. Spread: 10–15 ft.
Magnificent in their forestlike stands in the wild, these huge yuccas are striking exclamation points in a naturalized southwestern landscape. The stiff blue-green leaves, 8–14 in. long, have yellow margins. Flower spikes are short (usually 3 ft.), with a candelabra of side branches graced by 1½-in., bell-shaped, fragrant, creamy white flowers. Blooms in April and May. *Y. rostrata* and *Y. thompsoniana* are smaller, with similar foliage.

How to Grow

Full sun. Does well in poor or dry soil and heat. Sold as seeds, in containers, and bare root. Growth from seed is slow. Transplants easily; make certain you are buying legally collected plants (permits are required for collection). Space 10–12 ft. apart for forest effect. Remove old flower stems in fall. Dried leaves, which absorb moisture during rains and help sustain and insulate the plants, are best left in place, particularly in cold desert areas.

elata p. 184
Soaptree, palmilla, amole
WD. Evergreen shrub/tree. Zones 6–10
Height: 5–20 ft. Spread: to 10 ft.
An effective foil for lush desert tree and shrub plantings. Fine, stiffly arching leaves are gray to blue-green with white margins. Plants resemble coarse bunchgrass when young, gradually develop several heads on trunklike stems with age. Flowering stem is 3–7 ft. long, with 25–30 branches covered with clusters of night-fragrant creamy white flowers in May and June. Dried, the brown woody seed capsules are used in flower arrangements. Smaller yuccas include Spanish dagger, *Y. angustifolia*, to 6 ft. Datil, *Y. baccata*, has wider leaf blades, forms low thickets.

How to Grow

See *Y. brevifolia*. Transplant with care: a 3-ft. plant will have a 4-ft. or deeper root. If much of the pithy portion of the root is severed, the plant will turn completely brown and take a year to recover (keep dry).

filamentosa p. 184   *Pictured on facing page*
Beargrass, Adam's needle
CP EW. Evergreen shrub. Zones 5–9
Height: 5–6 ft. Spread: 5–6 ft.
A southeastern native, it is found on dry sandy soil at the edge of woodlands and along roadsides. Flower stalks rise from 2–3-ft.-high clumps of light green leaves. Clusters of 2–3-in. white flowers bloom in June. Leaves have a sharp point; site accordingly. 'Golden Sword' has gold-variegated leaves; 'Starburst', cream variegation; 'Ivory Tower', bright green leaves.

How to Grow

See *Y. brevifolia*. Sold in containers. Space 6–7 ft. apart.

glauca p. 185
Yucca, beargrass, soapweed, Spanish bayonet
GP WD. Evergreen shrub. Zones 3–8

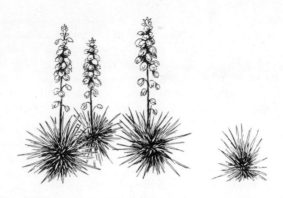

Height: 3–6 ft. Spread: 1½–2½ ft.
The cluster of narrow, bayonet-shaped basal leaves, green with whitish margins, contrasts sharply with surrounding fine-textured prairie plants. Around June a striking stalk, capped with a cluster of white bell-shaped flowers, rises well above the foliage.

How to Grow
See *Y. brevifolia.* Sold in containers. Plant spring or early fall.

whipplei *p. 185   Pictured above*
Whipple's yucca
CA. Evergreen shrub. Zones 7–9
Height: to 12 ft. Spread: 3–4 ft.
Gray-green to bluish spine-tipped leaves form a rosette about 2 ft. high. Flower stalks to 12 ft. bear hundreds of drooping, waxy, bell-shaped flowers, pale yellow or cream colored, in May and June. A perfect accent plant for a drought-tolerant planting of Matilija poppies and Cleveland sage.

How to Grow
See *Y. brevifolia.* Plant in fall.

Zauschneria
Zowsh'ner-i-a
Onagraceae. Evening primrose family

Description
A small group of California native perennials or subshrubs whose brilliant scarlet flowers brighten the landscape in summer and fall, when few other natives are in flower. Botanists have recently combined the four species in the genus with the

larger genus *Epilobium,* but gardeners and nurseries have been slow to follow suit.

californica p. 253
California fuchsia, hummingbird's trumpet (a.k.a. *Epilobium californica*)
CA. Perennial. Zones 8–10
Height: 1–2 ft. Spread: 1–2 ft.
A rangy plant that spreads widely and quickly, it is a good candidate for casual woodland gardens or informal borders. Long (1½–2-ft.) flower spikes rise above small gray-green or gray leaves. Trumpet-shaped flowers, 1½–2 in. long, bloom July–October; hummingbird favorites. Will grow on hot, dry slopes with a little cover from nearby shrubs; also thrives in cool exposures and light shade. 'Solidarity Pink' has pink flowers; 'Alba', white flowers. The montane form, *E. c.* subsp. *latifolium,* forms a low-growing mat, has wider leaves, and is hardier.

How to Grow
Sun or partial shade. Tolerates dry or poor soil, heat, and garden watering. Sold in containers. Plant in fall, space 18 in. apart for massed effect. Easy to increase by seed or division in fall or spring. Cut to ground after bloom; in mild areas, it will begin to regrow immediately.

Zinnia
Zin'i-a
Compositae. Daisy family

Description
The many showy annual hybrid forms of this smallish genus of North and South American plants are well known. Native

zinnias also have showy flowers and make wonderful low-maintenance mass plantings or ground covers.

grandiflora *p. 253   Pictured on p. 453*
Desert zinnia, Rocky Mountain zinnia
GP WD. Perennial. Zones 5–10
Height: 6–8 in. Spread: 10–12 in. (spreads)
Possibly the toughest low ground cover in the West, it provides a long season of colorful flowers on hot, exposed sites. Wiry, grasslike leaves are pale green, curing to tan in winter. A dense crop of bright yellow daisies, 1 in. across, blooms June–October. Flowers dry to a straw color. It spreads slowly by root sprouts, eventually forming a long-lived, dense, indestructible ground cover. Add verbena to young plantings for a wonderful color display while zinnia fills in. *Z. acerosa* has white flowers.

How to Grow
Full sun. Needs dry soil. Tolerates poor soil and heat. Sold in containers (seeds break easily when machine cleaned and are seldom commercially available). Plant in warm soil. Space plants 6–8 in. apart for fast cover, 12 in. apart if combined with other plants. Increase by division in spring. Mow 4 in. high in early spring.

Appendices

Further Reading

Once you get started with natural gardening, you'll want to expand your knowledge and horizons. The books on the following list are grouped by essay topic, but many will be of use outside the confines of our categories. Found in bookstores, through mail-order catalogs, or at the library, they will make a valuable addition to your basic gardening texts. In addition, contact local botanical gardens and arboretums and your Cooperative Extension Service for lists of the many informative books, pamphlets, and information sheets they offer.

Gardening Inspired by Nature

Landscaping with Nature. Jeff Cox. Emmaus, Pa.: Rodale Press, 1991.

Landscaping with Wildflowers and Native Plants. William Wilson. San Francisco: Ortho Books, 1985.

Landscaping with Wildflowers. Jim Wilson. Boston: Houghton Mifflin, 1992.

Natural Landscaping. John Diekelmann and Robert Schuster. New York: McGraw Hill, 1982.

The Natural Garden. Ken Druse. New York: Crown/Clarkson N. Potter, 1989.

The New American Landscape Gardener. Phoebe Leighton et al. Emmaus, Pa.: Rodale Press, 1987.

Eastern Woodlands

Herbaceous Perennial Plants: A Treatise on Their Identification, Culture and Garden Attributes. Alan Armitage. Athens, Ga.: Varsity Press, 1989.

Landscape Plants for Eastern North America. H. L. Flint. New York: John Wiley, 1983.

Manual of Woody Landscape Plants: Their Identification, Ornamental Characteristics, Culture, Propagation and Uses, 4th ed. Michael Dirr. Champaign, Ill.: Stipes Publishing Co., 1990.

Wildflowers of the Southeastern United States. Wilbur H. Duncan and Leonard E. Foote. Athens, Ga.: University of Georgia Press, 1975.

Taylor's Guide to Gardening in the South. Rita Buchanan and Roger Holmes, eds. Boston: Houghton Mifflin, 1992.

Coastal Plain

Gardening with Native Wildflowers. Samuel B. Jones, Jr., and Leonard E. Foote. Portland, Oreg.: Timber Press, 1990.

Landscape Plants of the Southeast. R. G. Halfacre and A. R. Shawcroft. Raleigh, N.C.: Sparks Press, 1989.

Native Shrubs and Woody Vines of the Southeast: Landscaping Uses and Identification. Leonard E. Foote and Samuel B. Jones, Jr. Portland, Oreg.: Timber Press, 1989.

Trees and Shrubs for the Southeast. B. E. Wigginton. Athens, Ga.: University of Georgia Press, 1963.

Trees of Georgia and Adjacent States. C. L. Brown and L. K. Kirkman. Portland, Oreg.: Timber Press, 1989.

Great Plains

How to Manage Small Prairie Fires. Wayne Pauly. Madison, Wis.: Dane County Environmental Council, 1985. Available from Dane County Parks Dept., 4318 Robertson Rd., Madison, Wis. 53714.

Jewels of the Plains: Wild Flowers of the Great Plains Grasslands and Hills. Claude A. Barr. Minneapolis: University of Minnesota Press, 1983.

Landscaping with Native Texas Plants. Sally Wasowski and Julie Ryan. Austin, Tex.: Texas Monthly Press, 1984.

Native Texas Plants: Landscaping Region by Region. Sally Wasowski and Andy Wasowski. Austin, Tex.: Texas Monthly Press, 1988.

North American Prairie. J. E. Weaver. Lincoln, Nebr.: Johnsen Publishing Co., 1954.

Prairie Wildflowers. R. Currah, A. Smreciu, and M. Van Dyk. Edmonton, Alberta: University of Alberta, 1983.

The Wildflower Gardener's Guide: Midwest, Great Plains, and Canadian Prairies Edition. H. W. Art. Pownal, Vt.: Storey Communications, 1991.

Western Mountains and Pacific Northwest

The Audubon Society Field Guide to North American Wild Flowers. Richard Spellenberg. New York: Chanticleer Press, 1979.

Flora of the Pacific Northwest: An Illustrated Manual. C. Leo Hitchcock and Arthur Cronquist. Seattle: University of Washington Press, 1973.

Rocky Mountain Alpines. Second Interim International Rock Garden Plant Conference. Portland, Oreg.: Timber Press, 1986.

Rocky Mountain Wild Flowers. A. E. Porsild. Ottawa: National Museums of Canada, 1979.

Trees and Shrubs for Pacific Northwest Gardens, 2nd ed. John A. Grant and Carol L. Grant. Portland, Oreg.: Timber Press, 1990.

Wild Flowers of Western America. Robert and Margaret Orr. New York: Chanticleer Press, 1981.

Western Deserts

Southwestern Landscaping with Native Plants. Judith Phillips. Santa Fe: Museum of New Mexico Press, 1987.

Taylor's Guide to Water-Saving Gardening. Boston: Houghton Mifflin, 1990.

Trees and Shrubs of the Southwestern Deserts. Lyman Benson and Robert A. Darrow. Tucson: University of Arizona Press, 1981.

The Xeriscape Flower Gardener: A Waterwise Guide for the Rocky Mountain Region. Jim Knopf. Boulder: Johnson Books, 1991.

California Floristic Region

A Field Guide to Pacific States Wildflowers. Charles Niehaus. Boston: Houghton Mifflin, 1981.

California Native Trees and Shrubs for Garden and Environmental Use in Southern California. Lee W. Lenz and John Dourley. Claremont, Calif.: Rancho Santa Ana Botanic Garden, 1981.

Complete Garden Guide to the Native Perennials of California. Glenn Keator. San Francisco: Chronicle Books, 1990.

Gardener's Guide to California Wildflowers. Kevin Connelly. Sun Valley, Calif.: Theodore Payne Foundation, 1991.

Growing California Native Plants. Marjorie G. Schmidt. Berkeley: University of California Press, 1980.

Hardy Californians. Lester Rowntree. Salt Lake City: Peregrine Smith, 1980 (reprint of 1936 edition).

Sunset Western Garden Book. Editors of Sunset Books and Sunset Magazine. Menlo Park, Calif.: Lane Publishing Co., 1988.

Taylor's Guide to Gardening in the Southwest. Roger Holmes and Rita Buchanan, eds. Boston: Houghton Mifflin, 1992.

Gardening for Wildlife: Birds and Butterflies

Attracting Backyard Wildlife. William J. Merilees. Stillwater, Minn.: Voyageur Press, 1989.

The Audubon Society Guide to Attracting Birds. Stephen W. Kress. New York: Scribner's, 1985.

The Backyard Naturalist. Craig E. Tufts. Washington, D.C.: The National Wildlife Federation, 1988.

Backyard Wildlife Habitat Information Packet. National Wildlife Federation (1400 16th St. NW, Washington, D.C. 20036-2266).

The Butterfly Garden: Creating Beautiful Gardens to Attract Butterflies. Jerry Sedenko. New York: Villard Books, 1991.

Butterfly Gardening: Creating Summer Magic in Your Garden. Xerxes Society/Smithsonian Institution. San Francisco: Sierra Club Books and National Wildlife Federation Books, 1990.

Butterfly Gardening for the South: Cultivating Plants That Attract Butterflies. Geyata Ajilvsgi. Dallas: Taylor Publishing Co., 1991.

How to Attract Hummingbirds and Butterflies. John Dennis and Mathew Tekulsky. San Ramon, Calif.: Ortho Books, 1991.

Landscaping for Wildlife. Carrol L. Henderson. Minneapolis: Minnesota Dept. of Natural Resources, 1987.

The Wildlife Gardener. John V. Dennis. New York: Knopf, 1985.

How to Grow Wildflowers and Native Plants

Collecting, Processing and Germinating Seeds of Wildland Plants. James A. Young and Cheryl Young. Portland, Oreg.: Timber Press, 1986.

Directory to Resources on Wildflower Propagation. G. A. Sullivan and R. H. Daley. St. Louis: National Council of State Garden Clubs, 1981.

A Garden of Wildflowers: 101 Native Species and How to Grow Them. Henry Art. Pownal, Vt.: Storey Communications, 1986.

Gardening with Wildflowers and Native Plants, rev. ed. (*Plants and Gardens,* vol. 45/1). Claire E. Sawyers, ed. Brooklyn, N.Y.: Brooklyn Botanic Garden, 1989.

Growing and Propagating Showy Native Woody Plants. Richard Bir. Chapel Hill, N.C.: University of North Carolina Press, 1992.

Growing and Propagating Wildflowers. Harry Phillips. Chapel Hill, N.C.: University of North Carolina Press, 1985.

Handbook of Wild Flower Cultivation. Kathryn S. Taylor and Stephen F. Hamblin. New York: Collier/Macmillan, 1963.

Meadows and Meadow Gardening. Framingham, Mass.: New England Wild Flower Society, 1990.

Native Plants for Woodland Gardens: Selection, Design and Culture. Framingham, Mass.: New England Wild Flower Society, 1987.

Propagation of Wildflowers. Will C. Curtis, revised by William E. Brumbach. Framingham, Mass.: New England Wild Flower Society, 1986.

The New Wild Flowers and How to Grow Them. Edwin F. Steffek. Portland, Oreg.: Timber Press, 1983.

The Wildflower Meadow Book: A Gardener's Guide. Laura C. Martin. Chester, Conn.: Globe Pequot Press, 1990.

Organic Control of Pests and Diseases

Common-Sense Pest Control. William Olkowski, Sheila Daar, and Helga Olkowski. Newtown, Conn.: Taunton Press, 1991.

Pests of the Garden and Small Farm. Mary Louise Flint. Oakland, Calif.: Statewide Integrated Pest Management Project (University of California, 67-1 San Pablo Ave., Oakland, Calif. 94608-1239), 1990.

Rodale's Chemical-Free Yard and Garden. Fern M. Bradley. Emmaus, Pa.: Rodale Press, 1991.

Rodale's Garden Insect, Disease and Weed Identification Guide. Miranda Smith and Anna Carr. Emmaus, Pa.: Rodale Press, 1988.

The Encyclopedia of Natural Insect and Disease Control. Roger B. Yepson, Jr. Emmaus, Pa.: Rodale Press, 1984.

Sources

Gardening by Mail. Barbara Barton. Boston: Houghton Mifflin, 1990.

Wildflower Handbook. ed. Annie Paulson. National Wildflower Research Center. Austin, Tex.: Texas Monthly Press, 1989.

Nursery Sources, Native Plants and Wildflowers. New England Wild Flower Society. (A regularly updated listing available at Garden in the Woods, Book Shop, 180 Hemenway Rd., Framingham, Mass. 01701-2699.)

Taylor's Guide to Specialty Nurseries. Barbara Barton. Boston: Houghton Mifflin, 1993.

Sources of Supply

The recent interest in wildflowers and native plants has been nurtured by an ever-increasing number of specialist nurseries. In this listing, we can offer only a sampling of those nurseries, which now number in the hundreds. (See "Further Reading" for books providing more extensive listings.) We encourage you to seek out local nurseries, botanical gardens, and arboretums, where the staff will be familiar with the plants and problems of your area. (After the listings of plant and seed suppliers by state is a list of suppliers of organic controls for pests and diseases.)

Many nurseries are concerned about the effects of collecting plants from the wild and have embarked on propagation programs. Don't hesitate to ask the nursery where their plants come from. And remember that "nursery grown" plants may have been collected — ask how the plants were propagated. Don't be too quick to judge, however. Nursery propagation of many native plants is relatively new, and reputable nurseries may sell both propagated and collected plants.

Some of the nurseries listed here sell only through the mail, others sell on site. Some have display gardens open to the public. Some sell a wide range of plants, others are more specialized. We've indicated this information in each entry (see the Key below), but you should call the nursery to confirm it before ordering or making a trip there.

Key:
MO: mail order
Nu: on-site sale
Gdn: display garden
[S]: seeds
[P]: plants
appt: some restriction, call to make sure

ALABAMA

Magnolia Nursery & Display Garden [P]
12615 Roberts Rd.
Chunchula, AL 36521

205 675-4696
Southeastern natives
Catalog: $2
MO, Nu (appt), Gdn (appt)

ARIZONA

Desert Enterprises [S]
P.O. Box 23
Morristown, AZ 85342
602 388-2448
Cacti, desert shrubs, grasses, trees, wildflowers
Catalog: free
MO

Hubbs Brothers Seed Company [S]
40 N. 56th St.
Phoenix, AZ 85034
602 267-8132
Plants of Sonoran and Mohave deserts
Catalog: free
MO, retail store

CALIFORNIA

Clyde Robin Seed Co. [S]
P.O. Box 2366
Castro Valley, CA 94546
415 785-0425
Shrubs, trees, wildflowers
Catalog: free
MO

Greenlee Nursery [P,S]
301 E. Franklin Ave.
Pomona, CA 91766
714 629-9045
Grasses
Catalog: $5 (free price list)
MO, Nu (appt)

Larner Seeds [P,S]
P.O. Box 407
235 Grove
Bolinas, CA 94924
415 868-9407
Grasses, shrubs, trees, vines, wildflowers
Catalog: $2
MO, Nu (appt), Gdn (appt)

Las Pilitas Nursery [P,S]
Star Route, Box 23X
Las Pilitas Rd.
Santa Margarita, CA 93453
805 438-5992
Shrubs, trees, wildflowers
Catalog: $4 (free price list)
MO, Nu (appt), Gdn (appt)

The Living Desert [P]
47900 Portola Ave.
Palm Desert, CA 92260
619 346-5694
Grasses, shrubs, trees, wildflowers
Catalog: monthly price list
Nu, Gdn

Mockingbird Nursery [P]
1670 Jackson St.
Riverside, CA 92504
714 780-3571
Shrubs, trees
Catalog: free
Nu (appt)

Moon Mountain Wildflowers [S]
P.O. Box 34
864 Nappa Ave.
Morro Bay, CA 93442
Wildflowers
Catalog: $2
MO

The Theodore Payne Foundation [P,S]
10459 Tuxford St.
Sun Valley, CA 91352
818 768-1802
Grasses, shrubs, trees, wildflowers
Catalog: $2
MO (seed only), Nu, Gdn

Wildwood Nursery [P,S]
P.O. Box 1334
3975 Emerald Ave. [in La Verne]
Claremont, CA 91711
714 593-4093 or 621-2112
Grasses, shrubs, trees, wildflowers
Catalog: $1
MO, Nu, Gdn

Yerba Buena Nursery [P,S]
19500 Skyline Blvd.
Woodside, CA 94062
415 851-1668
Ferns, grasses, shrubs, trees, wildflowers
Catalog: $1
Nu

C O L O R A D O

Neils Lunceford [P,S]
Box 2130
740 Blue River Pkwy.
Silverthorne, CO 80498
303 468-0340
High-altitude grasses, shrubs, trees, wildflowers
Catalog: free plant list
MO, Nu, Gdn

D E L A W A R E

Winterthur Museum and Gardens [P]
Kennet Pike, Rte. 52
Winterthur, DE 19735
302 888-4600
Catalog: $1
Shrubs, trees, wildflowers
MO, Nu

F L O R I D A

Blake's Nursery [P]
Rte. 2, Box 971
Madison, FL 32340
904 971-5003
Catalog: free price list with SASE
Shrubs, trees
MO, Nu (appt), Gdn (appt)

Native Nurseries [P,S]
1661 Centerville Rd.
Tallahassee, FL 32308
904 386-8882
Shrubs, trees, wildflowers
Nu, Gdn

GEORGIA

Goodness Grows [P]
P.O. Box 311
Highway 77 North
Lexington, GA 30648
404 743-5055
Grasses, wildflowers
Nu, Gdn

Piccadilly Farm [P]
1971 Whippoorwill Rd.
Bishop, GA 30621
404 769-6516
Shrubs, trees, wildflowers
Catalog: $1.00
Nu (appt), Gdn (appt)

Transplant Nursery [P]
Rte. 2, Parkertown Rd.
Lavonia, GA 30553
404 356-1658
Shrubs
Catalog: $1
MO, Nu, Gdn

IDAHO

High Altitude Gardens [S]
P.O. Box 4238
500 Bell Dr. 7
Ketchum, ID 83340
208 726-3221
Grasses, wildflowers
Catalog: $2
MO, Nu (appt), Gdn (appt)

Northplan/Mountain Seed [S]
P.O. Box 9107
Moscow, ID 83843-1607
208 882-8040
Shrubs, trees, wildflowers
Catalog: native seed list: long SASE
MO

I O W A

Ion Exchange [P,S]
Rte. 1, Box 48C
Harpers Ferry, IA 52146
319 535-7231
Grasses, wildflowers
Catalog: free
MO

Smith Nursery Co. [P,S]
P.O. Box 515
Charles City, IA 50616
515 228-3239
Shrubs, trees
Catalog: free price list
MO

I L L I N O I S

Bluestem Prairie Nursery [P, S]
Route 2, Box 92
Hillsboro, IL 62049
217 532-6344
Wildflowers of Illinois prairie
Catalog: free
MO

Lafayette Home Nursery [P,S]
R.R. 1, Box 1A
Lafayette, IL 61449
309 995-3311
Grasses, shrubs, trees, wildflowers
Catalog: free
MO, Nu (appt), Gdn (appt)

The Propagator's Private Stock [P]
8805 Kemman Rd.
Hebron, IL 60034
No phone
Shrubs, small trees, wildflowers
Catalog: free
MO

K A N S A S

Sharp Bros. Seed Co. [S]
P.O. Box 140

Healy, KS 67850
316 398-2231
Grasses, wildflowers
Catalog: $5
MO

LOUISIANA

Gulf Coast Plantsmen [P]
15680 Perkins Rd.
Baton Rouge, LA 70810
504 751-0395
Shrubs, trees, wildflowers for lower South
Catalog: none
Nu (appt)

Louisiana Nursery [P]
Rte. 7, Box 43
Opelousas, LA 70570
318 948-3696
Shrubs, trees, wildflowers
Catalog: $5
MO, Nu (appt), Gdn (appt)

MARYLAND

Environmental Concern [P,S]
P.O. Box P
210 West Chew Ave.
St. Michaels, MD 21663
301 745-9620
Wetland plants: grasses, shrubs, trees, wildflowers
Catalog: free
MO, Nu (appt)

Kurt Bluemel [P,S]
2740 Greene La.
Baldwin, MD 21013
301 557-7229
Grasses, wildflowers
Catalog: $2
MO

MINNESOTA

Landscape Alternatives [P,S]
1465 Pascal St.
St. Paul, MN 55108

612 488-3142
Grasses, wildflowers of Minnesota and prairie
Catalog: $1
MO, Nu (appt), Gdn (appt)

Prairie Moon Nursery [P,S]
Rte. 3, Box 163
Winona, MN 55987
507 452-1362
Grasses, wildflowers of prairie, woodland, and wetland
Catalog: $2
MO, Nu (appt), Gdn (appt)

M I S S O U R I

Missouri Wildflowers Nursery [P,S]
9814 Pleasant Hill Rd.
Jefferson City, MO 65109
314 496-3492
Grasses, wildflowers of Missouri
Catalog: $1
MO, Nu (appt)

M O N T A N A

Valley Nursery [P]
P.O. Box 4845
21801 N. Montana Ave.
Helena, MT 59604
406 442-8460
Hardy shrubs, trees
Catalog: list with SASE
MO, Nu, Gdn

N E B R A S K A

Bluebird Nursery [P,S]
P.O. Box 460
519 Bryan St.
Clarkson, NE 68629
402 892-3457
Grasses, shrubs, trees, wildflowers
Catalog: free
MO, Nu (appt), Gdn (appt)

NEW JERSEY

Lofts Seed [S]
Chimney Rock Rd.
Bound Brook, NJ 08805
908 560-1590
Grasses, wildflowers
Catalog: free
MO, Nu (appt)

NEW MEXICO

Agua Fria Nursery [P]
1409 Agua Fria St.
Santa Fe, NM 87501
505 983-4831
Wildflowers
Nu

Bernardo Beach Native Plant Farm [P,S]
520 Montano Rd. N.W.
Albuquerque, NM 87107
505 345-6248
Shrubs, trees, wildflowers
Catalog: none
Nu

Desert Moon Nursery [P]
P.O. Box 600
Veguita, NM 87062
505 864-0614
Natives, drought-tolerant plants
Catalog: $1
MO, Nu (appt), Gdn (appt)

Plants of the Southwest [P,S]
930 Baca St.
Santa Fe, NM 87501
505 983-1548
Grasses, shrubs, trees, wildflowers
Catalog: $1.50
MO, Nu

NORTH CAROLINA

Holbrook Farm & Nursery [P]
P.O. Box 368
115 Lance Rd.

Fletcher, NC 28732
704 891-7790
Shrubs, trees, wildflowers
Catalog: $2
MO, Nu, Gdn

Niche Gardens [P]
1111 Dawson Rd.
Chapel Hill, NC 27516
919 967-0078
Wildflowers of Southeast
Catalog: $3
MO, Nu (appt), Gdn (appt)

O R E G O N

Forest Farm [P]
990 Tetherow Rd.
Williams, OR 97544-9599
503 846-6963
Shrubs, trees, wildflowers
Catalog: $3
MO, Nu (appt)

Siskiyou Rare Plant Nursery [P]
2825 Cummings Rd.
Medford, OR 97501
503 772-6846
Wildflowers, dwarf shrubs and trees for rock gardens
Catalog: $2
MO, Nu (appt), Gdn (appt)

P E N N S Y L V A N I A

Jacob's Ladder Natural Gardens [P]
1375 Consho. State Rd.
P.O. Box 145
Gladwyne, PA 19035
215 525-6773
Shrubs, trees, wildflowers
Catalog: free
Nu

Musser Forests [P]
P.O. Box 340
Rte. 119 North
Indiana, PA 15701
412 465-5686

Shrubs, trees
Catalog: free
MO, Nu

SOUTH CAROLINA

Woodlanders, Inc. [P]
1128 Colleton Ave.
Aiken, SC 29801
803 648-7522
Shrubs, trees, wildflowers
Catalog: $1
MO, Nu (appt), Gdn (appt)

TENNESSEE

Native Gardens [P,S]
5737 Fisher La.
Greenback, TN 37742
615 856-3350
Shrubs, trees, wildflowers
Catalog: $2
MO, Nu (appt), Gdn (appt)

Sunlight Gardens [P]
Rte. 1, Box 600-A
Andersonville, TN 37705
615 494-8237
Wildflowers
Catalog: $2
MO, Nu (appt)

TEXAS

Antique Rose Emporium [P]
Rte. 5, Box 143
Brenham, TX 77833
409 836-9051
Shrubs, trees, wildflowers
Catalog: $5
MO, Nu, Gdn

The Lowrey Nursery [P]
2323 Sleepy Hollow Rd.
Conroe, TX 77385
713 367-4076
Grasses, shrubs, trees, wildflowers

Catalog: none
Nu (appt)

Turner Seed Co. [S]
Rte. 1, Box 292
Breckenridge, TX 76424
817 559-2065
Grasses, wildflowers (by the pound)
Catalog: free: long SASE
MO

Wildseed, Inc. [S]
P.O. Box 308
Eagle Lake, TX 77434
409 234-7353 or 800 848-0078
Grasses, wildflowers
Catalog: free
MO, Nu (appt), Gdn (appt)

Yucca Do Nursery [P]
P.O. Box 655
Waller, TX 77484
409 826-6363
Native Texas plants
Catalog: $3
MO

VIRGINIA

Andre Viette Farm and Nursery [P]
Rte. 1, Box 16
Fishersville, VA 22939
703 943-2315
Wildflowers
Catalog: $2
MO, Nu, Gdn

VERMONT

Vermont Wildflower Farm [S]
U.S. Rte. 7
Charlotte, VT 05445
802 425-3500
Wildflowers
Catalog: free
MO, Nu, Gdn

WASHINGTON

Plants of the Wild [P,S]
P.O. Box 866
Willard Field
Tekoa, WA 99033
509 284-2848
Grasses, shrubs, trees, wildflowers
Catalog: $1
MO, Nu (appt), Gdn (appt)

WISCONSIN

Country Wetlands Nursery and Consulting, Ltd. [P,S]
South 75, West 20755 Field Dr.
Muskego, WI 53150
414 679-1268
Grasses, shrubs, trees, wildflowers
Catalog: $2
MO, Nu (appt), Gdn (appt)

Little Valley Farm [P,S]
R.R. 3, Box 544
Spring Green, WI 53588
608 935-3324
Shrubs, vines, wildflowers of midwest
Catalog: free with first-class stamp
MO, Nu (appt)

Prairie Nursery [P,S]
P.O. Box 306
3291 Dyke Ave.
Westfield, WI 53964
608 296-3679
Grasses, wildflowers
Catalog: $3
MO, Gdn (appt)

Mail-Order Suppliers of Organic Pest Controls

Gardener's Supply
128 Intervale Rd.
Burlington, VT 05401
802 863-1700
Catalog: free

Gardens Alive!
5100 Schenley Pl.
Lawrenceburg, IN 47025
812 537-8650
Catalog: free

Harmony Farm Supply
P.O. Box 460
Graton, CA 95444
707 823-9125
Catalog: $2

Necessary Trading Co.
One Nature's Way
New Castle, VA 24127
703 864-5103
Catalog: free

Peaceful Valley Farm Supply
P.O. Box 2209
Grass Valley, CA 95945
916 272-4769
Catalog: $2

Rincon-Vitova Insectaries
P.O. Box 95
Oak View, CA 93022
800 248-2847
Catalog: free price sheets

Ringer Corp.
9959 Valley View Rd.
Eden Prairie, MN 55344-3585
800 654-1047
Catalog: free

Public Gardens

One of the best ways to learn about wildflowers and native plants and how to use them imaginatively is to see superb plantings and gardens at first hand. Here is a selection from the many excellent possibilities around the country. Be sure to phone or write ahead for opening times, admission fees, and travel directions.

Eastern Woodlands

CONNECTICUT

Connecticut Arboretum
Connecticut College
P.O. Box 5625
New London, CT 06320
203 439-2144
370 acres, woodland landscape

DELAWARE

Winterthur Museum and Gardens
Kennet Pike, Rte. 52
Winterthur, DE 19735
302 888-4600
200 acres of naturalized gardens

INDIANA

Hayes Regional Arboretum
801 Elks Rd.
Richmond, IN 47374
317 962-3745
350 acres, native plants in woodland settings

MASSACHUSETTS

Garden in the Woods
New England Wild Flower Society

180 Hemenway Rd.
Framingham, MA 01701
508 877-7630
45 acres, woodland and meadow

NEW YORK

Bayard Cutting Arboretum
P.O. Box 466
Montauk Hwy.
Oakdale, NY 11709
516 581-1002
Naturalistic landscape, wildflower gardens

NORTH CAROLINA

Blomquist Garden of Native Plants
Sarah P. Duke Gardens
Duke University
Durham, NC 27706
919 684-3698
55 acres, woodland and other gardens

Botanical Gardens at Asheville
151 W. T. Weaver Blvd.
Asheville, NC 28802
704 252-5190
10 acres, native plants in natural setting

North Carolina Botanical Garden
Old Mason Farm Rd.
P.O. Box 3375 Totten Center-UNC
Chapel Hill, NC 27599
919 962-0522
300 acres, native southeastern plants

OHIO

Holden Arboretum
9500 Sperry Rd.
Mentor, OH 44060
216 946-4400
3,100 acres, display gardens of woody plants and wildflowers

Toledo Botanical Garden
5403 Elmer Dr.
Toledo, OH 43615

419 536-8365
60 acres, native gardens

PENNSYLVANIA

Bowman's Hill Wildflower Preserve
Washington Crossing Historic Park
Rte. 32, 2 miles south of New Hope
P.O. Box 103
Washington Crossing, PA 18977
215 862-2924
100 acres, recreated Pennsylvania habitats

Brandywine River Museum and Conservancy
Rte. 1 and Rte. 100
P.O. Box 141
Chadds Ford, PA 19317
215 388-2700
Wildflower gardens, river walk

Coastal Plain

ALABAMA

Auburn University Arboretum
Garden St.
Auburn, AL 36830
205 844-5770
13 acres, native Alabama trees and shrubs

The Birmingham Botanical Garden
2612 Lane Park Rd.
Birmingham, AL 35223
205 879-1227
67 acres, many displays

GEORGIA

Callaway Gardens
U.S. Hwy. 27 South
P.O. Box 2000
Pine Mountain, GA 31822
404 663-2281
2,500 acres, naturalistic gardens

Georgia Southern University Botanical Garden
1211 Fair Rd.

Statesboro, GA 30458
912 681-9129
9½ acres woodland and developed plantings

MISSISSIPPI

The Crosby Arboretum
3702 Hardy St.
Hattiesburg, MS 39402
601 261-3137
64 acres, native plants and trees

TEXAS

Armand Bayou Nature Center
P.O. Box 58828
8500 Bay Area Blvd.
Houston, TX 77258
713 474-2551
1,900 acres, Texas coastal prairie, woodland, and bayou

Mercer Arboretum and Botanic Gardens
22306 Aldine-Westfield Rd.
Humble, TX 77338
713 443-8731
12 developed acres, native plants

Great Plains

ILLINOIS

Chicago Botanic Garden
Highland Park
P.O. Box 400
Glencoe, IL 60022
708 835-5440

Lincoln Memorial Garden and Nature Center
2301 E. Lake Dr.
Springfield, IL 62707
217 529-1111
Native Illinois plants recreate 19th-century landscape

Morton Arboretum
Rte. 53
Lisle, IL 60532

708 968-0074
Prairie restoration and woody plants

KANSAS

Dyck Arboretum of the Plains
Hesston College
P.O. Box 3000
Hesston, KS 67062
316 327-8127
Native Kansas prairie and adapted plants

MINNESOTA

Minnesota Landscape Arboretum
3675 Arboretum Dr.
Chanhassen, MN 55317
612 443-2460
950 acres, native prairie, wildflowers

OKLAHOMA

U.S. Southern Great Plains Field Station
2000 18th St.
Woodward, OK 73801
405 256-7449
Trees, shrubs, wildflowers

TEXAS

Dallas Arboretum and Botanical Garden
8525 Garland Rd.
Dallas, TX 75218
214 327-8263
22 acres, Texas and southeastern natives

San Antonio Botanical Center
555 Funston Pl.
San Antonio, TX 78209
512 821-5115
33 acres, formal gardens, native plantings

WISCONSIN

Schlitz Audubon Center
1111 E. Brown Deer Rd.
Milwaukee, WI 53217

414 352-2880
6 miles of trails, woodland and prairie

University of Wisconsin Arboretum
1207 Seminole Hwy.
Madison, WI 53711
608 263-7888
1,280 acres, woodland and prairie

Western Mountains and the Pacific Northwest

CALIFORNIA

Strybing Arboretum and Botanical Gardens
Golden Gate Park, 9th Ave. at Lincoln Way
San Francisco, CA 94122
415 661-1316
70 acres, California natives and adapted plants

COLORADO

Chautauqua Park
Baseline Rd. and 7th
P.O. Box 791 (Boulder Parks and Recreation)
Boulder, CO 80306
303 441-3408 (Ranger Station)
Mountain habitats, trails

Denver Botanic Garden
909 York
Denver, CO 80206.
303 331-4010
Alpine and other gardens

Oxley Homestead
24425 Currant Dr.
Golden, CO 80401
303 526-9463
Native plants in residential landscapes

OREGON

Berry Botanic Garden
11505 S.W. Summerville Ave.
Portland, OR 97219
503 636-4112
6 acres, display garden, woodland walk

Western Deserts

ARIZONA

The Arboretum at Flagstaff
P.O. Box 670
South Woody Mountain Rd.
Flagstaff, AZ 86002
602 774-1441
200 acres, demonstration gardens, research on water-efficient plants

Arizona-Sonora Desert Museum
2021 N. Kinney Rd.
Tucson, AZ 85743
602 883-2702 or 883-1380
186 acres, native plants in natural habitats; demonstration garden

Boyce Thompson Southwestern Arboretum
P.O. Box AB
Superior, AZ 85273
602 689-2811 or 689-2723
35 acres, including arid-land plants, demonstration gardens

Desert Botanical Garden
1201 N. Galvin Pkwy.
Phoenix, AZ 85008
602 941-2867
145 acres, many displays including demonstration gardens

Tohono Chul Park
7366 N. Paseo del Norte
Tucson, AZ 85704
602 575-8468 or 742-6455
36 acres, including demonstration gardens

NEVADA

Desert Demonstration Garden
3701 Alta Dr.
c/o Las Vegas Valley Water District
3700 West Charleston
Las Vegas, NV 89153
702 258-3205
2½ acres, low-water demonstration garden

Ethel M Botanic Garden
2 Cactus Garden Dr.
Henderson, NV 89014
702 458-8864
2 acres, dry-climate garden

University of Nevada Las Vegas Arboretum
4505 Maryland Pkwy.
Las Vegas, NV 89154
702 739-3392
Displays and xeriscape demonstration garden

NEW MEXICO

Albuquerque Xeriscape Garden
Osuna and Wyoming, NE
Albuquerque, NM
505 857-8650
Demonstration garden

Bosque del Apache National Wildlife Refuge Visitor's Center
P.O. Box 1246
Socorro, NM 87801
505 835-1828
Landscaped with native plants

TEXAS

Cactus Gardens
Judge Roy Bean Visitor's Center
Langtry, TX 78871
915 291-3340
Native trees, shrubs, cactus

Chihuahua Desert Visitor's Center
P.O. Box 1334
Texas Hwy. 118 (north of Alpine)
Alpine, TX 79831
915 837-8370
Desert gardens

Texas A & M Experiment Station
1380 A & M Circle
El Paso, TX 79927
915 859-9111
Xeriscape garden

Wilderness Park Museum
4301 Woodrow Bean–Transmountain Rd.

El Paso, TX 79924
915 755-4332
Chihuahuan desert garden

California Floristic Province

Descanso Gardens
1418 Descanso Dr.
La Canada, CA 91011
818 952-4400 or 952-4401
165 acres, camellia heaven, other displays

Lummis Home State Historical Monument
200 East Ave. 43
Los Angeles, CA 90031
213 222-0546
2 acres, low-water, low-maintenance garden

Rancho Santa Ana Botanic Garden
1500 N. College Ave.
Claremont, CA 91711
714 625-8767
85 acres, California native plants, demonstration gardens

Regional Parks Botanic Garden
S. Park Dr. and Wildcat Canyon Rd.
Tilden Park, CA
510 841-8732
10 acres, display of California plant communities

Santa Barbara Botanic Garden
1212 Mission Canyon Rd.
Santa Barbara, CA 93105
805 682-4726
65 acres, California native plants, demonstration garden

**The Theodore Payne Foundation for Wildflowers
and Native Plants**
10459 Tuxford St.
Sun Valley, CA 91352
818 768-1802
21 acres of gardens and a retail nursery

University of California Botanical Garden
Strawberry Canyon and Centennial Dr.
Berkeley, CA 94720
510 642-3352
30 acres, California natives and adapted plants

Photo Credits

David Benner
110–11

Rita Buchanan
166A

C. Colston Burrell
112–13, 143B, 190A, 207A, 229A, 261A

David Cavagnaro
106–7, 129B, 134B, 158B, 161A, 192A, 205B, 231A, 232B, 242B, 254–55, 260A,B

Thomas E. Eltzroth
152A, 180B, 204A, 229B, 265B

Barbara Emerson
114–15

Derek Fell
120A, 131A, 135B, 136A, 139A, 142B, 163A

Charles Marden Fitch
125B, 208B

Judy Glattstein
168B

Pamela Harper
116–17, 123A, 130A, 132A, 133A, 135A, 138A, 140–41, 142A, 144A, 145B, 147B, 148B, 149A,B, 150A,B, 151A,B, 153A, 154B, 157A,B, 159B, 162B, 164A,B, 165A,B, 167A, 168A, 169A,B, 170A,B, 171A,B, 172A,B, 173A,B, 174A, 175A,B, 177A,B, 178A,B, 179A, 180A, 181B, 183A,B, 184B, 186–87, 188A,B, 189A,B, 190B, 191B, 192B, 193A,B, 194A, 195A,B, 196A,B, 198A, 199A,B, 200A,B, 201A, 202A,B, 203A,B, 205A, 206A,B, 209B, 210B, 211A, 213B, 214A,B, 216A,B, 217A, 218A, 219A,B, 222A,B, 223A,B, 224A, 225A,

226B, 230A, 231B, 232A, 233A,B, 235A,B, 237A,B, 238A,B, 239A,B, 240A,B, 241A,B, 242A, 243A,B, 244A,B, 245A, 246A, 247A,B, 248B, 249A,B, 250A,B, 251A, 252A,B, 253A, 257A, 258A, 264B, 266A, 267A

Robert E. Heapes
154A, 265A

Saxon Holt
146B, 159A, 185B, 220B, 225B, 234B, 236A, 257B

Horticultural Photography, Corvallis, Oregon
128A

Kristi Jones
230B

Sam Jones
143A, 144B, 162A, 181A, 182A, 210B, 236B

Robert E. Lyons
123B, 129A, 156B, 174B, 204B, 211B, 221A, 245B, 251B

Charles Mann
108–9, 121B, 125A, 147A, 153B, 160B, 176A, 184A, 208A, 215A, 224B, 226A, 227B, 234A, 253B, 256A,B, 259A,B, 261B

Frederick McGourty
167B

Scott Millard
145A, 148A, 155A, 166B, 179B, 210A

Monrovia Nursery Co.
134A

Suzi Moore
156A

Jerry Pavia
118–19, 133B, 158A, 194B, 197A, 198B, 220A, 246B

Joanne Pavia
152B, 155B, 218B

Joy Spurr
122B, 130B, 131B, 136B, 146A, 212B, 215B, 227A

Index